Ignatius, Liborio Sinscalchi

The Meditations of St. Ignatius

Ignatius, Liborio Sinscalchi
The Meditations of St. Ignatius
ISBN/EAN: 9783744660389
Printed in Europe, USA, Canada, Australia, Japan
Cover: Foto ©Lupo / pixelio.de

More available books at **www.hansebooks.com**

THE

MEDITATIONS

OF

ST. IGNATIUS;

OR,

The "Spiritual Exercises" Expounded,

BY

FATHER LIBORIO SINISCALCHI,
OF THE SOCIETY OF JESUS.

TRANSLATED FROM THE ITALIAN
AND REVISED BY A CATHOLIC CLERGYMAN.

PHILADELPHIA:
PETER F. CUNNINGHAM & SON,
Catholic Booksellers,
817 ARCH STREET.

WE approve of the publication of the Meditations of St. Ignatius, expounded by Father Liborio Siniscalchi, by our enterprising publisher Mr. Peter F. Cunningham, and recommend their use to the faithful of our diocese.

✠ JAMES F. WOOD,
BISHOP OF PHILADELPHIA.

January 8, 1862.

Entered according to Act of Congress, in the year 1862, by
PETER F. CUNNINGHAM,
in the Clerk's Office of the District Court of the United States for the Eastern District of Pennsylvania.

TO THE

GLORIOUS PATIARCH

SAINT JOACHIM;

FATHER OF

THE EVER IMMACULATE VIRGIN MARY,

CONCEIVED WITHOUT SIN,

MOTHER OF GOD,

THIS TRANSLATION OF THE

SPIRITUAL EXERCISES OF SAINT IGNATIUS

IS HUMBLY DEDICATED.

PREFACE

TO THE AMERICAN EDITION.

This excellent work is well known throughout Catholic countries on the Continent. It has been everywhere received by pious and learned men, as one of the best and most edifying collection of Meditations of all those prepared after the plan of the "Spiritual Exercises" of St. Ignatius.

The only translation of this book into English, so far as we know, was published in Dublin, in the year 1849. It seems to have been prepared from a French copy, and contains not only the peculiarities of the original, but also the forms and idioms of the French language. Even with these drawbacks, the intrinsic value of the work made it spread widely, and the Dublin editions, we learn, are entirely exhausted.

The Author will be found somewhat singular in his illustrations and forms of expression. But his very singularity adds strength to his great thoughts, and stamps them on the mind of his reader. Whilst we have followed the Dublin translation, or rather revised it, we have not felt at liberty to destroy the right of the author to speak in his own way.

This translation is literal almost to great faultiness; and it is, as far as possible, an English echo of the Italian original. It was impossible to make the book more English, without rendering a less faithful translation.

Of the merit of these Meditations it is unnecessary to say anything. They have won recommendation from those most competent to form a proper judgment. The deep, solid, practical thought of the writer is unquestionable.

We offer this work to the American Catholic public with confidence, because we believe it will be welcomed in every pious household, and prized by every one who "loves to know the ways of God."

J. B. B.

TRANSLATOR'S INTRODUCTION.

TO THE READER.

THE SPIRITUAL EXERCISES of St. Ignatius were published at Rome in the year 1548. Though the saint was at that time unacquainted with learning any further than barely to read and write, yet this book is so full of excellent maxims and instructions, that it is most clear that the Holy Ghost supplied abundantly what was wanting in him of human learning. The Meditations of St. Ignatius are altogether new, and written upon a different plan from writers who preceded him. He appoints, for the foundation of these exercises, a morning meditation on the end for which we are created, that we fully convince ourselves that nothing is to be valued or sought after save as it conduces to the honor and service of God. The meditations on the fall of the angels, and of man, on the future punishments of sin, and on the last things, show us the general effects of sin. To point out the particular disorders of our passions, and to purge our hearts from them, he represents to us the two standards of Christ and the Devil, and all men ranging themselves under the one or the other, that we may be moved ardently to make our choice with the generous souls that follow Christ. Then he proposes what the resolution requires, and how we are to express in ourselves the perfect image of our Saviour, by the three degrees of humility, by meditating on the mysteries of Christ's life.

By meditating on Christ's sufferings, he will have us learn the heroic virtues of meekness and charity, and by them to fortify our souls against contradictions; and by reflecting on his glorious mysteries, and on the happiness of Divine love, he teaches us to unite our hearts closely to God.

Behold the plan of this work. To St. Ignatius we are indebted for this excellent method of meditation on the great truths of eternity. They are adapted not only to the ecclesiastics and religious, but also to Christians engaged in the world; for the great truths of Christianity are the same for all.

Those who are anxious to know more concerning the Exercises of St. Ignatius, may read the life of this Saint, written by Bartolo, or in "Alban Butler's Lives," from which work the above is taken.

We dedicate this translation to the father of the Blessed Virgin, St. Joachim; and implore his intercession for our readers and ourselves.

CONTENTS.

Med.		Page
	Preface to the American Edition,	5
	Translator's Introduction,	7
I.	Necessity of Fervor in Making the Spiritual Exercises,	11
II.	On the End of Man,	31
III.	On the Great Affair of Salvation. How much it imports Man to Attain his End, and be Saved,	50
IV.	On the Punishment of Sin,	69
V.	On the Malice of Mortal Sin,	90
VI.	On Venial Sin,	115
VII.	On Purgatory,	135
VIII.	On Death,	151
IX.	On the Death of the Just,	174
X.	On the Particular Judgment,	192
XI.	On the General Judgment,	211
XII.	On Hell,	229
XIII.	On the Eternity of the Damned,	252
XIV.	On the Prodigal Son,	269
XV.	On the Two Standards,	289
XVI.	On the Incarnation and Nativity of Jesus Christ,	308
XVII.	On the Institution of the Most Holy Sacrament of the Eucharist,	323
XVIII.	On the Passion,	343
XIX.	On the Sorrows of Mary at the Foot of the Cross,	363
XX.	On Heaven,	378
XXI.	On the Love of God,	397
XXII.	Of the Spiritual Fruit we should draw from the Exercises,	412

A COURSE OF SPIRITUAL EXERCISES.

MEDITATION I.

INTRODUCTION.

Of what importance it is to make the spiritual exercises with fervor.

WHEN the impious king, Antiochus, entered the temple of Jerusalem to lay it waste, his first act was to remove the golden altar and the candlestick, which was also of gold.

The Devil acts in the same manner when he intends to deprive of spiritual good that soul which is the temple of the living God: he takes from it the altar—that is, fervor of mind; he removes from it the candlestick—that is, the light which makes known the eternal maxims.

The Devil cannot take from the soul the light of faith: he, however, removes the light of consideration; so that the soul may not reflect on what it believes. As it is of no avail to open the eyes in the dark, so, says St. Augustine, "it is of no advantage to be near the light if the eyes are closed." The eternal maxims, considered in.the light of faith, are most clear; yet, if we do not

open the eyes of the mind to meditate on them, we
live as if we were perfectly blind: thus we shall
precipitate ourselves into every vice.

If men were to consider the shortness of life,
the uncertainty of death, the vanity of the world;
that they are between two eternities, one most
happy, the other most miserable; it is certain they
would all be saints. Why are they not so? They
do not reflect. Gamblers, not reflecting on the
immense sums they lose, easily risk their properties: so those who do not consider the importance
of salvation, easily lose their souls. What is still
more lamentable is, that they think least on eternity, who should consider it most profoundly—
those who are most deeply rooted in vice, and, for
the same reason, in greatest peril of damnation.
Thus the same occurs to them as befel Jonas. God
commanded this prophet to go and preach in Nineveh. He disobeyed, and went to Thersis. Suddenly there arose a tempest; thunder rolled; the
mariners cried out; merchandise was thrown overboard. In the meantime Jonas, whose disobedience
caused all these evils, slept soundly, and would
not have awakened, had not one of the mariners
descended to him, saying, "Ah, sluggard! is this
the time to sleep? We all labor in the shipwreck,
and thou sleepest!"

Sloth is daily visible in the world. There are
so many whose souls are full of vices, that our Lord,
in order to rouse them, places constantly before
their eyes sudden deaths, earthquakes, thunderbolts, misfortunes; while they, with greater sins
than others, play or sleep, without being aware that
they are on the brink of a precipice—that it is as

likely for them to die of an unforeseen accident, as to be damned.

Ah! miserable creatures, blind wretches, who sleep over the interests of your eternal salvation! Jesus Christ watches for you, and with infinite benignity comes to awake you. " Why are you oppressed with sleep? Arise, and invoke the Lord thy God."

What manner of life is yours? It is so long a period since you ceased to live as a Christian. This is the hour to arise from sleep. Let us open our eyes, and listen to the voice of Christ. " This is the acceptable time, now is the day of salvation." Let us profit well by the grace that God confers on us at this season.

" We beg of you, brethren, not to receive the grace of God in vain."—(I. *Thess.*, iv.) To this end the present meditation is directed. In it we will consider, first; Of how great consequence it is to perform the spiritual exercises with fervor in order to correct our vices; second, How important it is to advance in virtue; third, How we are to profit by these spiritual exercises.

FIRST PRELUDE.

Let us imagine that our angel-guardian takes us by the hand, and introduces us into these exercises, saying, as the angel did to Abraham (*Gen.*, x. 12): " Leave thy lands, relatives, and the house of thy father, and come to the land I will show thee." Separate thyself for a time from all terrestrial affairs, and come with me to meditate on what concerns thy eternity.

THE SECOND PRELUDE

will be to say to God: " Show me thy ways, O Lord, and direct me in thy paths."—(*Ps.*, xlii.) My God, enlighten my mind to know well the way of my eternal salvation, and I will be attentive to thy voice. " I will hear what the Lord God will speak to me; for He will speak peace to His people, and to His saints."—(*Pslm.*, 84.)

FIRST POINT.

How important it is to make the exercises with fervor in order to amend our faults. Two things are necessary for man to live well and holily: namely, to avoid evil and to do good. For this end the Spiritual Exercises of St. Ignatius are most powerful and efficacious. For these exercises act on the soul, as the cleansing and ornamenting of the rooms of a palace. How is a chamber put in order? The floor is well swept, each corner is dusted, what is disorderly is set right, every thing is put into its place, and all that can be added to embellish it is procured: thus we act in the exercises with the soul.

At a period when we are at leisure, in a sequestered spot, with a clear light from God, we review the secret windings of our conscience—its evil habits, our past faults in cleansing ourselves by penance—then we think seriously of commencing a new life, Christian and holy.

It appears king David acted thus when he said: " I exercised myself in cleansing the irregularities of my mind." He afterwards explains in what manner he did this; and it is precisely what is done in these exercises. 1. "I meditated with my heart," here was meditation; 2. "I thought on the days of old," here was examination of past life; 3. "I raised my voice to the Lord," here was mental prayer; 4. "I sought my God and was delighted," here was the unitive way; 5. Finally, "And I said: 'now I begin,' this is a change from the right hand of the Most High," here is the fruit drawn; that is, a serious change of life. Thus acted holy David;—what we also are to do in the holy exercises.

Jansenius, a learned commentator, on this passage, "I was exercised and I swept my spirit,"—(*Ps.*, 76,) says that David acted thus to cleanse his soul by penance. Genebrard says, he did so, "to direct his soul to virtue." For the same intentions we should act; for the exercises are most efficacious to purify the soul from all stain, and introduce it to all that is good. They are most powerful to sanctify the most hardened and obstinate sinners. As light remedies are not sufficient for grievous maladies, we must adopt those which physicians style great ones. For poisonous cancers, prepared oils are not sufficient; we must use fire and iron. So, for certain souls deeply rooted in vice, slight motives will not suffice, but the strong maxims of hell and eternity are necessary. These peals of thunder can arouse sinners from their profound lethargy; these dexterous bridles can keep in order certain furious passions, and act so that man may not plunge himself into wickedness. For this reason the Holy Spirit admonishes us always to keep our minds on the maxims of eternity, if we do not wish to fall into sin. "In all thy works,

remember thy last end, and thou shalt never sin."
—(*Eccl.*, vii.)

Sophia, a holy matron, mother of S. Clement, bishop of Ancyra, seeing the cruel persecutions of Dioclesian and Maximian, and fearing that her son might prevaricate, animated him with the maxim of eternity. "Son," said she, "I admonish you that here there is question of eternity." With this stimulus, he suffered under Dioclesian, Maximian, and Maximus, from eight inhuman judges, from the hands of innumerable executioners, so great torments, that Nicephorus, his historian, writes, that, since the creation of the world, there never was a martyr more tormented.

What are we doing in the spiritual exercises? We meditate at leisure and seriously, not one alone, but all the truths of eternity. If each of them well considered suffices to make a person holy, all united, what strength will they not have in converting an obstinate heart? It is not suitable to allege, that during the course of the year we can consider these truths, by meditating, reading, or hearing sermons.

What is there then more in the exercises? I answer, according to Galen, that the most powerful remedies are of little or no avail when they are not taken with the necessary precautions, namely, to observe a proper regulation of diet, to remain in the house, avoid cold air and similar things. "The best medicine is useless without dieting."

For the soul to profit by the great antidote of eternal truths, they must be meditated on in holy retirement, far from the affairs of the world, and with the assistance of a wise director. This is done in these exercises.

As medicine is of no avail to those who take no precaution against cold or unsuitable diet, so those who are in the midst of entertainments, games, and lawsuits, cannot well fix their minds on eternal truths, which, for that reason, cannot make much impression.

The seed thrown on the ground by the evangelical sower was perfectly good: however, that portion which fell on stones, no sooner appeared than it was sunburnt; that which fell among thorns scarcely arose when it was choked with brambles; and the seed that fell on the public road was trodden on by passengers. So the evangelical truths are always the same. If they occur to a distracted mind, occupied with a thousand affairs and interests, or to one exposed to vanity or worldly affections, for a time they may make slight impression, but then immediately vanish.

2. During the remainder of the year it seldom happens that these truths are heard from preachers in so striking a manner as they are laid before us in the exercises, so that they are here as so many drawn swords, which strike more deeply; besides, God communicates himself more or less with Heavenly lights, according to our dispositions; and where can a person be better disposed to be enlightened than in the exercises?

To intimate the law to the Israelites, God guided them into the desert, that there, without disturbance, they might better hear his voice: there also he nourished them with manna, which may be called a lively representation of the exercises; as that was very small, but of great virtue and flavor, so the sentiments which are here meditated on, are short, but of great virtue and efficacy. Men can never better hear the voice of God, and taste the manna of spiritual consolations, than in the desert of holy retreat.

For these reasons those who enter the exercises feel as if they were entering a new world, in which they open their eyes to perceive what, perhaps, they have never learned, unless in a confused manner. He who thought only of acquiring dignity, and becoming a great captain, learns that all is vanity, and that he was born solely to be saved. He who thought liberty consists in worldly pastimes and customs, knows now, that they are grievous evils, capable of provoking the thunders of divine justice: from this clear knowledge they are contrite and confused.

As one viewing the stars through a telescope, or an ant through a microscope, in amaze, can scarcely believe the stars so great, or the ant furnished with so many limbs, so from this clear knowledge of eternity, many conversions result from these exercises.

Michael Lewis, a German, was sent by his father, a Baron, to the court of Lorraine, there to learn the French language. He gave himself up to every vice, particularly gaming; having lost all his money, in despair he called the Devil to his assistance, who immediately appeared in the form of a youth, who filled his hands with money, saying: Spend and play as much as you please: I will always give you as much money as you wish, provided you are content to be my faithful friend: he then induced him to write, with his blood, a billet, renouncing his soul. As one precipice usually draws into another, this impious man, returning to his country, gave himself up to such vicious courses, that he attempted to murder his father and mother, also himself. The miserable parents being in great affliction, and not knowing to what cause to attribute their son's conduct, made many inquiries, and at length succeeded in discovering the fact of renunciation which their son made to the malignant spirit. To remedy so much impiety, his brother, a canon, under some pretext, conducted him to the Fathers of the Society of Jesus, at Molesme. They immediately made him begin the spiritual exercises, to dispose him for a general confession. Then all Hell was armed against him. The Devil first appeared to him in the form of a lion, to tear him to pieces; then, as a compassionate man, who tried to make him dislike the fathers, and be annoyed at what they said. He firmly resisted all these assaults, and with many tears made a general confession—during which he often fainted through contrition and horror of his misdeeds; he revoked the contract he had made with the Devil; pronounced the profession of faith; finally, hearing the votive Mass of St. Ignatius, in his chapel, he saw the Devil, against his will, restoring the billet of renunciation; thus being disburdened, he continued to lead a very Christian life (*Bartoli lib.* v. *vitæ S. Ignatii.*) Such are the admirable conversions which often happen in the exercises from the lively knowledge acquired of the eternal truths.

Enter then, O Christian soul, into yourself; repass in mind the disorderly life you have hitherto led; see how your conscience has become an immense chaos of iniquity; see how much you require these exercises. Here, you have to consider your most important affair, that is, to be saved. What great thing is it, after having spent an entire year in temporal affairs, now to spend eight days in the wants of the soul? If you knew, for certain, that these exercises were to be the last of your life—that at their termination, you were immediately to die, with what fervor would you not perform them? Who knows whether these are not the last admonitions and assistance God will give you?

Our Lord, in anger after so many sins, may turn away from you and abandon you; yet he does not. On the contrary, as a loving father, he runs to you, though you fly from him; he calls you to penance, and seems to say to you, as he did to the sick man in the Gospel, who for thirty years languished at the pond of probation, "Wouldst thou be healed?" Do you really wish to be cured of the evils of your soul? If you wish it, I desire it also, and I am ready to assist you, by my grace, to enlighten your mind, and inflame your will. Be courageous. "Wouldst thou be healed?" O infinite goodness of God! O charity beyond limits! Will you be so foolish as to allow God to do so much for you, and on your part do nothing?

SECOND POINT.

How necessary it is to perform the holy exercises with fervor, in order to advance in virtue.

As these exercises are necessary for the wicked to reform their evil ways, they are equally so for the just, to persevere and advance in virtue.

Genebrard on the seventy-sixth Psalm, "I was exercised and I swept my spirit," says, that David exercised himself in reviewing the state of his soul, daily to increase in virtue. On account of human weakness, even the most virtuous and holy relent and grow cold after their first fervor. As smiths, the better to work their iron, frequently replace it in the furnace, to be softened by the fire; and gardeners, to preserve a fine row of cedars and myrtles, frequently cut off the superfluous leaves and blossoms; so to preserve a soul in the fervor of virtue, it must often replace itself in the furnace of the exercises, and here, enlightened by God on its defects, divest itself of them and amend. Great fruit is continually observed from the exercises, in those communities where they are annually made. St. Jane Frances de Chantal, the first plant of the order of the Visitation, said, that from long experience of what happened in the monastery of Holy Virgins, she observed that the spiritual exercises were for them, like water on the flowers of their virtues, to make them increase. A vase of flowers not watered for several days, appears languishing—the plant decays, the leaves dry up, the stems wither, and the flowers have not strength to shoot forth from the branches; however, scarcely are they refreshed with water than they become at once vigorous and beautiful. The plant again grows, the leaves assume their verdure, the buds shoot forth, and soon flowers appear. In the same manner, in religious communities, previous to the exercises, the fervor of prayer, charity, and regular observance grow cold; but these being made, all are renewed: more attention is given to prayer, greater assiduity in the choir, greater charity, more exact obedience, precisely as if celestial dew of graces had descended on the flowers of these virtues. It cannot be otherwise, for in the devout solitude of the exercises, Jesus Christ speaks intimately to the heart. Oh! how much more efficacious and powerful is the internal voice of Jesus Christ, than all that men could say. "I will lead her into solitude, and there I will speak to her heart." God speaks to man in many ways; he speaks to the ears, by means of sermons; to the eyes, by placing before them the corpse of a parent or friend; and he speaks, as it were, to the whole body, by sickness; but in the exercises he speaks to the heart, and what does he say to it? Sometimes he seems to speak, as he did to Adam after prevaricating: "Adam, where art thou?" See to what a miserable state the soul is reduced—"Where art thou?" At other times he says, with the angel to Lot, at the burning of Sodom (*Genes.*, xix. 12): "Hasten to be saved." Already Hell is open to punish your sins—procure your salvation quickly. What was said to the deceased youth can also be here applied: "Young man, I say to thee arise."—(*Luke*, vii. 14.) Ah! unhappy wretch, dead to God and to grace, once more revive and be again renewed. "Come to me all you who labor and are burdened, and I will refresh you." Poor souls, who groan under the weight of innumerable sins, come to me and I will comfort you. "Open to me, my sister, my spouse."—(*Cant.*, v. 2.) Ah! obstinate soul, how long have I been knocking at the door of your heart, and will you be always deaf to my voice? Deign to open it to me that I may enter with my grace and my love.

What heart then can be so inflexible as not to yield to the penetrating voice of Jesus Christ? Hence arise those strong resolutions which, each day, are made in the exercises, to give one's self to God, and to advance in every Christian virtue. King Ferdinand having sent twelve noble Bohemians to Rome, recommended them to St. Ignatius, to be instructed in a spiritual life. The saint having received them cordially, placed them in the exercises; they imbibed so much fervor in them, that the twelve became religious of the Society of Jesus. Oh! how efficacious are the exercises for making a person not only good, but a saint. Finally, let us add from experience, God wishes to communicate his graces and mercies, especially during retreat; as the Blessed Virgin and the saints grant favors more easily to those who venerate their miraculous pictures than to others. As God and the Blessed Virgin taught these exercises to St. Ignatius, it appears they more strongly assist those who amend their lives. We have a bright example in Marina d' Escobar. This most pious lady had long begged of the Blessed Virgin to obtain from her Son some particular graces she desired for her soul. After many tears and lamentations, finally, Mary sent an angel on her part, indicating that during the spiritual exercises of St. Ignatius all favors should be granted. Hence, we easily conclude, our Lord communicates himself more abundantly during the exercises; for, those graces which he could have bestowed on Marina at any period, he, however, would not confer but in retreat. If, then, this be true, O religious soul! reflect a little on yourself; observe if your soul has grown cold in devotion— if it do not commit evil, at least it does not operate good. If from long indulgence in tepidity you know not how to advance one step in virtue, rouse yourself: now is the time to resume past fervor; if you do it not at this holy and retired period, it will be almost impossible to do it hereafter. Our Lord gives you an opportunity not only to destroy all that is vicious, but to constitute a new and more virtuous mode of life. He acts as the pious and valiant Judas Maccabeus, who having subjugated his enemies, purposed renewing and purifying the Temple of God, which had been profaned by infidels (I. *Mach.*, iv. 36.) Having gone with his soldiers to Mount Sion, where the Temple stood, he found it plundered, on fire, the altars ruined, and the doors half burnt. Having bitterly deplored these abominations with tears and the ashes of penance, he replaced the altars, restored the ruins, and having selected pious and religious priests, with solemn ceremonies the whole was sanctified by them. Now, do you also say, " Come, let us ascend to these holy exercises." " Let us purify and renew the sanctuary." Let us think seriously of reforming our manners, making our prayer with fervor, once more frequenting the sacraments, recommencing those devotions we omitted, practising more charity towards God and our neighbor. This is the fruit that can be drawn from the exercises.

THIRD POINT.

In what manner the spiritual exercises can be profitably made. The manner of drawing fruit from the spiritual exercises can be reduced. 1. To make them in earnest. 2. With recollection. 3. With tranquillity and submission to the will of God.

1. They must be performed in earnest.

Many wonder at themselves and say, they have frequently made the spiritual exercises, without reaping any of the fruit which is attributed to them. In truth, they do not speak justly; of which they have often given proof. Having performed the exercises, observing an exterior composure and retirement, they have not, in reality, penetrated the eternal truths, and endeavored to practise what they had meditated; thus, it is not surprising that they were little benefitted. He who considers a picture of St. Mary Magdalen weeping, grasping a cruel scourge, does not run either to wipe away the tears, or to remove from her that instrument of penance, for he is aware it is only a picture. Of many who make the exercises. the thirty-eighth Psalm appears to be verified. "Surely man passeth as an image." To judge from appearances, they seem to make the exercises: they are modest, devout, contrite, but neither the mind is well persuaded of the eternal truths, nor the heart well resolved to give itself to God. It is then necessary to make these exercises in earnest; therefore, every one after having heard them explained by the director, should thus discourse with himself. What I have heard, is it true or not? If it be true, why do I delay without coming to a conclusion? Having made a courageous resolution, come to the practice of what has been proposed. To this end, St. Ignatius, being enlightened by God, called these instructions, not spiritual meditations, but spiritual exercises; for it would avail little to meditate on them with tenderness and compunction, if what has been meditated on, is not practised or exercised.

2. They must be made with recollection, both with relation to God and to ourselves. As to what relates to God, it is said (*Isa.*, xxiv. 15): "Glorify the name of the Lord God of Israel in the islands of the sea." God appears to show himself more beneficent to those who, retired from the affairs of the world, seem like so many islands separated from the continent. As the Holy Ghost descended in the supping-room, the doors being shut where the apostles were in retreat; and as the manna descended on the Israelites when they were in the desert, so the divine Spirit, and the manna of celestial consolations are more abundantly communicated in the exercises, because of greater solitude. Concerning ourselves, this retreat is also very necessary; for the mind, if not entirely divested of terrestrial thoughts, cannot be disposed for those relating to the spirit. As water, in fountains not well enclosed, cannot ascend on high, so the soul when not well enclosed in solitude, cannot ascend to the contemplation of Heavenly things. "My soul, like waters, ascends aloft," says St. Gregory, *Pastor*, Bk. 3rd. To make the exercises well, we must observe the saying of St. Augustine, *Ser.* 15, *de verb. Apost.*, c. ix.—"Take thyself from thyself; remove every impediment." During this time, we should not think of friends, family, parents, or any temporal interest; not receive visits, letters, or news; but say to all temporal things what Jesus Christ said to his apostles at Gethsemane (*Matth.*, xxvi. 36): "Stay here while I go and pray." "Remain in peace without, for I must now think of my soul and eternity:" of the rest, we can speak at the conclusion of the exercises. Finally, they should be made with great tranquillity of

soul, and not admit the deceits of the Devil, who, in order to prevent the fruit of the exercises, tries by all means to disturb those who make them.

3. St. Ignatius being at Manresa, intent on these meditations, the Devil tried to annoy him with various illusions. He appeared in the air with a fantastical appearance, as a serpent shining with various colors, and very curious to behold. The saint, being aware it was the Old Serpent that was tempting him, turned it into ridicule, and beating it with a stick, sent it away (*Nolar V. S. Ign.*, c., xliii). The Devil disquiets some, inducing them to dislike solitude as insupportable. Let them reflect on the sufferings of a sick person, who is condemned by physicians to remain thirty or forty days, without taking the air. So much, however, is willingly done for the health of the body. And for the salvation of the soul, a retreat of eight days cannot be endured, even with the liberty of taking the air in a garden. Besides, there is this difference between spiritual and temporal enjoyments; the latter appear more sweet, but are full of bitterness; the former appear disagreeable and bitter, but are found full of sweetness. The Prophet says, "Taste and see how sweet God is"— (*Ps.* iii. 39.) Make a trial of applying yourself to prayer; *taste*, you will then find what interior consolation God communicates to his servants. The Devil tempts others with the appearance of a greater good, such as to settle the conscience; for this purpose he distracts them entirely from the meditations, and keeps them quite occupied with a thousand scrupulosities, thinking of the sins of their past life. Oh! what a deceit! The fruits of the exercises are not scruples, but the reformation of

manners: so that we must spend the time, first, in imprinting on our minds the eternal truths; then, in making strong resolutions with the will. As to what relates to conscience, at the end of the exercises communicate with a wise director, and obey him in all things. It is also necessary to abandon self with perfect indifference into the hands of God, being disposed to do whatever he inspires, and always to say: "Lord, what wilt thou have me do?" "Speak, Lord, for thy servant heareth."

There are some who would improve by the exercises, on condition, however, that they should always retain their attachments, or employments. Who are we, who wish to give a law to the divine disposition? How do we know what is good or hurtful to us? To have chalk or marble well wrought, it must be left to the sculptor to form according to his pleasure. In order that man may attain his eternal salvation, he should not second his own inclinations, but obey the divine will made known to him, either by interior illustrations, or explained by prudent priests, directors of souls. You who wish to enter the exercises, dispose yourselves to make use of these recommendations which are so necessary to draw fruit from them: persuade yourselves of this great truth, that, to attain salvation, you must suffer some inconvenience. "God, who created you without your consent, will not save you without your coöperation." This saying of St. Augustine is celebrated. Now that God, as it were, extends from Heaven his hand to assist us, and to draw us out of the depth of our iniquities, let us also raise our hand and cling to his beneficent right hand. "We gave a year to the body, let us give a day to the soul." These are the beautiful words of St. Peter Chrysologus. Every father of a family treats the eldest son better than the younger ones: now, the soul with regard to the body, is more than elder, it is like a mistress in comparison to a servant; it is then only right it should be treated much better than the body. At least let us treat them equally; let us bestow on the soul these entire eight days. Reflect then, O religious soul, on this saying of *Ecclesiasticus*, x., " Son, keep thy soul in meekness, and give honor according to its desert." Remember to treat your soul better and with more respect, for it deserves it. For the past, doubtless, you have bestowed more love on a dog, and preserved with greater care a crystal vase than your soul. Change then your ideas, and restore to it the honor you have taken away.

COLLOQUY.

My good God, how much hast thou done, and how much dost thou yet do, to save and sanctify my soul! What a great benefit dost thou grant me in these exercises, to remain eight days in retreat, and far from every trouble, to think on my eternity! If I do not now amend, even if I do not become a saint, who can I complain of, but solely of myself, who, by my obduracy, have rendered vain the assistance of thy grace? O my God, prostrate on the earth I thank thee for so much goodness towards a miserable person. I bless thy charity a thousand times. I exalt thy mercies, and admire the benignity with which thou sufferest my ingratitude; for when I am thoughtless of my soul, thou thinkest of it from Heaven; whilst I fly from thee thou callest me, and thou awaitest my return to penance.

3*

Ah! my God, how good thou art!—infinitely good. Now indeed I would be more than a monster of ingratitude, if I did not surrender to so many benefits. Behold me at thy feet, humbled and contrite. I ask pardon from the bottom of my heart for all the offences I have committed. Forgive, O Lord, forgive. I acted as a prodigal son: wilt thou act as a loving father, and in these holy exercises enlighten my mind, inflame my heart, defend me from temptations, and grant me the grace to perform them with fervor and fruit. In the mean time I place myself in thy divine hands, like soft wax, that thou mayest act and dispose of me according to thy greater glory and the good of my soul, repeating from my heart those words of thy servant St. Ignatius: " Receive, O Lord, my entire liberty, memory, understanding, and my whole will. All that I have and possess, thou hast given me, and to thee I restore them. Give me only thy love and thy grace, and I will be satisfied; I desire nothing more."

MEDITATION II.

On the End of Man.

INTRODUCTION.

THE Patriarch St. Ignatius has given two very significant names to this most important meditation: 1. He called it the fundamental meditation, as it is the basis of what is to be meditated on and resolved on during the exercises. He has also called it the first meditation, not only because by it a beginning is given to the other meditations; but still more, as in all sciences, natural or theological, there are certain first principles, sure maxims, from which arguments are deduced and consequences drawn of the most important doctrines: so by the knowledge of the end for which we were created by God, and for which we are in the world, consequences are to be taken for the regulation of our lives. Aristotle, *Phys.*, text, 89, says: " The end is the cause of causes; it is the rule, and as it were the helm of human actions, the centre to which turn as so many lines all the affairs and cares of the world." " The end." says St. Hilary, " is that to which all tends." In this, man differs from the brute creation; animals, in all their actions, have no end; man, if he be sensible, always acts with consideration and for an end.

This being supposed, what end had God in creating us? Why are we in the world? This is the great point on which we have now to meditate, and on which Cardinal Pallavicino (the famous author of the History of the Council of Trent) meditated for twenty-two years. In order to comprehend it well, we may suppose the doctrine of philosophers, who distinguish between the immediate and the last end. The immediate end is what is spoken of at the moment; the last end, is the last view for which we operate : thus, whoever goes to Rome to obtain a prelacy, has for immediate end to arrive at Rome, and for ultimate end the prelacy. The immediate end for which man is created, is to serve God here on Earth. This will be the first point of this meditation. 2. The ultimate end, is to enjoy God in Heaven, and be saved. This will be the second. 3. The end of all the other unreasonable creatures created by God, is to serve man. This will be the third part.

The better to understand these important truths, the following preludes are inserted.

FIRST PRELUDE.

Imagine you see God creating man, descending into the field of Damascus, taking a handful of earth, animating it with his divine breath, and forming Adam.

SECOND PRELUDE.

With a heart full of compunction say : My God, my Creator, I present myself before thy divine Majesty, with the blind man in the Gospel, and I ask of thee light. " Lord, that I may see." I have lived so long like a mole, with my eyes shut and buried under ground. I have been in the world as a blind person who walks groping along, not knowing whither he is going. Ah ! Lord, this is the grace I beg. " Lord, that I may see." Let me know once in truth—(*Job*, vi. 11). " What is my end."

FIRST POINT.

The immediate end of man is to serve God here on Earth. As God, by his sole goodness, willed to be the principle of our being, so he also wished to be the end of our labors and happiness (*Apoc.*, i. 8): "I am the beginning and the end." One hundred years ago, and for a preceding eternity, what was each of us? Nothing. Where did we remain? In nothing. The world existed a hundred years ago such as it now is; there was no want of us. How did we receive this soul, this body, this life, which we enjoy? Even our mothers, who brought us forth, did not know it. Hence said the mother of the Maccabees (II. *Mac.*, vii. 22): "I know not how you were formed in my womb; for I gave you not breath, nor soul, nor life, nor did I frame the limbs of any one of you: but the Creator of the world." That God, then, who created the world, has created us also; nor could he create us but for himself. Philosophers teach, that to draw a creature from nonentity, infinite power is necessary, and this is found in God alone. Faith not only teaches us, but reason also dictates to us, that God alone has created us; from him we acknowledge our being, and all the good we have.

If God has created us, for what end did he do so? Every intellectual agent operates from choice, and for an end; only fools act by chance or by natural instinct, like beasts. God, then, being infinite wisdom, in creating man, necessarily had an end worthy of himself. What, then, was it?

Did God, then, intend, in creating man, that he should only enjoy the pleasures of this world?

MEDITATION II.

Or, that he should advance to worldly honors—become eminent in literature—a great captain—a great sovereign? Certainly not. He could not do so for many evident reasons. First, because the end should be more noble than the means, as Aristotle teaches. II. *Phys.* The statue of a celebrated sculptor was never intended to be erected in a stable, but in a temple or gallery: the soul of man being most noble, immortal, and little less than the angels, it cannot have for its end the goods of this Earth, which are most vile. If man were created, as St. Augustine says, to eat and drink, and satisfy the senses, what difference would there be between him and the beasts? According to the doctrine of the angelical St. Thomas, the end of man is that which fully satisfies his desires.

What earthly good ever fully satisfied the desire of man? None. Who enjoyed the pleasures of the world more than Solomon? Yet he declared them all to be vanity: "Vanity of vanities." A bird being created to fly, though it find itself in a golden cage, in a royal saloon, does not experience any enjoyment until it spreads its wings in the country. So man, never being satisfied with Earthly things, cannot have for his end the enjoyment of temporal goods; if so, the Author of Nature would have given him a vain end, insufficient to satisfy his desires. What, then, is the end of man, more noble than himself; that declares him superior to the animal creation, and that satisfies the vastness of his desires? Here it is—God. First, Man has for immediate end to serve God. What more noble, surpassing all our merits and desires? Open, then, your understanding and comprehend it well, my soul; you are not created for Earth, but for

Heaven; not to serve the world, but God. From these great truths, as from the first principle of celestial doctrine, we draw many consequences. First, How great was the goodness of God towards us? We were created without any merit on our own part, through his sole love; we were loved from eternity, before we were in the world, consequently, previously to our being able to merit the divine love: " I have loved thee with an everlasting love." In creating us, we were preferred to thousands who might have been placed in the world and served God more faithfully; though it was foreseen we should be disloyal, we were, however, preferred to others of much greater merit. If a father foresaw the bad end of a wicked son, he would not wish to bring him forth to light. Yet God, notwithstanding his foresight of our ingratitude, created us, not amongst infidels, where we should have been lost, but in the bosom of the faith; not disabled, nor lame, like many, but furnished with the many prerogatives we possess. O love beyond comparison! Finally, in creating us, he enriched us with many gifts which we never could have imagined or desired. If God had said to any of us, previous to our creation: " I wish to create you in the best manner you desire, mention what you wish?" Who should have thought of answering: " Lord, I wish thee to give me a soul stamped with the image of the divinity; to have for my end to enjoy God eternally. I desire to be born in a world where the beautiful Heavens, the luminous planets, the well harmonized elements, shall be employed for me. I wish for my pleasure —seas, rivers, woods, gardens, plants, and flowers: for nourishment—birds, wild fowl, fish, and fruits:

for my treasure—gold, silver, and all kinds of precious jewels?"

Who, then, should have thought of such noble things as God has bestowed upon us? He, then, in creating us, by an excess of goodness, has enriched us infinitely more than we could have wished or imagined. What thanks, benediction, and love do we owe him? If we do not make him this return, how monstrous is our ingratitude? We are, as it were, worse than cinders are with regard to fire; they have birth in fire, and are as it were allied to it; notwithstanding, nothing resists it more than they do: fire boils vegetables, liquefies iron, burns stones; cinders alone resist it: they are not illuminated or enkindled by the flame; on the contrary they stifle and extinguish it: so it is with an ungrateful man (*Sap.*, xv. 10): "For his heart is ashes, and his hope vain Earth, and his life more base than clay, inasmuch as he knew not his Maker." He is created by God, and is like the Son of God, yet he is worse than cinders with regard to fire; he will not allow himself to be enlightened and inflamed with the love of his Creator—he rather opposes his will, and renders fruitless the designs of God in creating him.

The second consequence is, that if we belong entirely to God, we no longer belong to ourselves. The beautiful saying of St. Augustine, *Tract* 25 *in Jo.*, "We should be entirely of God and for God." St. Bernard well says, *Tract de dilect.*, "To him to whom we know we are indebted for all, we should give all our love." A tree in a garden belongs entirely to its owner: all therein contained is for his service—flowers, fruits and timber; whatever is thence taken away is a theft. The slave bought by his master belongs entirely to him, all his actions are directed to his master's service; yet neither the gardener nor the master gave a being to the tree or the slave. How much more then man, who has received his being from God, should belong entirely to him, should employ in his service all his thoughts, affections, and actions? If he give a part to the world or the Devil, he certainly commits a theft. Thus a Christian child in India, well answered a tyrant who requested his rosary, threatening to behead him if he did not take it off his neck. "How," said the child, "if the rosary appertain to God, can you wish me to give it to an enemy of God?" We should also often repeat the same. If my thoughts appertain to God, how can I give them to vanity? If my heart belongs to the Creator, how can I give it to creatures?

The third consequence is, if we do not fulfil the end of serving God, for which we were created, we are quite useless in this world. A key made for opening a door, if it do not open it, is thrown away. A tree planted to bear fruit and not fructifying, is condemned to the fire. He then, who does not employ his soul for the end of serving God, for which it was given him, keeps it in vain. "He hath taken his soul in vain."—(*Ps.*, ii. 34). According to the explanation of St. Bernard—(*Ser. in Ps.*, xxiii.) "He has lived in vain, or has not lived at all, whose life is other than that for which he received his soul." Ah! how many are there in the world, though solely and purposely created to serve God, serve creatures, serve the world, serve the Devil, but not God! "I have said, I will not serve." On the contrary, they act in such a manner, that God himself, the first cause of their operations, serves for their wickedness. (*Isa.*, xliii.)—" Thou hast made me serve you in your sins." All these merit the punishment given by Christ to the fig tree not bearing fruit: for that reason he condemned it to the axe and fire—(*Luke*, xiii. 7.) " Why cumbereth it the ground: cut it down." God could say to them—" What are you doing in the world? Go to eternal fire, and let another St. Teresa and St. Francis of Assisium come to serve me."

SECOND POINT.

The ultimate end of man is, to enjoy God in Heaven. God would have granted man a great favor, had he given him for his ultimate end, to serve him, and as a reward for his services, the incomparable honor of having served a God. It would have been a great thing for man to serve an angel, whose ultimate end is, to be a most sublime spirit, as irrational creatures have for end to serve man. Oh! how much greater has been the goodness of God towards us! He has given us for immediate end to serve him, and for ultimate end to enjoy him, and be saved: therefore, it is he alone can satisfy human desires, and having enjoyed him, there is nothing more to be desired. The angelic doctor says (12 *qu.* 2, *ar.* 8.) " It would not be an ultimate end, if after it, there was anything to be desired." The same holy doctor concludes, " that temporal things are not our end, but Christ." We have not here a lasting city, but where Christ is. " Let us go out and meet him." Not being able to enjoy God without saving ourselves, our Lord has united the interests of his glory with our salvation. Man following his last end, reunites himself with his first principle, in the precise manner that the genealogy of Christ, described by *St. Luke*, iii. 23 and 38, commences and terminates with a beautiful circle to the same God. Whence it begins. " And Jesus himself," &c., terminates " who was of Adam, who was of God." Abbot Rupert concludes, " The beginning and the end is joined, and the circle made." This end of engaging and saving oneself is most just; first, it being conformable to all laws, that the creature should be entirely turned towards the love and enjoyment of the Creator. Second, the end is most noble; man has the same end as the angels; he has the same God; in his actions, he has no other end than God and his glory. What an honor for a prince to be heir of a kingdom! A lady to be chosen for the spouse of a king! A golden chalice to be made to preserve the divine blood! How much greater honor for man to be destined for an eternal kingdom, and specially created for the enjoyment of God! Third, it is a most easy end: in order to gain it, it suffices really to wish it. To be rich or noble, it is not sufficient to will it; but to be saved, and become a saint, it is sufficient to will it with resolution. " Will it, and you do it," says St. Augustine, in *Ps.* xcii.

Finally, it is a most necessary end: for God wills that man should attain it. If he do not obtain Paradise; for which he was created, he receives in punishment eternal damnation. If water do not reach the sea, which is its end, it is not for that destroyed or consumed ; but, should man not arrive at Heaven, which is his end, he is condemned to the abyss. Thence we conclude, that man born for God, should conceive a holy ambition, and not debase his affections with terrestrial things, with desires of worldly pleasures, like a mere animal. Cleopatra and Marc Antony for amusement went to fish; the queen, while seated at a golden poop, cast the fishing-rod into the water, while dexterous swimmers immediately fastened to her rod some large fish, which she drew up with great joy; as the same did not happen to the king, he was a little annoyed, but the sly Cleopatra consoled him with adulation, saying: " Do not be angry, O sire, that the fish do not come to your rod; you are born for a much more noble end, to fish for kings and empires." Ah! man, know that you are born to enjoy the beatific vision, the King of kings, to take possession of an eternal kingdom.

In all our actions, we should have in view only to please God, and to do all for him, as the heliotrope turns towards the sun, and the needle floating in the mariner's compass always points to the pole. I do not say temporal affairs should be neglected. A person who sails in a ship, whether he eat or sleep, does not for that stop his course, but has always the helm turned to the prefixed course; thus, even in our indifferent actions, we should have in view to please God, and fulfil his holy will. " Whether you eat, or drink, or sleep, or whatever else you do, do all for the glory of God." In fine, we should always incline towards our last end, which is God, without ever allowing ourselves to be turned away by any human pleasure, like a river running to the sea. It passes through flowery meadows, and in nowise dazzled by these beauties, it passes in haste, repeating with its murmuring, " To the sea, to the sea :" it passes near the walls of strongly fortified places, and illustrious cities; nowise stopped by their magnificence, it flows on, saying, " To the sea, to the sea ;" its streams glide under beautiful arches of royal bridges, and without attending to their superb structure, it continues on to the sea. Thus is man to go to his end. If the world try to attract him with vain honors; No, he should say, these are not my end, to God, to God; if the Devil wish to deceive him with worldly pleasures; No, he should say, these are not my end, to God, to God. " I am born for a better purpose than to be the slave of my body." Seneca also said it.

How distressing is the disorder of those, who do not act for this end, being deceived by the false goods of this world. They are like the crow mentioned in Genesis, which being sent by Noah out of the ark, to trace a spot of ground already dry after the late deluge; it, however, did not do so; on the contrary, it was completely occupied in devouring dead bodies. Ah! how many are there though born to enjoy God, and to be saved, do all they can to please the Devil, and be damned.

The celebrated Sir Thomas Moore, having unexpectedly entered the cabinet where his daughter was dressing for a festival, he observed, that to have a more genteel appearance, she caused herself to be tied with a cord, the knot of which, two of her maids were by degrees endeavoring to tighten. Sir Thomas seeing this cruel martyrdom, sustained by his daughter for the vanities of the world, sighed, and turning to her, said: " Daughter, God would do you a great injury not to send you to Hell, as you labor so much to be damned." Oh! to how many in the world could this be repeated, who for interest and ambition, which conduct them to Hell, labor and suffer much more than the good do to practise Christian virtues that lead to Paradise.

THIRD POINT.

The end of other creatures is to serve man, to procure for him the means necessary to attain his end, and be saved.

As the end of man is to serve God, and be saved, so the end of all other creatures is to serve man, and to be for him so many means to attain eternal salvation. Aristotle says: "We are the end of all else." Who could believe it? Irrational creatures perfectly accomplish their obligation of serving man: the heavens, sun, moon, and planets do not cease their course: elements, plants, beasts never omit to administer to man, not only what is necessary for his livelihood, but whatever he may wish for relief or pleasure. Man, on the contrary, though gifted with reason, does not fulfil his end of serving God; but perverting the order of Divine Wisdom, in the creatures given to him as means to be saved, by an awful abuse, he employs them as means to be damned, placing his end in the enjoyment of creatures, which should only serve as means. He commits two great outrages, one to the Creator, on whom he turns his back; the other to the creatures, by obliging them to concur against their will in offending the common Creator. St. Bonaventure heard the heavens, the elements, and all in the world resenting so great a wrong, and crying out against the sinner: he then adds: Let the Earth exclaim against the sinner; why does it longer support him or suffer the weight of his sins? The waters—why do they not swallow him up? The air—why does it permit him to breathe? The stones—why do they not bury him alive? Hell—why does it not consume him? Finally, all creatures cry out he does not serve his God: we therefore are no longer obliged to serve him. Let us then open our eyes for once, and learn to make good use of creatures, as means, and in the manner most conducive to our salvation.

This is the great consequence drawn by St. Ignatius. As the pilgrim does not mind whether the road be agreeable or difficult, but solely whether it lead to the prefixed term: as the sick person does not consider whether the medicine be more or less disagreeable, so that it contribute to his cure: so in the use of creatures we should always have in view what contributes most to our salvation.

If adversity be more useful to us than prosperity, seclusion than liberty, crosses than pleasures, we should embrace them. If what is more dear to us than the pupil of the eye be an occasion of scandal, we should deprive ourselves of it. God has given us innumerable means, natural and supernatural, for our salvation. King Nebuchadnezzar, having destined the three children for the honor of remaining in his presence, provided them with a noble governor to nourish them with royal food. So God, having destined man for the great honor of being in his presence in Heaven, provided him with natural means of memory, to remember the divine benefits; understanding, to know what is good; a will, to embrace it; health, to sustain the sweet burden of the evangelical law; wealth, to enrich himself by almsgiving; nobility, to become more agreeable to the King of kings. Besides other supernatural means—the holy sacraments, spiritual books, sermons, good example, churches, oratories, priests. Even the evils of the body—sickness, disasters, persecutions—are sent for the good of the soul, to arouse it.

Besides these general means, how many special ones are provided for each individual! How many lights, inspirations, remorse of conscience, opportunities of living well! "What more, then," says our Lord, by his prophet, "could I do to my vineyard, that I have not done?" With fewer helps than God has given you, how many have become saints!

No Christian, therefore, is excusable if he be not saved. Innumerable are those who are lost. Why? Because many do not avail themselves of such means. They resemble the insects called centipedes, which, notwithstanding their numerous feet, are slow and indolent in walking; or like sea fish, which, notwithstanding their being in salt water, are still fresh. "Men are as the fish of the sea," said the prophet Habacuc (i. 14). By many pretexts and dissimulation, they disengage themselves from acting well. In the Church there are sacraments, and they do not avail themselves of them, saying: "They have not time." For prayer they have not sufficient understanding. They pretend to be poor, in order not to give alms. They have not sufficient health to do Christian penance. To exempt themselves from devout exercises, they put them off with affectation. O God! what folly!

Others take the means for the end, and the end for the means. Oh! what disorder!

Creatures are as it were a ladder whereby to ascend to the knowledge and love of the Creator. Man should tread on them, and he acts in a contrary manner: he places this ladder on his head, wishing creatures for the object of his enjoyment and the end of his desires.

What more? The body, which is vile, should serve the soul, which is mistress and the heiress of Paradise: yet wicked man makes the soul serve the body: provided the body enjoys a momentary pleasure, he does not mind the soul's being eternally injured, which is a disorder similar to that which Solomon so much deplored: "I have seen servants upon horses, and princes walking on the ground as servants."—(*Eccl.*, x.)

Finally, others make use of means given them by God, against God, turning against him his own benefits. Nobility is used to become more proud; riches, to be more dissolute; beauty, to encourage vanity; knowledge, to become more wicked; sacraments, to increase sacrileges; churches, to multiply irreverences and excesses. O monstrous ingratitude. David had reason to lament it. "They were turned as a crooked bow."—*Ps.*, lxxvii.

History shudders, relating the diabolical impiety of a person in Flanders, who murdered a soldier with the same instrument with which the soldier a short time before had given him life, by cutting down the rope from which he was hanging, when on the point of expiring. What shall be said of those who make use of the benefits of God as arms to offend him and crucify him again? When the kings of the Goths armed a nobleman, the sword was so presented as to be received by the point, to indicate that it should never be turned against the king who had bestowed it. We should learn not to convert the means given us by God for our salvation, against our ultimate end, which is God.

Let each, entering into himself, reflect on the tenor of his present life; run over in thought, all the years he has been in the world, saying, (*Isa.*, xxxviii. 15): " I will recount to thee all my years in the bitterness of my soul." O God! what a monstrous way of living has mine been? I can also weep with St. Augustine, for not living for God, who is my end. I am a prodigy of iniquity, as a fire would be in the world, not ascending, or a stone not falling. I lived by chance, as a brute. " I wandered as a sheep that is lost." I was placed in the world to serve God; and not only have I not served him, but I have served his enemy, the Devil. I was created to be saved, and I mind every other thing but my salvation. For what end have I employed so many years of life? For tiresome interest, vain honor and passing pleasure; and for these I have undergone the greatest labors and solicitude. For God, my soul, and my salvation, I wearied spending one hour. Oh! days, months, years of my life, how ill have I employed you. " Remember all the years of thy life in the bitterness of thy soul." My soul, what are you doing? When will you open your eyes to occupy better the short remnant of your life? Have courage to make the same strong resolution as St. Dositheus. He is mentioned in the *Lives of the*

Holy Fathers, as being a youth of a delicate complexion and slender figure: yet, being excited by the examples of singular sanctity given by some holy religious in a monastery, he went in haste to the abbot St. Dorotheus, and casting himself at his feet, with tears and sighs begged to be admitted as his disciple, repeating these words: " I wish to save my soul." This prudent superior, thinking that his apparent delicacy rendered him incapable of bearing the severity of observances, said: " Ah! how willingly would I comply with the fervor of your desires, but your delicacy prevents our mutual consolation. Do you know the rigor of our observances?" " It is of no consequence," said the youth, sobbing; " all is little, for I am resolved to save my soul." " Well," added Dorotheus, " but God does not wish us to commit suicide." " Whether I live or whether I die," answered Dositheus, " I will not leave your feet until I obtain my request; for I wish to save my soul." " Oh! do as you please," replied Dorotheus; " I cannot, and I should not, admit you." In saying these words, he left Dositheus, who continued to repeat; " I wish to save my soul."

As he would not quit, the porter was obliged to remove him; but the holy youth, who was left outside in the evening, was found in the same place the following day, redoubling his sobs, and crying out: " I wish to save my soul."

Finally, the holy abbot, moved with compassion, admitted him among his religious, with whom he lived five years, leading so virtuous and exemplary a life, that he died a saint.

This strong resolution, then, I ought also to adopt. This is the active fruit to be drawn from this meditation. As I am resolved, cost what it may, to be saved, I wish at any rate to attain the end for which I was created. " I wish to save my soul." I was placed in this world solely to serve God, I will no longer serve vanity, pleasure, or interest. I was created to save my soul: whether I live or die, whatever the world may say, notwithstanding my passions, I will not attend to any thing else but this most important affair. " I wish to save my soul." What a subject of confusion for me, if irrational creatures punctually follow their end, and I, on the contrary, who am gifted with reason, deviate from mine. What a shame, that one born for the enjoyment of God in Paradise, should debase himself with vile pleasure. St. Bernard cries out with reason (*Ser.*, 24 *in Cant.*): " Blush to find joy here, since thou wert made for eternal joy."

No: I shall no longer be as I have been: if for so many years I was blind, and lived like an animal, it shall not be so in the future. I will act towards God in a grateful manner, who has destined me for so noble an end : to fulfil his designs I wish to have that sense which hitherto was wanting—namely, to spend my life for that which solely is of consequence, to assure my eternal salvation—" I wish to save my soul."

COLLOQUY.

My good God, the love of my soul, here I am at thy feet, humble and contrite, to protest to thee my resolute will to be saved, with thy assistance, cost what it may, and to turn towards thee, my last end, this soul which thou hast given me as my first beginning. " I wish to save my soul."

It is but too true that I walked many years out of the right path; for I did not consider this great end which thou hast given me as a guide to conduct me to Heaven. I have wandered away too far from thee, like the prodigal son, attracted by the pleasures of the world and the suggestions of the Devil. I have not the heart to consider this soul of mine so laden with faults, for it has walked amidst the wickedness of the world, as it were in obscurity, without the light of its great end. I recognize my errors in the most lively manner: I detest them; and I wish for tears of blood, to weep bitterly over them.

Deign, my God, to be moved to compassion. Thou who art the true way to Heaven—direct my steps, regulate my life with thy assistance, and my path in the right way of salvation. I place myself in thy hands, and as one blind I will allow myself to be conducted by thee whatsover way thou pleasest; for I wish to save my soul. If thou wishest me to be in the way of crosses and sufferings, here I am. "I will follow thee whithersoever thou goest." If thou wishest to conduct me by means of prayer, fasts and alms, I am ready for all; for I really wish to be saved, and I wish, in being saved, to enjoy and to love thee, to find in thee the plenitude of my desires for all eternity.

MEDITATION III.

How much it imports man to attain his end and be saved.

INTRODUCTION.

One of the most strange follies is certainly that related of Achitophel in the Second Book of Kings. Being in despair at his designs failing against King David, he went to his house; there, with all possible attention provided his people with everything necessary, made up his accounts, and placed his domestic concerns in order; after having adjusted with the most exact diligence all the affairs of his house, children, and goods, he hanged himself to a beam. (II. *Reg.*, xvii. 23). O foolish man! he provides for all besides himself. For what is of little consequence, the greatest solicitude is bestowed; and what is of greater moment than life itself, he not only has not the slightest thought of, but he makes a torment and a slaughter of. Oh! blind, extravagant, silly person. O God! would to Heaven that similar and even greater follies were not daily seen in mankind, who, as St. Jerome says, "In little things are cautious, in great things careless." How many are provident and attentive in temporal affairs, which are of little consequence; and negligent in the affairs of the soul, which are most important? For a law-suit, interest, and domestic cares, to arrive at a post of honor, for these, indeed, labor and fatigue are employed, and esteemed well spent: on the contrary, to gain for the soul an eternal kingdom, everything appears too difficult. St.

THE AFFAIR OF SALVATION.

John Chrysostom could not refrain from saying: "To share the kingdom of the Only Begotten, would you not rush against a thousand swords; would you not cast yourself into any fire?" Let us see by the light of faith how great this error is; let us seriously meditate how important it is for man to attain his end and be saved.

I will ponder three powerful motives which shall form the three points of my meditation. It imports man, above every other affair, to be saved. 1. The interest is great. 2. The success difficult. 3. The error, without remedy.

FIRST PRELUDE.

Imagine our good angel leading us by the hand, withdrawing us from the world, and guiding us to the throne of God, saying the words which the angel uttered to Lot when he drew him from Sodom, and delivered him from burning (*Gen.*, xix. 17): "Save thy soul."

SECOND PRELUDE.

Say to God from your heart (*Ps.*, cxviii. 94): "I am thine: save me." I am the work of thy hands, made purposely by thee that I might be saved: grant that I may for once understand this great truth—that the greatest error man can fall into is, to neglect the salvation of his soul. "The worst error," says St. Eucharius, "and the grossest ignorance, is to fail in any way about salvation."

FIRST POINT.

In the great affair about salvation, the interest is the most important. Good sense requires that the greatest labor and solicitude should be employed for matters of greatest moment and consequence. Even serpents are thus prudent; when assailed, they expose every part of the body to be wounded, with the exception of the head, which they protect by every possible means.

Who can doubt that the most precious thing man has is his soul? It is spiritual, eternal, stamped with the image of God, created by God with the breath of the divinity, to denote, as Tertullian says, "as breath proceeds from the heart, thus the soul emanates from the loving heart of God." Finally, created not with a simple fiat like other creatures, but with the full council of the three Divine Persons, who said: "Let us make man," to signify, as Tertullian remarks, that the most important affair which God had in the beginning of the world was to create the soul; and the most important affair of man is to save it. It is so noble, that to save it, the Redeemer, who is Infinite Wisdom, thought thirty-three years of labor well employed, even with the shedding of all the blood of his veins. We should here reflect on the sentence of Eusebius Emissenus: "What God has done for the salvation of all mankind, he would do for each soul in particular." Each person then is as much obliged to God as all mankind together. For the salvation of souls, the holy angels-guardian, those most sublime spirits, do not disdain to be our guides and masters. What efforts do the demons make to gain them? For one soul, they would willingly give the whole world. Thus the enemy said to the Redeemer in the desert: "I will give thee all the kingdoms of the Earth if thou wilt fall down and adore me." Hence Salvian justly remarks: "Whoever does not esteem his soul in the manner it deserves, does it a great injury, as the Devil makes very much account of it." What a great affair is the salvation of the soul? How great folly it is to sell it to the Devil, not for an entire world, but worse than Adam, for a momentary pleasure? It would certainly be a great injustice to the soul if man were required to do for it as much as he does for the body; for the noble soul is the queen and heiress of Paradise, while the body is a most vile slave made of earth. Yet, would to Heaven that, to save the spiritual life of the soul we were to do half that man does to save the life of the body. If a physician tell a patient to swallow bitter medicine, he does so; to be enclosed in a heated apartment for several days, to have an arm removed, or a foot bled, he submits; but if a priest tell him, for the cure of his soul, to say a short prayer, to fast, to give alms, to make the spiritual exercises for a few days, he can do nothing of all this. It seems intolerable. O God! what injustice. To enable the body to live in delight how much is done? what time spent, and labor endured? For the immortal soul nothing is done.

Socrates relates of an aged, holy man named Bambo, that meeting a vain woman in Alexandria covered with ribbons and jewels, walking like a proud peahen amidst the acclamations of the people, he began to weep bitterly; being asked why he wept, he responded: "I weep for two reasons; because this person to please the body, is about to lose the soul; 2. I am reflecting that I do not for God and my soul the half of what she does for the world and her body."

Man not only prefers the body to the soul, but

to please the body, abuses the benefits received from the soul. Sight is derived from the soul; yet, by unchaste looks, man wounds the soul. The motion of the tongue arises from the soul; yet with blasphemies it offends the soul. Hearing comes from the soul; yet, by listening to murmuring, it transfixes the soul. O lamentable abuse! When we treat of saving the soul, we do not speak of a friend, or connexion, or father; we treat of your own soul; this most important affair entirely concerns yourself; for this reason the apostle says: "Brethren, we pray and beseech you in the Lord Jesus, that as you have received of us, how you ought to walk and to please God, so also you would walk, that you may abound the more. For you know what precepts I have given to you by the Lord Jesus. For this is the will of God, your sanctification"—(1 *Thess.*, iv.) If you acquire any other good in the world, either honors, or riches, that good is not entirely yours; the greater part will belong to your children or heirs; but if you save your soul, all the good will be your own. "If thou be wise, thou shalt be so to thyself"— (*Prov.*, ix.) Does not this excite you to apply with all your strength to so great an affair? You have great love for yourself, which is admissible, but with reason, procuring for yourself what is most useful and important. I beg of you, with tears, to have compassion on yourself. O God! to what are we reduced? To love self well, and this is not granted. Your soul is your own, and an only one. "Deliver, O God, my soul from the sword; my *only one* from the hand of the dog"—(*Ps.*, xxi.) If, by misfortune, you lose your soul, you have no other to enjoy God. The father who has an only son, sole heir of his possessions, oh! with what solicitude he guards him! What care he takes of his health if he have a slight illness? how much he makes of it? how many physicians he consults? how many remedies he administers? Why all this? He is the only one; if he lose him, his chief prop is lost, and all the hope of his succession. The soul of man is also the only one: having lost it, all is lost; with what jealousy then should it be guarded? With these sentiments Benedict XII. answered a king, who begged of him an unjust thing. "If I had two souls," said he, "I would give one for that sovereign; having but one, it is not right that I should lose it." "One thing is necessary"—(*Luc.*, x.) If the soul be lost, it cannot be acquired by giving anything in exchange. "What shall a man give in exchange for his soul?"

Alphonsus of Arragon condemned a criminal to death. His sister offered a son instead of her brother, saying, "I may have another son, but never another brother." If a man lose his soul, not only has he no other soul to save, but he has nothing to compensate for the loss of his only soul. What a subject for meditation? There is question of saving this only soul, which is eternal: its perdition will likewise be eternal. Every other evil in life is temporal; if it were even to last so long as life, it would only be an evil of a few years. To lose the soul is an evil to last for eternity.

The angelic St. Thomas observes, that a great and sensible man does not spare any expense for what can only be done once, such as nuptials, or what is to last a long time, as edifices. Who then is not aware that the consequences of salvation are eternal? With what attention therefore and solicitude should it be treated? Finally, the affair of salvation is the greatest of all affairs, as everything depends on it. Understand it well. Were you the most miserable and unfortunate being in the world, save your soul—you will have done all things. On the contrary, were you the richest and most happy person and be damned, you have lost everything. "What doth it profit a man to gain the world, if he lose his own soul?" This is the great evangelical truth, with which, in the University of Paris, St. Ignatius converted St. Francis Xavier. "What will it avail a man to gain the whole world and lose his own soul?" What does it injure Lazarus, that he spent the few short years of his mortal life in distress and disease, if he is now in joy in Heaven, in the bosom of Abraham, and happy for all eternity? What benefit was it to the glutton to have enjoyed, for a few short years, all the pleasures of the earth, if he is now, and will be for eternity, in the most profound abyss of Hell?" Dearly beloved, let us here pause and listen to the voice of God, who thus speaks: "You think only of becoming rich, honored, learned; if after obtaining your desire, you are damned, of what use will your riches be?" "What will it profit?" An ingenious Spaniard formed a design, in which he painted a ring without a precious stone, then he added, the motto, "the best is wanting." Know, then, that were you in the possession of all the goods of the earth, and lose your soul, the best is wanting, and all is lost. Is it not madness to lose all, for a light and momentary pleasure of the body?

It is related that a certain rich man, on his death-bed, left in his will, his immeasurable riches to him who, in the opinion of wise men, was considered the greatest fool in the world. After his death, several in the city pretended to the great inheritance; but, as the testator named the greatest fool in the world, not in the city, the executors searched in various countries. Having arrived at a city in India, they saw in the midst of a great crowd, a miserable man loaded with chains, whom they were conducting to an elevated scaffold, to be there tormented with excessive torture, and finally executed. They inquired who he was: being answered he was the king. "What! the king," said they, astounded. "Know," added the citizens, " this is our custom, to elect annually a new king; he only is chosen who is contented to reign but one year, with the express contract of being afterwards tormented and executed in the manner you are now going to witness." The astonishment of the strangers increasing, they added : " Is it possible any one should be found, who, for one year's reign, chooses so horrible torments and death? If such a person exist, who can deny that this is the greatest fool in the world? Oh! then, let all the rich inheritance be given to him." However doubtful this statement may be, it is certain, that whoever does not care about losing his soul, with an eternal death, amidst eternal torments, for the enjoyment, not of one year's reign, but of brief worldly pleasures, is certainly the greatest fool the sun ever saw. What do you say, my soul? What do you resolve? Is it possible that the light of so clear a truth should not recal the senses.

SECOND POINT.

The success is most difficult. The affair of salvation is of so great importance that, even were the success most easy, we should, nevertheless, live in the greatest apprehension and solicitude, even from the remote peril of not gaining what is of greatest consequence. Suppose several thousand persons assembled in an extensive place. An angel from Heaven descends and exclaims: " In one hour, one here is to die suddenly;" would not every heart beat at this intelligence, saying within himself: " It is true, amidst so many, it would be severe that I should be the unfortunate person; but, as I may be the individual, that suffices to perplex me?" How much greater then must be the apprehension and fear of a Christian, reflecting that it is most difficult to be saved; so much so, that it is not one only that is lost amongst so many, but many are lost, and few are saved. " Many are called, but few are chosen."

Father Anthony Baldinucci, a celebrated missioner of the Society of Jesus, was preaching in one of his missions, in the diocess of Veletri, to an immense audience, collected in an extensive field, surrounded with high trees, which, with luxuriant foliage and extensive branches, obscured the rays of the sun. It was in the month of April. Suddenly, the preacher stopped, profound silence prevailed; the father, in an ecstacy, remained immovable, with his eyes raised to Heaven, and his arms extended. At this view, the astounded multitude could not imagine what had happened to the holy preacher, who, after some time, returned to himself, exclaiming, in a strong and awful

THE AFFAIR OF SALVATION.

voice: "My people, think well of salvation, for a great many are damned. God recently opened the eyes of my mind, and I saw souls fall into Hell, in as great numbers as the dry leaves fall from the trees in winter." The people being horrified at this recital, sobbed aloud; still greater was their dismay when they saw all the leaves fall from the trees under which they reposed, as if to prove the truth of what the servant of God preached. Ah! how difficult it is to be saved! How difficult! Blind worldlings cannot persuade themselves of it, yet it is the truth. This great difficulty of salvation proceeds from different causes.

The salvation of man depends on two wills; namely, on the will of God, who assists by his grace, and on the will of man, corresponding to the grace of God. As to the will of God, no one can doubt that we always have sufficient help to be saved. "God wishes all men to be saved." When man has rejected many graces and calls from God, "it is uncertain," says St. Bernard, "that God will afterwards renew strong and powerful assistance." We have always reason to fear our will, being inconstant, indocile, inclined to evil, and easily dazzled with worldly pleasures; thus it is easy to observe the risk to be encountered in the affair of salvation.

The second reason is, because a place is held with difficulty, if it have enemies within and without: within, rebellious and tumultuous citizens; without, a powerful army that oppresses and combats it. Man has within and without him very strong enemies, that seek with all their strength to prevent his eternal salvation. Within, he has the tumult of passions, the strength of bad habits, which draw him to evil, bad inclinations, and irregular appetites. He is besieged from without by invisible enemies, the demons, who with continual temptations and a thousand stratagems surround him. His visible enemies are, so many scandalous companions, so many perilous occasions, which frequently shake the virtue of the most constant. See the difficulty of salvation, surrounded as we are by such terrible besiegers.

Finally, the third reason is, that the happy or unhappy termination of our salvation depends on the one sole moment of death, which occurs but once. " O moment on which eternity depends." At that extreme moment, man has to pass from time to eternity; if this be not happy, he falls without retrieve down the eternal precipice. Oh! what alarm! what dismay! A soldier is condemned with other accomplices to play at dice under a scaffold, with this condition, that if he fail, he shall be hanged. O God! with what fear does he shake the dice in his hand; with what fear does he throw them on the table, reflecting that his life or death depends on a moment? Should we not be horrified and agonized, thinking that eternal life or eternal death depends on the one last moment. This great thought caused the primitive saints of the Church to tremble. St. Mary Magdalen de Pazzi died as she had lived, a saint: she had so joyful a countenance, so peaceable a soul, exhaling so many sweet affections to her celestial spouse, that she occasioned a holy emulation in the witnesses of her death. Suddenly she became sad, her countenance became pale, and turning to her confessor, with a trembling voice

THE AFFAIR OF SALVATION. 61

she said: "Father, father, do you think I shall be saved?" The confessor dismayed at this question, answered: "Oh, how can you doubt of it, after having led so innocent and penitential a life? How can you doubt that God, who enriched you with so many special favors in life, should fail to conduct you to the eternal joys of Heaven?" "All that is true," answered the saint, trembling and weeping, "all that is true, however I am not secure. What do you think then—shall I be saved?" Ah! where are certain worldlings, who enjoying delights, and following their caprice solely, reciting carelessly a few times the "Our Father," and practising a few small acts of devotion, if they think by these means to take possession of Paradise? Ah! how much they deceive themselves: if they wish to purchase Heaven at so vile a price, certainly God will not sell it at so cheap a rate. On the contrary, he has declared, that to be saved is so difficult an affair, that it resembles a hidden treasure. The kingdom of Heaven is like to a treasure hidden in a field. It is as laborious as to draw a net to the shore, and as hazardous as to conquer a kingdom by force of arms. The kingdom of Heaven suffers violence, and none but the violent bear it away.

The simple lay brother, blessed Giles, of the Seraphic Order, by means of acute irony strongly admonished two prelates who lived too much at their ease. Having gone to visit him, they earnestly begged of him to pray to God for them, to which request Giles answered: "What do you want with my poor prayers, since you can pray so much better for yourselves. You have much more faith and hope than I have, the very virtues for successful prayer." "How is it possible," they replied, "that such virtues should be more eminent in us, than in you, who are a religious?" Giles continued, "do you not believe and hope to be saved?" "Certainly," they responded. "Then," added the saint, "you have more faith and confidence than I have, since you, having riches, honors, and pleasures, certainly believe and hope you shall obtain the eternal enjoyments of Paradise; and I, on the contrary, from many sufferings, much poverty and want, strongly doubt and fear that I shall pass to the eternal torments of Hell." With this great lesson he dismissed them, rendering them more careful and timid in the great affair of eternal salvation. My soul, here enter into yourself, and seriously reflect what is to become of your salvation, if you continue the life you now lead?

If to be saved is so difficult to the just, who live remote from dangerous occasions, entirely occupied with God, what will become of those who lead the lives of epicureans, only thinking of satisfying their senses and caprices, who do not take one step for God and for eternity? You may say, that the good thief was saved, though a great sinner. I answer, this was a miracle of the mercy of God.

Do you wish to found the hope of your salvation on a miracle?

Two persons dying at the side of Jesus Christ crucified, while he was dying for them, on that great day of man's redemption, on which was offered to the Eternal Father the sacrifice of his expiring Son, who would not think that each of them was to be saved—that one hundred thousand persons should have been saved, if so many had been in such fortunate circumstances? Oh! what extreme fear should it occasion? Of those two robbers, one alone was saved, the other eternally damned. God willed the salvation of one, that no one should despair: he permitted the loss of the other, that no one should presume. God did not give many examples of the wicked repenting and being saved. They wish to enjoy Paradise on Earth and in Heaven, but "the desires of the wicked shall perish." A plan so agreeable to them cannot succeed.

THIRD POINT.

The error is without remedy. We could forgive negligence in the arduous affair of salvation, if having once failed, the fault could be corrected. This is precisely what is worst and most painful in the affairs of the soul. The same maxim is held as in the experiments of war: we cannot err twice. The first loss is irreparable. If a man let his foot slip into the abyss, he cannot return; he must remain there forever. If a law suit be lost, it can be ameliorated by appealing to a superior tribunal. If riches be lost, they can be regained by new commerce. If health be lost, it can be restored by remedies. But if the soul be lost, the loss is eternal, irreparable, both with regard to God and man. With regard to God, for the decree made by him, of the damnation of that soul, is eternal and irrevocable. God wills that the fruit of the redemption should benefit the living, who are travellers on Earth, not the dead, who are at the termination of their course; so that it is said: "Out of Hell there is no redemption."

On the part of the man, the loss of the soul is

irreparable: during life, man can merit or demerit. but being dead in the disgrace of God, " Time shall be no more." He will suffer in Hell, but he will not satisfy for his misdeeds. Theologians say, that in Hell there is no satisfaction. Oh! what a great point is this. It should horrify us more than it did the seraphic Teresa of Mount Carmel, who being once seen weeping bitterly, and being asked the reason, replied : " I weep for these three great causes, which like most acute thorns transpierce my mind; namely, one God, one death, and one soul. One God, who being displeased, we have no other to whom we can have recourse. One death, which being once ill made, cannot be repeated. One soul, which being once lost, cannot be regained. One God, one death, and one soul! why should you be surprised that I weep?"

If in the loss of the soul, we could only give to God an equivalent compensation for its ransom; but, O God! what can a man give in exchange for his soul? Hear, O great God of terrible majesty, hear. This soul is damned for refusing to manifest in confession its hideous disorders: now the soul is ready to declare them in a public church, to publish them with the sound of trumpet, and to expose them to the whole world. " No," answers God, " it is no longer time." " Time shall be no more." Lord, this soul is damned for usury, now it offers to give all its possessions to the poor. It is damned for indulging too much in the pleasures of the body; now it offers itself to a continual immolation until the day of judgment. " No, no," answers the Lord, " it is no longer time." To repurchase this lost soul, the price of the whole world would not suffice, or the martyrdom of all mankind. What will a man give in exchange for his soul? Oh! what terror, what alarm! King Darius, in his last campaign and battle with the great Macedonian, was not only defeated, but the queen, his consort, was made prisoner. Darius, desirous to spend for her ransom as much gold as should be required, was answered by Alexander, that there was not in the world as much gold as would suffice—that there was no other way of ransoming the queen, but by the king's becoming prisoner in her stead.

The soul of man was queen and heiress of Paradise. When it was lost by the sin of Adam, it was necessary to redeem it, that the King of Heaven, not only should be girded with cords, but fastened to a cross. St. Bernardine said: "For thee, my soul, God himself was seized and bound; to give thee life he was condemned to death." If to redeem a lost soul, the infinite price was required of all the blood of a crucified God, how is it possible that a miserable man can ransom his soul, though he should shed torrents of tears, or surrender his life with the martyrs? What exchange can a man give for his soul? The loss of the soul is an error, which, considered in any light, is irreparable. If, then, the affair of salvation be so important, is it not a duty to apply our thoughts to it with the greatest solicitude? We should suffer for it every inconvenience, even the agonies of death. "Strive for justice for thy soul; and even unto death fight for justice." (*Eccles.*, iv.) Do we wait to have hereafter an eternal and useless repentance; since the evil committed will be without remedy?

Oh! if the many wicked wretches, already dead, could raise themselves from their tombs, what would they say? They would utter with many sighs, "We have wandered from the way of truth." Miserable creatures that we are, who mistook the road which led to our own end. "We have wandered." We minded nothing but the affairs of the world—we thought we did everything in making ourselves rich and great; now, we find that we have done nothing since we have not attained salvation. "We have wandered." How many are there, who cry in despair in Hell. "We fools esteemed their life vain, and their end without honor." Oh! foolish and blind that we were. Who are they that are called foolish? Who could believe it? A Demosthenes, an Aristotle, many politicians, who were oracles at court; many persons, who, by a miracle of economy, multiplied their rents by the hundred, elevated their families, and left their sons heirs of estates: these are all foolish creatures. "Yes," they respond, "we were foolish for knowing everything else; we were ignorant of what was most important, namely, to save ourselves. The truly wise were those whom we esteemed ignorant—those simple females, those devout beggars, those rustic monks, who, knowing nothing of economy or politics, knew, however, how to gain Heaven."

I conclude, beloved, beseeching you with tears, as St. Nilus besought the emperor Otho III., who, as Baronius relates, excited by the fame of the great sanctity in which St. Nilus lived, went to visit him in his poor hermitage: after venerating him as a saint, and imploring the assistance of his prayers, he showed him numerous costly gifts, but the humble servant of God refused each of them. Otho, anxiously requested that Nilus would ask some favor best suited for himself or others. St. Nilus answered, "Oh! yes, willingly, and when your majesty deigns to grant my petition, I shall be obliged to you during life." "Ask, then," said the emperor, "whatever you please, for I promise not to deny your request." The saint then, extending his hand with holy intrepidity, several times shook the purple which Otho had on his chest, saying, "Sire, the favor which I ardently beg of you is this: save your soul, save your soul." This favor I also beg of you, beloved, save your soul. Reflect deeply that this is the most important affair that you have in this world. Fix well in your mind this great maxim: "He obtains all, who, losing everything else, is saved; he loses all, who, gaining everything else, is lost.

COLLOQUY.

"Most sweet Redeemer;" "God of Mercies," our last end, first author of salvation (*Ps.*, lxvii. 21); as the Psalmist entitled thee; "God of salvation," as St. Jerome called thee. bathed in tears, we have recourse to thee, not to ask of thee temporal graces for the body, but solely to beg for the eternal salvation of our souls. These were created by thee for Heaven. and in order to save them thou hast shed all the blood of thy veins. Do not permit it to be lost through our wickedness. Thou seest well how dangerous the world is in which we live. It is a sea full of tempests and shipwrecks, of many temptations and many perilous occasions. Each of us is, as it were, a frail vessel which cannot withstand so many risks of being lost. Hence we have recourse to thee, and we cry out with the holy apostles: "Lord, save us, or we perish." Guide us with thy grace, strengthen us with thy help, and making use of thy infinite mercy say to us: "It is I; fear not." We cannot have hope in our own merits. We have it entirely in thy infinite goodness, and in the most precious blood thou didst shed for us;

> "Thou didst Mary's guilt forgive,
> Didst the dying thief receive;
> Hence hope within me live."—*Dies Iræ.*

The happy success of our death is in thy hands, on which our eternity depends. Be moved, O good God, with mercy towards us; grant us, through thy sole goodness, that last final grace, which we cannot merit on any account.

> "King of dreadful Majesty,
> Who dost freely justify,
> Fount of Pity, save thou me."—*Dies Iræ.*

And thus saved, we shall eternally sing in Heaven, and exalt the excess of thy infinite mercy. "I will sing the mercies of the Lord forever." Amen.

MEDITATION IV.

On the Punishment of Sin.

INTRODUCTION.

A TERRIBLE and exemplary chastisement of sin was inflicted by God, in the Old Testament, as read in the Book of *Numbers*, xxv. 4. The Almighty, intending to punish and to astound the people of Israel for their idolatry, that they might not relapse into the same perfidy, commanded Moses to erect a number of gibbets opposite the sun, that on them the princes and most distinguished personages of Israel should die, as so many trophies of his justice, and memorable instances of his anger, to curb all sacrilegious wickedness, not only in those present, but in their posterity.

Oh! how much more terrible is the catastrophe we have now to meditate upon. It was executed by God himself, not only to punish those who prevaricated, but to frighten mankind, that they should not transgress by mortal sin, which alone impedes the acquisition of God, our last end.

God then, *himself*, not by means of other ministers, most severely punished in Heaven, Lucifer, the first of all the angels; in the terrestrial Paradise, Adam, the first of all mankind; and on Calvary, the first of all the faithful, the Redeemer, for sins not his own. May it please God, that we also may conceive a just and necessary fear, at so terrible a consideration.

The Redeemer made use of this means to curb

pride and vanity in the minds of the apostles, who once came to him in great joy, saying: "The devils also are subject to us." Lest they should entertain vain complacency, our Lord reminded them of the fall of proud Lucifer; "I saw Satan, like lightning, falling from Heaven"—(*Luc.* x.) If, then, God made use of this thought for the benefit of his apostles, let us also avail ourselves of it for the good of our souls, and, in three points, meditate on three horrible theatres of divine justice, namely, in Heaven, in the terrestrial Paradise, and on Calvary. From Heaven, God expelled Lucifer, for *one sole sin of thought*. In the terrestrial Paradise, God condemned Adam and Eve to atrocious pains, *for one sole sin of deed.* On Calvary, the Redeemer died on a cross for the sins of the world, *in thought, word, and deed.*

FIRST PRELUDE.

Imagine you see God irritated, seated on a cloud, with a grasp of thunder-bolts in his hand, chasing away Lucifer and his followers, and precipitating them into the abyss.

SECOND PRELUDE.

Great God of terrible majesty, deign to transfix my obdurate heart with thy holy fear; if thy benefits cannot excite me to serve thee well, at least, may thy chastisements do so.

Ah! my good God, give me light to know well how terribly thou dealest with sinners, and to learn at the expense of others, how to shun thy anger.

PUNISHMENT OF SIN.

FIRST POINT.

The chastisement inflicted by God in Heaven on Lucifer, the first of all the angels, for one sole sin of thought.

The first and most beautiful works that issued from the hand of Divine Omnipotence, were the angels of Heaven; most sublime spirits, the least of whom exceeds in perfection the greatest of all men. Amongst those angels the first place was held by Lucifer, thus called from the brightness of his singular prerogatives, for which his name is given to that bright star, which always precedes the rising sun, and follows its setting. He was in so high a place in Heaven, that many doctors assert he was more elevated than St. Michael the archangel. Under the figure of the king of Tyre, that eulogium was made in *Ezechiel*, xxviii. 12. " Thou wast the seal of resemblance, full of wisdom, and perfect in beauty: thou wast in the pleasures of the Paradise of God, every precious stone was thy covering." As Lucifer was the first to be enriched with the greatest gifts of God, so he was the first in the greatest ingratitude and impious felony. God could have said to him, what Jacob said to Reuben, after his sin: " Reuben, my first born, thou art my strength, and the beginning of my sorrow, excelling in gifts, greater in command" —(*Gen.*, xlix.) God kept the angels, after their creation, in the state of probation a short space of time—some theologians say, for quarter of an hour. Lucifer, abusing his free will, foolishly dared to rebel against his sovereign, and sin grievously against his great benefactor. What sin did he commit? The sin was only of thought. St. Bonaventure believes it to have been of vain complacency, seeing himself adorned with so many sublime gifts. It appears that God explains himself in *Ezechiel*, xxxiii.: "Thou hast sinned, and thy heart was lifted up with thy beauty; thou hast lost wisdom in thy beauty. I cast thee out from the mountain of God; therefore, I will bring forth a fire from the midst of thee, to devour thee." Scotus believes it to be a vain pretension—pretending to attain the beatific vision with the strength of nature, without the assistance of grace. St. Thomas says, it was an aversion from God, through pride; he was ambitious to be on a level with him, saying: "I will be like the Most High." However this may be, no sooner had the miserable creature sinned, no sooner had he consented to his proud thought, than God changed his first love into wrath: "Ah! unhappy wretch," said he, "away from my sight, go to the abyss, I do not wish to behold you any longer."

1. God punishes him suddenly, without granting him any indulgence, without giving him any time to reflect or do penance for his sin.

The Devil once said, by means of a possessed person, that if God would give him a little time to repent, he would wish to do more than all mankind; but this time God has not granted him, and never will.

2. God punishes him himself, notwithstanding the war made with Lucifer by St. Michael, when a great battle was fought in Heaven. God himself wishes to show Paradise how he can act, armed with thunderbolts against those who rebel. The Prophet David astounded, exclaims: "O great

God, how terrible thou art? How heavy is thy avenging hand?"

God punishes in the weightiest manner, without heeding that he was his first work; without having any regard to the nobility of his being; not minding that this was the first fault, and consequently, more worthy of his clemency: he removes the supernatural gifts he had bestowed on him, he degrades him from his dignity, changes him into an ugly dragon: he precipitates him from the height of Heaven into the abyss, where he condemns him to eternal torments. What more? He punishes with him all his followers, who were no fewer than the third part of the angels. Even though thereby Paradise be depopulated, sin shall not remain unpunished. In this world, where the guilty are numerous, as in rebellions, the chiefs alone are chastised; or one out of every ten, as Suetonius mentions, was the custom of the Roman militia. God did not act thus with the angels; he willed them *all* to be lost, in eternal pains. O God! what terrors, what thunderbolts are these of an Infinite Justice! Let us then, beloved, reflect on this fact, which is of faith. Was it injustice in God, thus to punish Lucifer; or, did he act with too great rigor? "Shame," answer theologians, "these are blasphemies! On the contrary, God chastised him less than he deserved." Perhaps God condemned him to those pains from some sudden movement of passion; as it sometimes happens in this world, that a judge being in bad humor, or being prejudiced by some sinister apprehension, is precipitate in awarding an unjust sentence? No, this is also blasphemy; for God is not subject, as we are, to passion: whatever he does is with serenity and prudence. If God, judging the sin of Lucifer with all calmness and justice, esteemed it worthy of so great a penalty, how great an evil must sin be. Who is deceived in this, God or man? God, to consider it a great evil, or man to hold it for nothing? Ah! miserable that we are, the mistake is ours, for certainly God cannot be deceived.

3. How many balances has the divine justice in Heaven? Has he two—one to weigh the sin of the angels, and another to balance the sins of mankind? Oh! no, answers the pontiff St. Sixtus, the same God is judge of angels and of men: the same scales serve for the one and for the other. If it be so, says St. Bernard, judge now yourselves. *Sermon in Advent.* If God has punished with so much rigor the most sublime spirit of Paradise, will he forgive you, who are but a handful of earth? Will he pardon you, who are so much more guilty than Lucifer? He sinned but once; you one thousand times a thousand. He sinned only by thought; you by works and words. "He," reflects St. Anselm, "offended God only as his Creator; you offended him as Creator and Redeemer." He, in sinning, pretended to become like to God, but he did not contemn him; you, in sinning, despised him, postponing him to creatures. By chastising the angels, Heaven was almost made empty, and God did not heed it. If you are damned, Paradise will lose little or nothing. Will God act towards you, vile worm of the Earth, with a regard which he had not for the first princes of Heaven? Imagine you see a great king seated at table, who asks for a drink; instantly a massive golden cup is presented to him, filled with the best

wine. Before partaking of it, the king views the wine; seeing a small fly in it, he sickens, disdains it, and in a rage, throws the wine and golden cup out of the window. Shortly after he again asks for a drink, and an earthen vase, filled with miry water, is presented to him. What now will the king do? If with so much fury he threw out the golden cup, because a small fly was in it, what will he now do with the earthen vase?

The angels of Heaven were as golden vessels, on account of their nobility and charity. Because God saw in them an atom only of sin of thought, he cast them into the abyss. Men are as "vases of soiled clay," filled with the filth of a thousand sins: what then will God do with them? This great thought caused St. Gregory to shed torrents of tears, when he said, *De malis Ang.* "They were cast from Heaven that man might learn to fear; for what shall be done with the brazen vessel if the golden be broken by a scent of pride?"

Let us reflect that the sin of Lucifer, which caused him to suffer so many pains, was his *first* and *only* sin, and was *only of thought*. Ah! where are those who make so little account of sins of thought, and scarcely make any examination of them, and hardly ever confess them? Ah! where are those who, abusing divine goodness, say by word, or in heart: What great thing is it for once, and not more, to give way to passion? For once only, God will forgive. Ah! wretch, God did not forgive the sin of Lucifer, though only of thought, and will he easily forgive your first fault? Oh! how many sinners have been deceived by this vain hope! It is true God has acted so with many, but not with all. How great folly then is it to risk the great peril of being suddenly damned, by committing the first fault, which has happened not only to Lucifer, but to a thousand others. Witness the painful fact related by Father Engelgrave of a young student who was found in the morning suddenly dead in bed, having been stifled by vomiting blood. His afflicted parents immediately informed his confessor, one of the fathers of the Society of Jesus, who, having shown sentiments of great grief, began to console himself and others, saying: " Blessed is he ! he will certainly be saved, for I knew his conscience perfectly, also his piety, and I can attest he was an angel. However, I wish to offer immediate suffrage for him by celebrating." Having proceeded to the sacristry, and being vested, as he was going into the church he felt himself dragged back by his sacred vestments. He turned, and not seeing any one, he concluded he was mistaken, and turned to enter the sanctuary, but was again retained. Being astonished, he knew not how to proceed; when behold, a black hand appears in the air, and impetuously snaps the chalice from him. Raising his eyes he saw in the midst of flames the unfortunate youth, who having uttered a most horrible cry: " Ah! father," said he, " do not celebrate for me, for by the just judgment of God I am damned." The poor father was near dying with horror. " What!" said he, " were you not good and innocent? Or did you conceal from me in confession some grievous sin?" " No, no, father," answered the youth; " I was always good and innocent, as you knew me to be; I never concealed any sin in confession; yet learn precisely what occurred. Last night before I went to sleep

I was assailed by a violent temptation: I strongly resisted it by fervent protestations. A short time afterwards I was again more strongly attacked, and I overcame by recurring to the assistance of the Blessed Virgin and the saints. Finally, the third time the temptation was so strong, that I fell and consented for once only to commit sin. Shortly after, by the just judgment of God, being afflicted with a violent suffocation of blood, I miserably lost both the life of the body and that of the soul." After this speech he disappeared, leaving the father half dead with terror.

We should observe, that although the sin of Lucifer appears less grievous, being only in thought, yet, considering its quality and circumstances, it is worthy of the greatest punishment.

1. Being a sin of pride, sovereignly hated by God, and, as St. Thomas teaches, "the greatest of all sins;" for in all other sins man swerves from God either through ignorance or weakness, or allured by some good; but pride directly opposes God.

2. The sin was committed by a spirit most noble and most gifted by God; his ingratitude was therefore strangely magnified.

3. He sinned in so holy a place as Paradise, so he merited this pain. "In the land of the saints he worked iniquity, and he shall not see the glory of God"—(*Isa.*, xxvi. 10.)

4. It was a sin of scandal which caused the third part of the angels to prevaricate. "And his tail drew the third part of the stars of heaven"—(*Apoc.*, xii.) We should hence learn to conceive a holy fear of God, a sovereign horror of sin, particularly of pride. We should imagine our Lord

addresses us, as recorded in chapter xiii. of *St. Luke*, where having expressed to the multitude the rigor of divine justice, represented by the town of Siloe, which in its ruins destroyed eighteen persons, he added: " Unless you do penance, you shall all likewise perish."

Lucifer, like a tall edifice, by his fall caused the ruin of innumerable angels. Let us then learn not to fall into his sin, if we would not fall under the same ruins. " Let the destruction of the greater be a caution to the less," says St. Gregory (4 *in lib. Reg.* c. ii.) Ah! my God, deign to enlighten us. " The way of the wicked is darksome; they know not where they fall"—(*Prov.*, iv.) Replenish us with thy holy fear, strengthen us with thy holy grace, and grant that Hell may be only for the rebellious angels for whom thou didst create it. " Depart from me, ye cursed, into everlasting fire, prepared for the devil and his angels"— (*Matt.*, xxv. 41.)

SECOND POINT.

Chastisement inflicted by God on Adam, the first of all mankind, for one only sin of deed. Some may say in their hearts: It is true God has severely punished the angels in Heaven; but he will not act thus with men. Who is not aware of his having a particular affection for all mankind, even so far as to say: " My delight is to be with the children of men!" Ah! his loving predilection for man will not allow him to act thus with them! Let us now see how God has acted in chastising the sins of men, and especially of the first man, Adam, whom God created in the terrestrial Paradise, and gifted, as St. Thomas says, with wisdom, grace, and original justice. God created him universal monarch of the whole world, with a happiness never enjoyed by any other; for of all other sovereigns some were masters of this or that kingdom, but no more. Adam alone was master of the whole world, which at that period was infinitely happier and more beautiful than now. Then the Heavens were without thunderbolts; beasts without claws; plants without poison; and all creatures, even irrational, punctually obeyed Adam, insomuch that lions and tigers served him like spaniels. "He was ruler of the fishes of the sea, the birds of the air, and the beasts of the earth." He had no burden imposed on him by God, but one alone, very light—not to eat of the forbidden tree, under pain of being immediately condemned to death. Who then could have imagined but that Adam would have been most faithful to God, through justice to the King of kings, to whom he owed this slight tribute; through gratitude to him by whom he had been benefited, the command being so easy: yet it was otherwise. The Devil, under the form of a serpent, seduced Eve, then Adam: so that they both ate of the forbidden apple, and sinned grievously against God; as Salvian says, on the eighth day after the creation of Adam.

Let us meditate at leisure what was the sin of Adam: let us weigh its grievousness by the standard of moral theology. There is no doubt of its being a mortal sin, a grievous transgression of the divine commandments; yet among mortal sins, it is of much less weight than others.

1. As to the number, it was only one.
2. As to the matter, it was light; namely, one

apple; the subject was not intrinsically bad, but became so by being prohibited.

3. As to the period, it was before the incarnation and death of our Redeemer, consequently it had not the peculiar malice which our sins have, by being injurious to the blood of Christ.

4. St. Thomas reflects that Adam sinned without any experience of the divine rigor; he may have thought that his sin could easily obtain pardon.

5. St. Thomas notes that he sinned, not to outrage God, but to please Eve, whose sweet entreaties he would not resist.

Notwithstanding these considerations, which appear to lessen the grievousness of the sin of Adam, observe what was his chastisement. Scarcely had the miserable creature taken the forbidden apple, than immediately God in wrath came to the terrestrial Paradise to punish him. He did not avail himself of the cherub armed with fire, who was at the gate of Paradise, nor did he make use of any other celestial spirit; but he himself, the great God, with a voice of thunder exclaimed: "Adam, Adam, where art thou?" Adam in dismay takes to flight, and seeks refuge in a wood; but whither can he fly? Where hide himself from the anger of God, who coming before him, reproaches him with his crime; despoils him of all the gifts with which he had adorned him; degrades him from the empire of the universe; chases him and Eve from Paradise; curses the ground which sustains him, that in future it should produce thorns and briars; condemns him to death with all his descendants, and sentences him to labor in the sweat of his brow. God, not satisfied with punishing Adam so rigorously in his own person, extends the penalty of his sin to all his posterity.

The children of a father condemned for high treason cannot claim ancient dignities and dominions: thus Adam having been convicted of high treason, God willed that all his descendants should be despoiled of their original innocence, and condemned to the innumerable calamities, under which the world at present groans. "Adam left to his posterity only the inheritance of death"—*St. Zeno.* Cast a glance over the universe; considering its many evils and say with astonishment: All these are the effects of the sin of Adam and the fruits of his murderous apple.

A German prince wishing to dissuade an only son, whom he tenderly loved, from the determined resolution of going to war, after uselessly entreating him, with promises and reasons, finally, as a last resource, caused a battle scene to be painted. This large picture he suspended in his ante-chamber, with this motto: "The fruits of war." As soon as the youth beheld it, being horrified at the bloody massacres represented so plainly and sadly, he laid aside every military idea.

Consider the many hospitals. What mean so many spasms, ulcers, and agonies? Nothing else but the fruit of the sin of Adam. "The fruits of sin." Consider the gallies where so many miserable creatures are loaded with chains, treated like dogs, beaten, fed with biscuit and putrid water; and ask why so many disasters? "The fruits of sin." Consider the many law suits at tribunals, variances at courts, so many tears in domestic houses, famines, plagues, earthquakes, thunderbolts, conflagrations, desolations; and ask why all these? "The fruits of sin." O sin, accursed sin! how murderous you are! Reflect that Adam, driven out of the terrestrial Paradise, lived nine hundred years, always weeping and doing penance for his sin; which not sufficing to satisfy divine justice, the Divine Word became man, and died on the cross. After Adam had done nine hundred years of penance, after the blood and death of a God for sin, the penalty due to it still continues in the world. O God! what terror is this! O sin! O sin! My soul, enter into thyself, and bitterly deplore thy faults, far greater than the sin of Adam.

If a person were to take a small bottle of poisonous liquor, saying that he would poison the ocean by casting into it only two drops of that liquid, what would you exclaim? "Oh! what strong poison that must be." How much greater then must be that of mortal sin, since one alone, and not the most grievous, suffices to embitter the sea of the infinite mercy of God! If Adam deserved so many penalties for one sin, how many await you for your numerous and enormous sins? You may say that you sinned, not heeding the rigors of divine justice, not to outrage God, but not to displease the world. If these excuses did not exculpate Adam, who was the first and most noble of mankind, will they excuse you who have much less merit?

Finally, Adam sinned but once, and he did not persist in his sin: you, on the contrary, hardened and stubborn in malice, committed habitual faults, and almost considered it a necessity to sin. How much greater and more worthy of chastisement was your malice? The angelic doctor proposes this question: At the day of judgment, as the whole world is to be purged from sin by fire, is the terrestrial Paradise likewise to be cleansed from the sin of Adam, and Heaven from the sin of Lucifer? The holy doctor answers in the negative; for Adam being chased away immediately from the terrestrial Paradise, and Lucifer from Heaven, those holy places were not contaminated by their sins. On the contrary, as men for a long space of time have infected the Earth by their wickedness, it will be necessary to purge it with the fire of the last judgment. My soul, if you for so many years have been laden and infected with so many irregularities, how much more than Adam do you deserve to be purged by God with the fire of greatest chastisement?

Finally, though the sin of Adam, compared with some others, appears less, yet considered in its circumstances it is most grievous, and worthy of every punishment.

1. Because it was committed by the most noble man, and the most favored by God, so that his ingratitude was the greatest. St. Augustine says: "God did not give the angels time or grace after their sin to obtain pardon, as he afterwards did to Adam." Many of the people of Israel committed sin, allured by the Madianite women. The Priest Phineas was excited with zeal to avenge such mischief, with sword in hand. Against whom did he turn it? Against one only Israelite and one Madianite. Both were murdered in their sin, on account of their being of the first rank: the Israelite being son of a captain of the tribe of Simeon, and the Madianite, "a most noble princess," to show, as St. Peter Damian observes (*l. i. p.* 6),

"The nobler the criminals are, the worse are their carnal sins."

2. Adam displeased God rather than displease Eve. Thus he committed the greatest outrage to the Creator, postponing him to a most vile creature. "There is a deceitful balance in his hand." —(*Ose,* xii.)

3. Finally, he was the first of all mankind to give an example to others of sinning. Thus he became guilty of the innumerable sins which were afterwards committed by his descendants. "The sinner's guilt," says Salvian, "is multiplied by the number of those he draws into sin." Ah! if those persons could well understand this, who are the first to introduce certain customs which are the greatest abuses in the world. Miserable creatures! the thunderbolts of divine justice will fall on them. My good God, how terrible thou art towards sinners! And yet I have so often had the boldness to offend thee. May the infinite mercy of God be a thousand times blessed, that bears with me for so long a time, and awaits my repentance.

THIRD POINT.

Chastisement inflicted by God on the first of all the faithful—our Redeemer—for the sins of the world. Among the many thunderbolts which the divine justice hurled against sin, and the many chastisements given to sinners in Heaven, on Earth, or in Hell, there is not one so striking, and which should cause more terror, than the chastisement given to our Redeemer on Calvary, for the sins of the world. He was Redeemer; innocence itself, impeccable by nature. He was the only Son of the Eternal Father, consubstantial with him. He was of infinite dignity. The least outrage of his most holy humanity must be esteemed a greater evil than the ruin of all creatures.

Why did he enter the world as a culprit for all mankind, and take on him their sins? "He bore our sins in his body." Consider with what severity the Eternal Father punished him for sins not his own. He treated him, not as a son, but "as an enemy." He condemned him to be born in a stable in the midst of beasts; to live in hardship for thirty years, in the miserable shop of a carpenter. After three years of most laborious preaching, he ordained him to suffer a most awful passion of chains, whips, thorns, mockeries; and caused him to die naked on Calvary, on a cross, vilified between two thieves, as the worst malefactor in the world.

Although our Redeemer had agonized and sweat blood from every pore, foreseeing his future martyrdom; although three times he begged of his Eternal Father to have mercy on him—the Father not only refused his petition, but, in the garden, sent him an angel with a chalice of black wormwood. On Calvary he appeared to have entirely abandoned him, so that our Redeemer in his last agony repeated those words: "My God! my God! why hast thou deserted me?" O God! what more can be said to conceive an intense horror of sin?

The Eternal Father thought the life of a God well spent, to destroy the sins of the world. He himself punished a Son with this rigor, that sin might remain unpunished. What more can be said?

The King of Moab formed a most strange and tragical resolution, as related in the Fourth Book of Kings. Finding himself narrowly besieged by three enemies, namely, the kings of Juda, Isreal, and Edom, who surrounded him on all sides with most powerful troops, and having in vain attempted other means of becoming free, and not being willing, on any account, to surrender to the enemy, he had recourse to one of those means which despair alone could suggest. He attemped to terrify and put to flight the besiegers, by an act of unheard-of ferocity. For this purpose, having gone out on the highest point of the castle, opposite the army of the enemy, he seized by the arm his eldest son, heir to the kingdom; then, unsheathing a sword, he plunged it into his breast, and with a heart, not of a father, but of a murderer, he continued mangling the innocent child, who fell a victim to his fury.—(IV. *Kings* iii.) At this sight, the besiegers were so horrified, that they despaired of obtaining any advantage from so cruel and desperate a man: the siege was soon abandoned, and all departed to their own country.

What the King of Moab did so unadvisedly, the Eternal Father did with the most high counsel of Providence, when mankind made war with Heaven by sin. For, having attempted, in the Old Testament, to overthrow human wickedness by means of the deluge, fire, plagues, famine, and other chastisements, and man still remaining obstinate; and finally, the Divine Son, having taken on himself all the sins of the world, God caused him to die, crucified on Calvary, a victim of his justice. Human perfidy was vanquished, and the Jews were the crucifiers. "And all the multitude of them who were come together, to that sight, and saw the things which had passed, returned, striking their breasts."—(*Luke*, xxiii.) Oh! What! more can be said to explain the atrocity of sin, than that the divine justice could not be satisfied for the outrage received from sinners, but by the death of a God. If the Eternal Father could pardon the sin of man, he would have forgiven the appearance of it in his only Son. "He spared not even his own Son, but delivered him up for us all?"

If God had allowed one single wound to be inflicted on the body of Christ, he would thereby show greater rigor, than if he had buried a thousand worlds, and had precipitated into Hell all the angels and mankind together. The most holy humanity of our Redeemer, united to the Divinity, being of infinite dignity, is infinitely superior to all creatures.

What then was the rigor, to punish sin, not with one, but a thousand blows, a thousand agonies, even by the death of Christ?

St. Thomas of Villanova exclaims: "Will there be a man so daring, after this reflection, not to be horrified at the very name of mortal sin?"—(*Ser.* 2 *Adv.*) This relates to the Eternal Father. As to the divine Son, see what hatred he bears sin. He most willingly loses his life, provided sin should be destroyed.

Samson never showed in a more lively manner the great hatred he bore the Philistines, than when he prayed to die, provided they should die with him, and be buried under the ruins of the temple. Never did our Redeemer more clearly show the great evil of sin, than when, to give death to it, he did not refuse to die on the cross.

In conclusion, my soul, discourse thus with yourself. If divine justice has so rigorously punished a God made man, for sins not his own, how will he treat you, most vile worm of the Earth, for so many of your own sins?

If the fire of divine thunder has caused so many flames to arise, to operate on the green wood of the most holy humanity of the Redeemer, what fire will it not inflict on sinners, who, as dry wood, are prepared to burn in Hell? Had not our Redeemer, while ascending Calvary, reason to say to the Hebrew women who wept for his torments: "Weep not for me; reserve those tears for yourselves; you stand in greater need of them, having much more to satisfy to the divine justice for your own sins?" "Weep not for me, but for yourselves."

Ah! my God, what terrors are these for me! The reasons are so clear and striking to persuade me how great an evil sin is. If I do not surrender, it may with certainty be alleged, that I have lost either my senses or my faith.

COLLOQUY.

Most beloved spouse of my soul, how much do I owe thee for the light thou hast deigned to grant me in this holy meditation. Like a man who is aroused from sleep and opens his eyes to the light, it appears to me, I know what I never knew, namely, the sovereign evil of sin. Reflecting on its frightful punishments, I conceive a sovereign horror of sin. Ah! miserable me! How could I have been so blind for many years, as not to mind what I did in sinning? It is true, Lucifer sinned, Adam sinned; but neither had seen the chastisements of other sins committed before theirs. But I, more wicked, have committed much greater sins, and—what is the height of my iniquities—I have committed them, after knowing by faith the chastisements inflicted by God on creatures so much more noble than myself. Whilst actually suffering the misfortunes of the world, I knew by experience that these were the chastisements of Adam. Oh! miserable that I am! "I now know my folly." And now that I know them, O my God, what else can I do, than to have recourse to thee? "What shall I do? whither shall I fly, but to thee, my God?" I will act as Magdalen did, when she became aware of her wickedness. She wept bitterly, throwing herself at thy feet. With her I will shed tears of lively contrition. Weep then, my soul, weep for so many past sins; and do not stop sighing day or night, according to the advice of Jeremiah: "Let my eyes shed down tears, night and day, and let them not cease"—(*Jeremias*, cxiv.) After the destruction of Jerusalem, the miserable Jews were forbidden to enter the temple to weep over their own misfortunes, except once a year, after spending much money. It was "the day of tears." But we, after committing so many sins, are not only prohibited, but strongly advised to weep. Then, "Let us weep before the Lord." My God, lover of souls, hear our cries, whilst with tears we humbly implore pardon, pity, mercy. Remember that a God has died for our sins: "Look on the face of thy Anointed." The dying blood of Abel cried to Heaven for vengeance. The dying blood of Christ cries out pardon and mercy for us: "Look on the face of thy Anointed." I merit for my sins the greatest chastisement of your justice; but the blood of Christ has taken upon itself the punishment of my sins. Then, "Look on the face of thy Anointed, and have mercy on me." Amen.

MEDITATION V.

On the Malice of Mortal Sin.

INTRODUCTION.

St. Peter Damian relates a very tragical case of a traveller, who, having strayed for a long time in a dark wood, finally tired by the extent of his journey, rested on a beautiful grassy ascent. He seated himself on it to restore his weary limbs, and enjoy, in the shade of the spreading beech trees, the warbling of the birds. O God! while he thought he was securely seated on a stone, he had placed himself on the back of a formidable dragon, which was there extended and asleep. This monster, finding himself pressed on the back, resists, arises, and to the inexpressible terror of the pilgrim, raises its horrible head, opens its venomous jaws, and turning its black eyes towards the wretched traveller, catches him in its claws, tears him in pieces, and devours him. A great misfortune, surely, for this poor person. How much greater is that of sinners, who, while thinking themselves in the enjoyment of sweet repose in delights, riches, and the indulgence of their passions, are within the claws of a dragon much more fierce, which inflicts on them the death of the soul, an eternal death; and to crown their misfortune, they are not aware of their miserable state.

As the Philistines first blinded Samson, then ill treated him as they pleased; so the Devil, before depriving sinners of the life of the soul, blinds them in such a manner, that they no longer see the evil which they commit. Notwithstanding the daily chastisements inflicted by God on sinners, they say: What great harm is it to give way to passion? Only considering in sin, the mere appearance of a momentary pleasure, like the fish, says St. Austin, "that imbibes with the pleasing nectar of a passing delight the murderous bait of its own perdition."

Jeremiah weeping, exclaims: "Ah! blind and unhappy sinner, open your eyes for once, and consider in the light of faith how great an evil, how murderous a dragon, is that sin, which until now, you have considered a plaything, a nothing: thus you committed it with that facility with which men partake of a drink of fresh water. "They drink down iniquity like water." Deign for once to arouse yourself from sleep and open your eyes: "Know and see that it is a bitter and an evil thing to have left the Lord thy God"—(*Jeremiah*, ii. 1.) If you only knew the evil of mortal sin! It is the greatest evil in the world, whether viewed in regard to itself, or to God, or to the sinner who committed it. This will be the subject of this most important meditation, in which we shall consider three points.

1. Mortal sin is the greatest of all evils. 2. It is hated by God more than any other evil. 3. It is more pernicious to man than all other evils.

FIRST PRELUDE.

Imagine yourself in the presence of God, as a culprit guilty of grievous crimes, who presents himself to the judge loaded from head to foot with the heaviest chains. Our chains are precisely our very grievous sins. Or, let us place ourselves in the presence of God as so many infirm lepers, having our members covered with horrible cancers. Our cancers are our sins, which disgust and displease the eyes of the Most High.

SECOND PRELUDE.

My good God, behold at thy feet a monster of felony and ingratitude. I dare not appear before thee, seeing myself so disgusting on account of my iniquities. Yet thy infinite goodness animates me. It did not disdain to revivify the decayed body of Lazarus, though four days deceased. The mercy thou now showest me in giving me time and light to weep over my sins, makes me hope that thou wilt deign to grant my pardon. "Guilty, I mourn: I blush for my crimes. O God, spare thy suppliant."

FIRST POINT.

Mortal sin is the greatest of all evils. "Two things," says St. Augustine (in *Sent.*, 150), "are great in this world, namely, the sovereign good, that is God; and the sovereign evil, that is sin." God is infinite goodness, in comparison to whom all possible goods are nothing. Sin is infinite malice, in comparison to which all possible evils are nothing. Sin is of so much malice, that it comes in contradiction with whom? With God. Sin is not only the sovereign, but also the only true evil. It should not be committed, either to avoid any pain, or to attain any good.

Dragons and toads, how venomous soever they be, are created by God, and exalt his power. "Praise the Lord, ye dragons"—(*Ps.*, clxviii.) Not so with sinners. Sin is the sole evil: with this exception, there is no evil for the soul. St.

Chrysostom feared nothing in this world but sin. Eudoxia, his persecutor, used to say of him: "He is a man fearing sin only." It is, finally, an infinite evil, because it is an offence against an infinite God. The angelic doctor attests it (*Co.* 1, 2, *qu.* 87, *a.* 4). "As against God it is infinite." You will ask: In what does this great evil, this great venom consist? In a contempt of God. We read in the divine Scriptures: "They spurned me"— (*Isaias*, i.) "Through prevarication of the law, you dishonor God"—(*Rom.*, ii.) "He despised my judgments"—(*Ezechiel*, v.) In sinning man contemns God as his master, by not executing his commands. "Thou hast said, I will not serve." He contemns God as his King, not practising his laws; he contemns God as his Creator, not operating according to the end for which he was created; he despises God as his Father, showing himself ungrateful to his love; he contemns God as his Redeemer, rendering his blood useless; he despises God as God, destroys his majesty, as if God knew not how to revenge the outrages against himself.

This contempt increases immeasurably by comparison. According to the celebrated definition of St. Thomas (1, 2, *qu.* 87, *art.* 4), "the sinner turns his back on God to follow a most vile creature." Oh! what an affront. To contemn one prince in order to honor another prince, might have some excuse. If by possibility there could be another God, and by sinning a man should offend one to follow another, this might be supportable; but to turn one's back on the one only true God, who should be preferred to a thousand worlds —to please what? It is shameful to mention it—

a carcase. What contempt, what an insufferable wrong, for a handful of barley, or a mouthful of bread. Incomparable injury, says Jeremiah. "Be astonished, O Heavens, and you, inanimate creatures, be horrified"—(*Jer.*, ii. 12.)

This contempt is increased to infinitude by the vileness of him who commits it, and by the greatness of him who receives it. This is the theological argument by which the schools prove that sin is of infinite malice. The injury is the greater, inasmuch as he who offers it is less than he who receives it. If a peasant offend another peasant, his equal, or a prince outrage another prince, the offence could be considered light; but if the peasant offend a prince, the deed is most grievous. If the same peasant offend a king, the fault has no punishment equivalent to it.

Let us then reflect on sin. Who is the man that offends? A vile worm, a little dust. Who is the offended God? An infinite majesty, the King of kings. Who then can deny that sin is of infinite malice, being an offence offered by a most vile creature to an infinite majesty. This then was your boldness, O man: when you sinned you outraged a God. If an ant armed with a bit of straw wished to defy the sun in a duel, what rashness, what folly, would it be? The audacity of a sinner is greater, beyond comparison, who, with respect to God, is much less than an ant—a nothing. In sinning he unsheathes his sword against an omnipotent God.—(*Ps.*, xxxvi. 14). God thus contemned, cannot but be infinitely displeased.

Blanch relates that in the year 1392 a player at dice, from the many losses he had sustained, being in despair, declared, if he again lost at play (the mind shudders at his expression) he would seize the dagger against Christ. This impious man throws the dice and loses. He instantly unsheathes the sword he had by his side, and brandishes it against Heaven, thus blaspheming: "Hear me, Christ; I will not spare thee. I shall thrust this blade into thy side." What follows? Immediately three drops of blood fall from Heaven, in the form of a cross, on the gaming table. Then the earth opening under the sacrilegious wretch, two frightful demons appear and drag him soul and body into Hell.

Finally, he who sins offends God by contempt, which is multiplied by the number of the divine attributes. Hence holy David wept bitterly to have committed sins more numerous than the hairs of his head, or the sands of the sea.—(*Ps.*, xxxix. 6.) Not that his sins were so many as the hairs of the head or the sands of the sea, but each of his sins offending all the divine attributes, contained the malice of innumerable sins. Man in sinning offends in a particular manner the immensity of God, who being in every place is forced to be witness of these outrages.

St. Peter Damian tells us (*Opusc.*, c. 32) of a robber to whom Jesus appeared in the form of a beggar with long dishevelled hair. The robber, taking a pair of scissors to remove it, found two eyes at the back of his head. Then the beggar discovered himself. " I am Jesus, who look around everywhere. I saw the robbery which a short time since you committed."

2. The sinner offends the omnipotence of God,

using against himself his own gifts, namely, the senses and powers of the soul.

3. He offends the beneficence of God, outraging that God, who has given him a being, who preserves it, who at every moment could reduce him to nothing. Thus the sinner is worse than a rebel. Rebels have not received from their prince either the hand that does battle, or the arm that is directed against him. When the angel held Habacuc suspended by the hair over the lion's den—(*Dan.*, xiv. 35), if Habacuc had brandished a knife to wound the hand of the angel who sustained him, what folly and monstrous ingratitude would this be? God sustains the sinner on the verge of Hell by a hair, that is by the thread of a most frail life. What rashness then, by sinning, to wound the beneficent hand of God, who preserves him when his Creator could annihilate him or send him to perdition?

4. The sinner offends the goodness of God, who cannot but complain of the wrongs which he receives, saying: What have I done to thee, O man, thus to injure me? on the contrary, what good have I not conferred?

A city having rebelled against the Emperor Charles V., a noble chief of the sedition went to implore forgiveness at his feet; having discovered in the king excessive goodness in receiving him, he expired at his feet from pure grief for his felony. What then should the sinner do who returns to penance?

5. Not to mention other divine attributes, the *patience* of God is offended by the sinner, who is so long borne with, who sins so easily, and returns a thousand times to his sin. The most kind

hearted father in the world, after having several times forgiven a worthless son, finally expels him. God does not act thus; he pardons the sinner a hundred, a thousand times, insomuch, that St. Gertrude, having asked him what was the most agreeable manner of praising him, he answered: "In my long waiting for the sinner's return." The sinner, however, abuses this patience, not once only, but a thousand times. Open then your eyes, my soul, and consider what you have done in sinning: "Know and see." You, the most vile of creatures, contemned a God, and preferred to him a momentary pleasure; you contemned him infinitely, and offended all his attributes. Contempt is the most jealous offence that can be offered to man, because his honor is wounded, which is more estimable than life itself. Charles VII., King of France, had extraordinary love for one of his great and faithful captains; once excited by curiosity, he said to him: "Do you think it possible that anything in the world could make you rebel against me, who love you so much, and who in return am so beloved by you?" "Yes, Sire," answered the captain, "contempt might, so I hope you will not put me to the trial." If then a private individual would consider himself so much offended by contempt, how much more should a God consider himself outraged? When there is question of kings and sovereigns, every offence given to them by subjects is punished with death.

What punishment do you deserve who outraged the Monarch of all kings? What astonishment did your presumption cause to all Paradise, who witnessed at the same moment God adored by the seraphim, and despised by a vile worm, such as you? Will you say you did not sin through contempt of God, but to satisfy caprice? That sinful action with which you wish to gratify yourself, was a contempt of God, if not directly, at least interpretatively, as St. Thomas says (1 *l.*, *qu.* 73). When a noble son contracts a base alliance, he does so from fancy, not through contempt of his father; who, notwithstanding considers himself offended in the highest degree. You ask, " What evil do we offer to God by offending him?" I answer, in effect no harm soever is done against him, for he is not capable of receiving intrinsic injury; but in affection, great evil is proposed by contempt. All the evil a creature can do is effected; that is—*to disobey God.* What harm is done to a king when his portrait is disfigured, or his laws contemned?

Dishonor, disobedience, and contempt are, however, held as great evils. My soul, by offending God, you committed the greatest of all evils. If you understand it well, how horrified you must be, and how bitterly you should weep. Finally, if we consider the malice of mortal sin, committed by a Christian, it wonderfully increases its grievousness. It is a great evil for a pagan or a Turk to sin, who has not the light of faith, and who has not received from God so many graces as you; but for a Christian to commit it, born in the bosom of the Church, cleansed by baptism, and sanctified by so many sacraments—that he should fail in the promise made at baptism, entirely to renounce Satan, saying: " I renounce Satan and all his pomps;" that he should prove himself ungrateful after so many benefits from God—oh! this is certainly the summit of all evils.

A Christian believes that God, to redeem him, died for his sins; yet he does not cease with fresh blows to renew his passion and death, and scourge him again by his dishonesty, crown him with thorns by his pride, and crucify him by his ostentation. Who then can say how much his iniquities are redoubled and increased beyond measure? St. Augustine said, that for a Gentile's sin one Hell sufficed; for a Christian sinner a thousand would be wanted. St. Jerome attests that in Hell a Christian is much more atrociously tormented than an idolator. For believers that cruel furnace, like that of Babylon, "Is multiplied sevenfold." Wretched me! How much heavier will my sins weigh in the balance of God than those of others!

SECOND POINT.

Mortal sin is hated by God more than any other evil. It is undoubted that the first and infallible rule of the just man is the divine will. Whatever is willed or loved by God, cannot be but good; and what is hated by God cannot but be evil. To conceive then what a great evil mortal sin is, let us observe how much God hates it.

1. He hates it solely and sovereignly, with all the wrath of his heart, more than any other evil in the world; because in every creature, whether asps or toads, God sees some good, and considers some communication of his perfections; "whereas sin is a pure evil, without mixture of any good," as St. Ambrose defines it.

2. He hates it essentially and through necessity: for, as St. Thomas teaches (1, 2 *qu.* 29, *art.* 1), "Hatred proceeds from love." As much then as

God loves himself, so much does he abominate sin, which directly opposes his love. Besides, loving immensely the soul of man, he cannot but hate sin, which makes man his enemy, and does him injury.

3. He hates it infinitely; for this is the nature of two opposite terms; in proportion as one approaches, the other recedes. Thus one who goes from Naples to Rome; the nearer he approaches the latter, the farther he removes from the former. God then loving himself in an infinite manner, it follows he should infinitely abominate sin, which is contradictory to his love of infinite holiness.

4. He hates it eternally. Thus, these two terms, God and sin, throughout eternity cannot be reconciled either by truce or peace. In a fog, cold and heat may be united; what is dry with what is damp; but never can supreme sanctity be united with the sum of human malice.

5. He hates it with abomination. "When you shall see the abomination of desolation"—(*Marc*, xiii.) He not only contemns sin and the sinner, but those foolish creatures that served the guilty and were instruments of their sins. Thus he commanded Moses (in the 13th of Deuteronomy), in the city in which he discovered the sin of idolatry, to put it to fire and sword. Life was not even granted to the beasts; the entire city was changed into an eternal sepulchre of its iniquities.

6. He hates it, finally, in union with all creatures in Heaven and on Earth. When a king deprives a person of his favor, and this individual becomes his enemy, he is soon hated by all the

courtiers of that king, even by his servants and vassals. Thus the sinner being hated by God, is also hated by Mary, the angels and saints; also by all creatures, who unwillingly serve an enemy of God, their Master. The sun would refuse to enlighten him, the Earth to support him, the elements would have him to be fulminated and destroyed.

Let us discourse together. Tell me, beloved, how great an evil must sin be, thus hated by God, who cannot err in his high and most just will? Can it be possible that a person will love more than himself that sin which God so much hates? How perfidious and rebellious a servant is the sinner who so much loves that sin which his Master hates, to contract a friendship with the Devil, the sworn enemy of God? Reflect, that a person after having committed a mortal sin, can say with truth: "I am hated by God; I have God for my enemy."

St. Chrysostom says (*Lib. de Provid.*): "Sin separates us from God, makes God our enemy." O terrible sentence, capable of making the hair stand on end, and of causing the blood to freeze in the veins of every sinner. "He who would not tremble and be horrified at it," says St. Chrysostom, "shows he does not know who God is."—(*Hom. 26, ad Popul.*) I have then for an enemy that God who can at each moment strike me with a thunderbolt, or a fit of apoplexy; who, by withdrawing his assistance, can at any instant reduce me to my former nothingness. I have for an enemy that God by whose omnipotence I am; by whose mercy I merit; by whose patience I am preserved. I have for an enemy the God of all riches: what then can succeed with me? The God of health: what medicine can then avail me? The God of all creatures: who then can screen me from their insults? They can say, *now*, that God is his enemy, let us persecute him. I have God for an enemy. Alas! if a harsh word, a suspected aversion from a prince, would suffice to take away sleep and life from his vassals, what effect should be produced on a sinner by the declared hatred of the King of kings? To flee the hatred of a prince, it suffices to abandon his dominions, and have recourse to the protection of another sovereign; but he who has God for an enemy. whither can he flee? Though he should hide himself in the Heavens, or in a profound abyss, everywhere he finds God, who can "cast body and soul into hell." Most terrible sentence, who can think of it without shuddering? A Roman, whose cause was discussed in the senate, hearing that he had Tullius for an enemy, to speak against him, in despair committed suicide.

Two gentlemen in Spain behaved with little decorum at church; in consequence of which they received from Philip II. this reprimand: "Do not appear any longer in my presence." Having returned home, they died of grief. A sinner knowing, by faith, that he has God for his enemy, should he not die with terror? Yet so many sinners, with this clear knowledge, not only do not die, but live, laugh, dance, and amuse themselves. O foolish and senseless creatures. My soul, if this be not folly, what then can we name it?

THIRD POINT.

Mortal sin is more destructive to man than any other evil. If all tyrants on Earth were to conspire against one man, all dragons, snakes, etc., they could not do him so much evil as a sinner does to himself by sinning. They could only take away the life of the body, not that of the soul. All the Devils in Hell could not do him so much harm, though they should have an unlimited license from God to injure him as much as they could: they could only incite, not oblige him to sin.

Divine justice cannot, in a direct way, do him so much harm, by all the power of its thunder, for it can never positively will that he should sin, but only permit it. The oracle of Tobias (i. 20.) is true. Sinners are the worst and most fatal enemies of themselves, as they do themselves temporal, spiritual, and eternal evil. According to the angelic doctor (2 *quest.*, 164, *art.*, 1), every actual sin causes the same effects in the sinner, as original sin did in the first of the human race. The latter injured man in body, soul, and throughout eternity. Actual sin acts likewise; it brings on him every temporal evil. What is the greatest injury that the most capital enemy, the most cruel assassin can do to man? Steal his riches, destroy his house, burn his farms, wound him in his members, take away his life in the most barbarous manner. Can he do more? No. Cain could not do more to Abel, nor Absalom to Ammon, nor all the tyrants of Rome to the many millions of martyrs.

The greatest of all evils that one man can

inflict on another, is the least of that evil which a sinner causes himself, by committing sin; for he renders himself the subject of the revengeful wrath of God, who showers on him all kinds of misfortunes and death.

God sheds on this world his formidable punishments, by many famines, earthquakes, conflagrations, plagues, desolations, to punish rebels. God himself declared (in *Deuteronomy*, xxviii.), that he would shower on sinners all his maledictions, so that they should never enjoy any good in their homes, affairs, or friends.

The true cause of all the misery we see in cities, and the many lamentations which are daily heard amongst the people, is not the influx of the planets, nor the changes of seasons, but sin. Kingdoms and most august empires are transferred from one nation to another by sins of fraud and injustice. Why do so many sudden and improvident deaths occur, even to stout youths, in the flower of their youth? On account of sin. This is clearly seen in what happened to the Emperor Anastasius. One night a person of formidable aspect, who held in his right hand a pen, and in his left an open book, with an angry countenance and terrible voice, exclaimed: "See how, being pained by your misdeeds, I efface from your life fourteen years." Anastasius being terrified, immediately arose, not well knowing whether it was a vision or a dream. In a few days the Heavens became cloudy, loud thunder was heard. The emperor, doubtless foreseeing misfortune, took flight through all the apartments of his palace, and went to conceal himself in a secret cabinet: there precisely a thunderbolt fell from Heaven, to terminate his life and wickedness. If sinners are found, who prosper in the world with the goods of fortune, this is precisely the summit of their own evils; for God allows them to thrive, like beasts, to conduct them afterwards to the most cruel slaughter. " Why doth the way of the wicked prosper?" asked Job (xxii. 3). God acts towards the impious, as Abigail counselled David to act with his enemies, namely, to surround them.—I. *Reg.*, xxv. A person with a sling does not throw the stone immediately, but goes round several times, to aim afterwards with greater velocity. In the same manner (*Ps.*, xi.), the wicked are surrounded by God, who defers the chastisement, to give it to them afterwards in a more heavy manner. Sin is the furnace, in which the arms of divine justice are fabricated, to wound the sinner with every sort of temporal evil. Sin is the armory of all spiritual evils of the soul, which are incomparably the worst and most numerous.

1. Mortal sin gives to the soul of man a death so much worse than the natural death of the body, that in comparison the latter may be called the shadow of death. As the body when separated from the soul, is frightful to behold, and decays; so the soul, when separated from God, though it may be that of the gayest and most pompous youth in the world, is more hideous and disgusting before God than a dead dog. It cannot be otherwise. For if one sin committed by the angels, who are most beautiful spirits, rendered them horrible devils, will not numerous grievous sins, committed by a vile creature, render him more odious to God than even the devils?

St. Augustine wept over the corpse of a man

dead to God by sin. "His body lives, but his soul is dead."

2. Mortal sin destroys the merits of all the good works performed before committing sin; though the sinner, for an entire century, had performed more penance than a Simeon Stylites, or an Hilarion. These good works never revive unless the soul is restored to grace. How great a loss, worthy to be lamented with tears of blood. Titus Livius relates of Manlius Capitolinus, a Roman captain, that after having bestowed on the republic many services, he acquired the glorious title of Father of the Country. He was accused of a capital offence. In order to defend his life, he carried into the midst of the senate all the crowns he had acquired by his valor: the naval crown, acquired in conflict at sea; the mural crown, for being the first to make the ascent to the enemy's walls; the camp, for having first rent asunder the trenches of the enemy; the civic, for having saved the life of a Roman citizen in battle; then, uncovered his breast scarred with wounds, after the many trials to which he had been exposed for the good of his country. "Is it possible," said he, "that so much glory should be eclipsed for one only fault?"

O God! how much more harm than this accrues to a soul for one sin, destroying in one moment the merit of many years, "like a heavy hail storm to a flourishing vine." A sinful soul may well lament with Jeremiah (*Thren.*, i. 12), and say of his sin: "It hath made a vintage of me."

3. Mortal sin deprives the soul of sanctifying grace, which is a supernatural gift of so much value, that each degree of it is worth more than

a kingdom, even a thousand kingdoms, as they are merely natural goods. Besides grace, it also deprives the soul of infused habits, of the dignity of child of God, and heir of Paradise, so that God immediately effaces its name from the book of life.

It is written of the Emperor Caius, that being one day indignant against his son for a fault he had committed, and troubled for his kingdom, stamping his feet on the ground, he said: "He is not my son, I do not recognize him for such." In the same manner it appears that God says from Heaven to the sinner: He is no longer mine.

4. Sin deprives the soul of quiet and peace; and produces most cruel remorse, which embitters every enjoyment of the sinner; so that even in the midst of feasts and dances, he hears a voice saying to him: " Woe to me, I am in disgrace with God: if a sudden death were to occur to me, it is certain I should be damned."

From the time Cain murdered his brother Abel, he was miserable. He no longer found peace; but a fugitive, he ran over the country, and knowing himself worthy of death for his great crime, he feared that all wished to murder him. How vain was this fear? There was no one but Adam his father, and Eve his mother. What then had he to fear? Could he fear his parents as enemies? No. Yet his fear was not vain, but just; for, being the enemy of the Creator, he had all creatures for enemies; and the cruel remorse for his sin made him suspect that the wild beasts, the serpents, and whatever was in the world, would put an end to him.

5. Sin clouds the mind of man, and blinds his reason. Blind and unreasonable, he rejoices an

animal more than a man. Lucifer, after his sin, was called the Dragon. David, after his sin, was aware that he was like a beast. "I am become as a beast." A sinner is even worse than the beasts, for they are not hated by God as the sinner is.

6. Sin renders man worse than a possessed person; for the latter is possessed by the Devil only in his body. The sinner is possessed in the soul, by as many devils as he has committed sins; thus he becomes the child and slave of the Devil, like a demon incarnate.

7. Finally, (to be silent on innumerable other evils,) sin destroys in a certain manner every good in the sinner; so that, properly speaking, he is reduced to nothing. The cause is clear. For having to assume reason from the first being, namely God, and the sinner being his enemy, he is truly nothing before God. Solomon says, that sinners are like so many pictures in prospective. In these you will see large fields, thick woods, and delicious gardens; nearer, shepherds, bullocks, droves of cattle, birds, rivers, and rivulets; at a short distance, sea and mountain views, which sweetly beguile the eye. But if the canvas be turned, nothing of all this will be seen; no seas, nor mountains, nor birds, nor flocks, nor rivers, nor trees. Such is the fate of the impious. Before men they appear something great, rich in apparel, retinue, and honors. The picture however being reversed—"they are not." Consider them as they are before God.

Besides temporal evils which sin brings on the body, besides those it produces in the soul, it also gives to the body and soul the completion of all evils; that is, eternal damnation in Hell. Of a man who is in mortal sin it may be said that he is suspended in the air " over the mouth of the abyss," which has its jaws open to swallow him. He is suspended by a thread; that is, the very frail thread of life. When this is broken, he immediately descends beneath to eternal ruin. O terror, who is not dismayed at the thought!

We read of a man bewitched with profane love, who promised his wicked accomplice, if she acceded to his wishes that he would grant any request she desired. The wretch asked him to precipitate himself from a high rock. The miserable man, blinded by passion, was about to consent to the request, but was sufficiently enlightened to demand a little time to consider the precipice. Scarcely had he arrived at the point of the rock, when seeing the profound abyss into which he was to fall, his blood freezing in his veins with horror, the ardor of the love he had conceived was entirely extinguished.

Blind, wretched sinner, I ask one favor of you. When the Devil tempts you to sin, have at least sufficient judgment, before consenting, to present yourself at the abyss of Hell, into which you are about to precipitate both your soul and body. I am certain you would not be so rash, or rather so foolish as to commit it. From what has been said, beloved, I wish you to draw the intended fruit of this meditation, namely, a great horror of sin. Reflect in a lively manner, on the horrible change that is made in the soul which commits sin. A short time before, being in the state of grace, the soul was a child of God, a spouse of Jesus Christ, a temple of the Holy Ghost, sister of angels, queen and heiress of Paradise, rich in merits and supernatural habits. Having committed the fault, oh! God, what a sad catastrophe! In one moment she loses all; is degraded from her former honors; is odious to God, to the saints, to all creatures, a chained slave of the Devil, a living portable Hell. "Thou shalt make them as an oven of fire, in the time of thy anger."—(*Ps.*, xx.) O God! what a frightful change. "A leap," says St. Bernard, "from the highest to the lowest, from a throne to the prison, from heaven to hell!"

St. Augustine cannot refrain from tears at this sight: torrents might be shed on the misfortune of a sinful soul. "You were the spouse of Christ, the temple of God, the dwelling place of the Holy Spirit. I mourn to say, *you were*. I weep that you are so no longer." All this! because by sin you lost God. Weeping, repeat what the miserable Jonas confessed of himself. A great tempest having arisen at sea, it was expedient to disburden the vessel of some of the inmates; the lot fell on the life of Jonas. Then the mariners interrogated him—(*Jon.*, i. 8). "Confess, O unhappy man, who you are? What great evil have you done? Whence do you come? Whither do you go?" "I will briefly tell you," answered Jonas; "neither my country nor profession causes so many evils, but my sin alone, by which I fly from the face of God." How can it be possible that he who is far from God shall not encounter every evil?

To conclude. I beseech whoever reads this to run over in thought all the years of his past life, and then exclaim: How then is it possible that I committed with so much facility so grievous an evil as that of mortal sin? What! Have I lost my senses? Have I lost faith? What has made me so cruel an enemy to myself?

My sins, *as to number*, have been countless. I began to sin as soon as I was capable of sinning—from the first use of reason. I then continued, without ever ceasing, always abusing divine patience. Scarcely is there a precept in the Church that I have not several times transgressed. I have sinned in every kind of thought, word, and deed: the multitude of my sins, divided amongst many men or angels, would suffice to damn them all. Who knows but, after so many sins, the measure may be filled up, after which God will not give me efficacious grace to be saved? Who knows but that for me, " the time is come; the day of slaughter is near." (*Ezech.*, c. vii.)

As to weight; who can tell the grievousness of my heinous sins? How vile they must appear in the eyes of God, since I am so fearful to mention them to a confessor, lest he should be scandalized!

As to the manner; I have sinned, knowing well the evil I was doing, contemning the voice of God and the remorse of conscience, when by so many titles I should, more than others, have been faithful to God, who has blessed me more than others.

Oh! if God wished to exert his justice towards me, he could have damned me as often as I committed sin. "A thousand times I would have been lost, if thou, O Lord, hadst willed," said St. Augustine, weeping. If he has not done so, it has been an excess of his infinite mercy, of which I was unworthy.

Now I understand why the saints had so great a horror of sin. St. Frances of Rome fainted, when she passed by a place where there was scandal given. St. Mary of Oignic had her feet scarified, for having inadvertently passed through a street in which dwelt a public sinner. Blessed John of God, to resist a grievous temptation, drove sharp reeds under his nails. Others burnt their fingers. Some removed their tongues with their teeth, and cast them before their tempters.

O God! how can I hold in so little account what the saints so much feared? Wretch that I am! I have not the lively faith that they had. Now I will execute the beautiful admonition of the Holy Ghost. I will have pity on myself and sin no more. In this case, the interest is all mine, not that of my relatives or friends. It would show great pride if I, who am bound to love my enemies, did not truly love myself.

COLLOQUY.

My God, my Creator, and my Redeemer, here at thy feet is a monster of ingratitude, a sink of iniquities. I am ashamed to appear before thee, so guilty do I find myself by my innumerable sins. "I know my iniquity." I am he who dared despise an infinite majesty. Blind as I was, I turned my back on the sovereign good to follow a most vile creature. Being foolish, I held for nothing the greatest of all evils—sin; insensible to so many lights and threats; rebellious to thy love; ungrateful for thy benefits. I know it but too well, and I confess it. "I know my iniquity." I would have done thee a great injury, if, after having loved me so much and blessed me, I had not loved and served thee in return with the most intense love.

What then is it, not to love thee, the Sovereign

MALICE OF MORTAL SIN.

Good, and to love that which did me so much injury?—not to serve thee, and to serve thy enemy the Devil? What shall it be, to have sold thee, worse than Judas, for a caprice? To have again crucified thee, worse than the Jews, not once, but a thousand times, by my sins?

Ah! miserable me! What have I done? How is it possible that I had the heart to commit such grievous sins? Yes, my God, I merit the greatest punishments for my many iniquities. I have but too well merited temporal and spiritual chastisements, as well as such as are eternal, and which thy justice thunders against sinners. "I know my iniquity."

Among these chastisements, the most intolerable to me is, to have thee for my enemy. Oh! this punishment indeed I cannot bear. In comparison to this, a thousand Hells seem to me as nothing. My God, the love of my soul "does not permit me to be separated from thee."

What good can I have far from thee? and of what use would the friendship of creatures be to me, if I have God for my enemy?—a God who hates sin. Deprive me of thy love, and then punish me with any other chastisement. Demand from me any other satisfaction:—I am most ready to give it. I know that thou requirest nothing more from poor sinners than tears and contrition. Here I am, quite contrite, to implore thy mercy. Pardon, my God, pardon. "Thou canst loose more than I can bind; thou canst pardon more than I can perpetrate." Pardon my many crimes. I have recourse to thee, who hast been offended. Pardon! my God, be merciful!

This clear knowledge which thou now givest me

of my wickedness, and this resolution to detest it, these are for me, a pledge of the forgiveness thou wilt accord to me. I abominate all my past disorders, and myself who committed them, resolving to commence a new life; and with the most lively affection I implore thy mercy to grant me, with the pardon of my past faults, a strong and powerful grace, never to commit them again. Amen.

MEDITATION VI.

On Venial Sin.

INTRODUCTION.

THE Jews made use of two sorts of weights and two sorts of scales. One was taken from the Sanctuary, and was true and just; the other was called a public weight, and was very fallacious. The divine Scripture says of Absalom, that when he sold his precious hair, he weighed it with the public weight, and sold it for no less than two hundred shekels.—II. *Reg.*, xiv. 26.

With two kinds of scales, then, we can weigh the sins of men. If they are placed in the public balance of sinners, it is deceitful. "In the hand of the wicked, a deceitful balance." The blind world says, that mortal sin is not so great an evil, and that venial sin is light and small—a nothing, and to be made little account of. We sometimes hear these questions: Is this a mortal sin? No. As it is not mortal, it little imports one. O blindness! justly deplored by St. Anthony of Padua: "Many do not weigh their sins in the scale of the Sanctuary, that is as they appear before God, and are regarded by his saints. They use the common scale of worldly opinion."—*Dom.* 4 *post Trin.*

Ah! if venial sin be weighed in the balance of the Sanctuary, and as the just held it, who were enlightened by God and faith, oh! how grievous it is! So grievous, that St. Catherine of Genoa, considering its deformity, almost died. St. Aloysius, thinking of it, fainted away. It is so grievous, that St. John Chrysostom (*Hom.* lxxxviii. *in*

Mat.) makes a very wonderful proposition. "Believe me," says the saint, "although venial sin is, without comparison, less in malice than mortal sin, still it causes greater fear: for mortal sin is a horrible monster, the aspect of which is sufficient to scare almost all who behold it; whereas venial sin is a hidden poison, which deceives the incautious, and by degrees makes them fall into mortal sin. To undeceive us in this respect, this meditation proposes three points:

1. What venial sin is in itself;' its intrinsic malice.
2. What damage it does to the soul.
3. What chastisements it receives from God.

According to the angelic doctor (1, 2, *qu.* 88, *ar.* 3), there are two sorts of venial sins. Some are committed through want of consideration, through human weakness, and proceed "from our corrupt condition." Others are committed with a deliberate will. I intend to treat of the second sort.

FIRST PRELUDE.

Let us imagine ourselves in the presence of God, like the poor man in the Gospel, who went from Jerusalem to Jericho. Having fallen into the hands of robbers, he was by them despoiled of what he had, severely wounded, and left in this sad state on the ground: thus only his life remained.

SECOND PRELUDE.

Say from the heart: My God, my celestial Samaritan, by my many venial sins, I see myself despoiled of supernatural goods, and wounded in my powers: it appears to me that I have nothing left but the sole life of grace. Ah! Lord, be moved to pity towards me. "Heal my soul, for I have sinned." With the oil of thy inspirations enlighten me to know the evil I have done; and with the wine of thy love render me fervent, that I may no longer displease thee.

FIRST POINT.

"*He is truly wise,*" says St. Bernard, "*who esteems things as they are.*" Let us, then, by the light of faith and with the assistance of theology, see what venial sin is in itself. St. Thomas (1, 2, *qu.* 72, *ar.* 5) says, " that mortal sin is an irregularity of the soul, by which, turning from the last end to adhere to some temporal good, the soul loses the principle of spiritual life, which is charity towards God, and grace. By venial sin the soul is disordered in adhering to some worldly good, but not so as to turn from the last end. Thus the vital principle of grace remains; we may say, the soul becomes infirm, but does not die.

This being presumed, I will thus discourse. It is true, venial sin does not contemn God, as mortal sin does; but it is also true that it does not hold him in that just estimation which he deserves: it does not oppose itself to the divine will. But in a certain manner, as St. Thomas says (1, 2, *qu.* 88, *art.* 1), it acts beside the law, rather than against the law. It is also true that it disgusts him, by not perfectly observing the divine precept. If so, how can it be called trivial? This saying appeared to St. Bonaventure to be a blasphemy. In venial sin we have to consider not so much the slight transgression of the divine commandments, as the infinite majesty of God, whose command is not executed with sufficient exactness.

If a man do not execute the divine will in a small thing, he commits a fault which has no excuse, since he could easily avoid the fault. It was a great sin in Adam not to obey God in a slight thing, such as to deprive himself of an apple. For a like fault Naaman was justly reprehended. He went from Samaria to the prophet Eliseus to be cured of his leprosy. The prophet, without receiving him, and even without speaking to him, sent him directions to go and bathe seven times in the Jordan. Naaman was indignant at this message. He was thus answered: "Sire, if to be cured, a very severe remedy were prescribed, surely you would adopt it: how much more readily should you acquiesce in the slight request to bathe in the limpid waters of the Jordan!"

This thought removes every excuse from the person who commits a venial sin. If to avoid it he had to labor much, or to overcome a great repugnance, he might be pitied if he failed. But what great strength is requisite to overcome in a slight thing? For this reason the fault is inexcusable.

Two things of great import are to be considered in venial sin. 1. *The person who is offended;* namely, God; our King; Redeemer: Father. 2. *The person who offends;* that is, a just soul, who by sanctifying grace is the adopted child and spouse of God. When there is question of a great personage, the least want of respect is a considerable slight. How indignant was Aman, the favorite of King Assuerus, that Mardochai, who was only a foot soldier, did not salute him! He went so far as to endeavor to have him put to death. An Arabian king condemned to death James Almanzorre, who returned conqueror from Spain, for having related to him *jestingly* what had happened to him on his route; namely, that having met a little girl alone and wandering in a wood, and having reprehended her for it, she answered: " So long as Almanzorre is a Spanish gentleman, I shall not fear for my virginity."—(*Boter. lib.* 1., *Dict, mir.*) Thus a laugh, more confidential than respectful, before a king, was considered a crime deserving death. Shall venial sin, which offends the majesty of God, be considered slight? " It is not so," exclaims St. Bernard (in *Reg. Monach.*) " It is never trivial to contemn the Deity, even in the smallest degree." The law of God Almighty should be kept as the apple of the eye, to which even a little straw causes pain and labor. " Son, keep my law as the apple of the eye"—(*Prov.*, vii. 2.)

If we consider in God the title of Father, what a disloyal and ungrateful son would he be who should thus express himself: " I will not take away the life of my father, nor even wound him mortally. Oh! no; but I will displease him from morning until night: I never will do anything to please him; on the contrary, I will always prick and wound him slightly." What an unworthy son would this be? I am precisely that most ungrateful child to a God who is to me so loving and beneficent a Father. I think nothing of continually displeasing him; he might justly reprehend me: " If I be Father, where is my love ?" I have become like to those Jews who did not crucify Jesus, but ridiculed, beat, and flagellated him. Should such impiety appear to me as nothing?

If the person who commits venial sin be considered, how much the crime increases! It is committed by a just soul, who by sanctifying grace is the friend of God, his spouse, and adopted child. Who is not aware that the slightest displeasure received from a friend—(how much more from a spouse or a child)—is always more keenly felt than even grievous offences received from a stranger or an enemy?

The patriarch Jacob could not enjoy peace, because Reuben, his eldest son, beloved by him as the apple of his eye, had committed a crime in his house. "Reuben, my first born, thou art my strength, and the beginning of my sorrow." (*Gen.*, xlix.) Our Redeemer, at the treason of Judas, appeared more displeased with the ingratitude of the person, than with the treason itself. By the mouth of his prophet he made this complaint: "If my enemy had reviled me, I would verily have borne with it: and if he that hated me had spoken great things against me, I would perhaps have hidden myself from him:—but thou, a man of one mind, my guide, my familiar." (*Pslm.*, liv) My soul, stop here; and reflect that you are much beloved by God, and have received many benefits from him. Are you so ungrateful as to displease him frequently, when he has not given you the slightest displeasure? With what reason does the Lord denominate this sort of injury (by *Zacharias*, xiii. 6) the greatest wound which he receives from his dearest children.

Notwithstanding all these considerations, some

will say that venial sin is certainly not a grievous fault. 1. I answer, venial sin is not a grievous fault in comparison to mortal sin. Absolutely in itself it is; as it displeases God. The Earth is a point in respect to Heaven; but it is not a point in itself; on the contrary it is a vast structure, twenty-four thousand miles in circumference. 2. If venial sin be light as a crime, who will say that it is light as an evil? It is so great an evil that to efface it the merits of the Redeemer are necessary. Our Lord has shed all the blood in his veins, not only for mortal sins, but also in satisfaction for those which are venial. In holy indulgences, the treasures of the blood of Jesus Christ are applied in satisfaction to the divine justice for both. Can that be called a small evil which the infinite wisdom of God esteemed worth shedding blood of infinite price to efface? It is so great an evil that there is nothing worse, except mortal sin. It is even a greater evil than Hell; for, according to Suarez (*de peccat. disp.* 2 *sect.* 5, *num.* 18), Hell being a pure pain, it might be chosen in some case; whereas venial sin being an evil proceeding from a fault committed, cannot be chosen in any case. Venial sin is so great an evil that it ought not to be committed, either to obtain any good, or to avoid any evil. If a person by uttering one single lie could save all infidels, and send all the damned to Paradise, he should not say it. O God! what an evil! How great is my confusion? One single venial sin should not be committed to purchase a kingdom, and I daily commit so many with so much ease, and for what—for nothing. Oh! shame!

Finally, should we even suppose, what in reality is not the case, that venial sin is a slight thing, in its criminal malice, we should reflect on the multitude of these faults committed from morning until night.

St. Augustine says: "If you fear not the weight, tremble at least for the number." If mortal sin is a thunderbolt which kills, so many venial sins are hail-stones which ruin the vineyard of the soul. Mortal sin is a tempestuous sea which causes shipwreck. Many venial sins are like drops uniting together, and also causing shipwreck. The effect is the same at last, however different the cause. (*St. Augustine, Ep.* 108, *ad Selecuc*). Whether this happens by a great sea which envelopes, or by many drops enclosed in the keel of the vessel, is of little matter when the ship sinks. Many venial sins do not form one mortal sin; but many venial sins dispose to mortal sin, and make the soul fall into it.

Mino says, in his *Sentences*, every bat has its shadow; and every small defect is subject to its particular penalty. The pains of innumerable defects united form a great and extreme punishment. My soul, here weep and lament with the holy penitent David: "My sins are multiplied beyond the hairs of my head." (*Ps.*, xxx. 13.) If in so many years of my life the venial sins I have committed are more numerous than the hairs of my head, if each of them—even a thought, an idle word—is to receive punishment, how great chastisement should I expect from divine justice!

SECOND POINT.

What damage venial sin does to the soul. The evils which venial sin brings to the soul are all great and worthy of consideration.

1. The stain which renders it odious in the sight of God. King Nebuchadnezzar expressly ordered his ministers to choose for royal pages well-formed youths who had "no defect nor any kind of stain." (*Dan.*, i. 4). Otherwise they could not be acceptable. God likewise wishes for just souls, without stain of guilt: otherwise he regards them with wrath. Men too are thus inclined. If a stain of oil or ink fall on a richly embroidered dress, its value is so much lessened, that, although there should not be any part of it torn, its price is lessened one half. A queen may be the most beautiful and majestic in the world: but if she receive the least cut or scar on the countenance, at once the estimation of her beauty is completely lost.

A soul enriched with virtuous habits and supernatural gifts, with sanctifying grace, though queen and heiress of an eternal kingdom, if stained with a venial fault, immediately becomes displeasing in the sight of God; and so deformed, that God no longer takes complacency in considering it. He contemns it, as we disdain a vile and disagreeable object. Is not this a serious evil?

What is related of a Spanish lady named Sancia Carriglia, is memorable. She had attained an eminent degree of virtue by means of that great master of spiritual life, John of Avila, her confessor. Conceiving a great desire to know the state of her soul, she begged of God for a long time to make it known to her. After many penances and prayers offered for this intention, at length one evening, being in her closet, an angel suddenly appeared to her, dressed like a hermit, carrying in his arms an infant covered from head to foot with small pustules, as if it had the measles, so that it excited compassion and disgust to behold it. Advancing towards the lady, he said: "This is your soul:" and immediately he disappeared.

The servant of God was so horrified and so wounded with sorrow, that she wept bitterly, saying: "Ah! wretch! what a frightful soul!" She continued weeping and sighing the whole night. On the following day she went in haste to her confessor, and with sighs and groans related what had happened.

The enlightened director enquired whether the child was living or dead. "Living," answered the servant of God. "Oh!" replied the director, "be consoled: as it was alive, it shows that your soul is living by sanctifying grace. As to its being full of little spots, it indicates that you have many faults and imperfections, which render you displeasing to Almighty God"—(*Thomas a Kempis. l.* II., *c.* xxi.; *Nierem Dif., l.* III., *c.* iii.

If God showed me my soul, it would appear so monstrous and deformed on account of my many venial sins, that it would terrify me.

2. Venial sin does not dispossess the soul of sanctifying grace, but it prevents actual graces, which our Lord would bestow were the soul faultless. Actual graces are certain illuminations to know what is good—certain efficacious inspirations to the heart to embrace it—compunction, spiritual sweetness in prayer, great courage in resisting temptations.

As a father, displeased with his son for frequently disobeying him, does not show him the same marks of affection as if he had been obedient—does not give him amusements or clothing suitable to his desire: so God, indignant for the ungrateful meanness of the man, who merely contents himself with not offending him mortally, and nothing more, deprives him, in punishment of his unworthiness, of his most special graces.

St. Martin acknowledges that he was deprived by God of the power of casting out demons, because for a short period he was forced, for the good of the faithful, to treat with the heretics of Ithaca, in the ordination of Felix, Bishop of Treves (*Sulp. Sev., lib.* III., *Dial.*)

Many lament and express surprise at not finding relish in prayer. They pray continually to God and to the saints, and are not heard. Why do they find themselves so weak and fragile at every temptation? Because they are continually displeasing God. How can they ever expect extraordinary graces, or that their petitions to Heaven should be easily heard? How is it possible for them to stand firm at the assaults of temptation, when they are abandoned by celestial assistance on account of their venial sins? They live in the grace of God; but they lead a life similar to consumptive persons, who are pale, languid, and emaciated, in whom but little life remains.

The greatest damage venial sin brings to the soul is, that it disposes to mortal sin. According to the angelic Doctor (1, 2, *qu.* 89, *art.* 1), this occurs in two ways: 1. Indirectly; for God withdrawing the more powerful assistance of his grace, the soul remains weak, and easily falls into mortal sin. 2. Directly: from the habit of several times committing slight faults, the soul is drawn by degrees into a great fault. Add what St. Thomas attests (1, 2, *qu.* 88, *ar.* 6, *ad.* 1), that "venial differs from mortal sin, as an imperfect thing in its kind differs from what is perfect"—"as a boy differs from a man."

No one would have near him long a young lion, lest the growth of his teeth and nails might endanger life. So every one should remove far from him venial sin, lest, resembling a young wild beast, it might afterwards become great and dangerous. The curiosity of Eve degenerated into great disobedience; too much affection for money led Judas to Deicide; the policy of Jeroboam ended in infidelity; and the love of Solomon terminated in idolatry. Oh! what matter of consideration is here!

Woe to you, Sinners, says Isaiah, weeping (vi. 10), who commit so many venial sins; you are working a rope for yourselves which will drag you first into mortal sin, and then into Hell. A similitude is drawn from ropes. A few threads twisted together form cords; these little cords twisted together form those large cables with which windlasses are turned and ships moved. Sinners, according to the remark of St. Augustine, multiplying venial sins, dispose themselves to mortal sin, which draws them to perdition. My soul, enter into yourself, and reflect on your numerous habitual defects. Fear and tremble. Remember what St. Teresa writes of herself in the thirty-second chapter of her *Life*. While wrapt in an ecstacy, she was led by an angel to witness the pains of Hell. "Consider that abyss," said the angel;

"see that little vacant place among the damned. Know that if in youth you had not avoided certain venial sins, from these you would have passed to mortal, and from them *hither.* You should have had an eternal punishment." O terror! O God! what will become of me if I do not renounce my frequent venial sins?

My soul, learn to believe wise confessors when they make great account of what appears to you but of little moment. Often they act like skilful pilots, who when the ship is sailing in the most prosperous manner, seeing from afar a small cloud in the Heavens, cry out: "Gather up the sails quickly; let us recommend ourselves to God, for a great storm is coming on." "Why so?" ask the inexperienced sailors. The pilot replies: "You will soon see arise from that small cloud, whirlwinds and rain; and the whole sea will be in commotion." "Behold a little cloud arose out of the sea like a man's foot. And he (Elias) said, Go up and say to Achab: Prepare thy chariot and go down, lest the rain prevent thee. And while he turned himself this way and that way, behold the heavens grew dark with clouds and wind, and there fell a great rain." (3*d Bk. Kings,* xviii.)

Frequently wise ministers, apprehending from small beginnings the worst consequences, admonish and reprehend. What answer do they receive? The same that certain persons gave in the time of St. Dorotheus: What great thing is this? What great evil is that? Thus they fall into ruin. "Thus the Devil leads them gradually from the least to the worst." (*S. Dorot. ser.* 3.) O deplorable blindness! O ruinous folly!

THIRD POINT.

The chastisement which venial sins receive from God. Punishment is like a shadow which follows the fault. From the size of the shadow we measure the body; so from the grievousness of the chastisements with which God punishes venial sin, we may clearly conjecture what its malice is. God being infinitely just, he justly proportions his chastisement. Being infinitely wise, he well knows what that proportion is. Being incapable of human weakness, he cannot chastise more than he ought, through passion, or false apprehension, or from ill regulated motive, as sometimes occurs amongst men.

1. How has God punished venial sin in this life, under the old and the new law? 2. How does he punish it after death?

As to the Old Testament; Moses, the favorite of God, who had constituted him the minister of Pharaoh, by the divine order went into Egypt to free the people of Israel from slavery. He was met on the road by an angel, who full of anger, wished to destroy him. For what sin of Moses did this happen? Simply because he had delayed circumcising his son who was with him. He had deferred it on account of the tender affection which he bore his child. This was only a venial sin. Sephora, his wife, circumcised him on the spot. Thus the anger of the angel was disarmed.

God sent a prophet to Bethel to king Jeroboam, with orders not to take refection of any description on the way, (III. *Reg.*, xiii.,) which he punctually executed. On his return he met a false prophet of venerable aspect, who deceived him, saying that he might come and dine at his house, as it was revealed to him by God that such was the divine will. The credulous prophet accepted his invitation. What sin did the prophet commit? It was certainly venial; yet immediately God caused a lion to issue forth from the forest to kill him. That we might understand that this had happened not because the beast was hungry, but from the fault of the prophet, the lion did not devour the body, but guarded it until it was interred. Through curiosity to see the burning of Sodom, the wife of Lot was converted into a pillar of salt. For a vain complacency which king David had concerning his flourishing army, he was punished with a plague, which in three days killed 70,000 persons. Nadab and Abihu, sons of Aaron, were destroyed by fire for having used in the censers unhallowed fire.—(*Levit.*, x.) An hundred similar examples are mentioned in the sacred writings.

Many authors remark that God seeming to pass over many mortal sins, is sometimes excited to chastise them when a venial sin is added to them; as in the case of Oza, who first sinned grievously by causing the ark to be drawn by bullocks, contrary to the prescription of the law, which required it to be carried by the Levites. He was not chastised by God for this. He afterwards sinned venially, sustaining with little reverence the ark which was about to fall. Immediately he was punished with death. St. Austin concludes (*l.* 2, *de Mir.* 8 *Scrip.*), that "small faults often prepare the way to punish great crimes." Moses also sinned grievously from diffidence, when God promised him an abundance of meat. "There are six hundred thousand footmen of this people, and sayest thou: I will give them flesh to eat a whole month? Shall then a multitude of sheep and oxen be killed, that it may suffice for their food? or shall the fishes of the sea be gathered together to fill them?"—(*Num.*, xi.) Yet he was not punished by God. He then sinned slightly by the tongue near the waters of contradiction, and he was immediately chastised by God. Can venial sin then be thought light, which not only draws on itself the punishment due to itself, but the punishment due to many past grievous sins? If we read the records of the New Testament, of the Church, we shall see the grievous punishments given by God, even in this life, for one venial sin. St. Jerome relates of St. Hilarion (in the third chapter of his *Life*), that for the distractions which were not sufficiently rejected by him at prayer, God permitted that a devil should scourge him.

St. Odo, abbot of Cluni, writes of St. Gerard, that God struck him blind for having once fixedly looked on a young girl. (*Life, book* I., *chap.* xx). Palladius mentions that a holy man who lived in great austerity, received from God, by an angel, for several years, the whitest bread, which lasted for many days. After some time he began to think he was better than others. God immediately punished him. He received black bread. St. Frances of Rome once suddenly felt a great blow. Turning round to see who had struck her, she beheld an angel with an angry countenance. He said: "I gave you the blow as a punishment for uselessly employing time which is so precious." Similar examples are recorded in sacred history.

The most atrocious pain which God inflicts on venial sin is after death. It is the sentence of the angelic St. Thomas (1, 2 *qu.* 87, *art.* 5) of the seraphic St. Bonaventure (in 4 *dist.* 4 *art. qu.* 3) followed by the general opinion of theologians, that if a sinner dies without the grace of God, and carries with him to Hell mortal sins, and a venial sin not remitted, he shall there suffer eternal pain for both. The reason is clear. In Hell there is no redemption; there is no remission even of a venial fault; there is no remission of the pain due to it. Venial sin! how great an evil, since a case may be found wherein it suffers an eternal punishment.

2. Venial sins, for which just souls did not penance in this life, are atoned for by the most severe pains of Purgatory. If any one while living, for a lie, was to be thrown into a burning furnace, what terror would it occasion! Yet, he would feel but for a few moments the pain of fire, as he must soon die. What torment then for a soul in Purgatory to be obliged to live for a long time in that fire, and in so active a fire, that in Scripture it is called spiritual and the quintessence of fire (*Isa.*, iv. 4.) "A fire so tormenting, that it is the same fire as Hell." So says St. Augustine. With this difference, that the fire for the damned is eternal; for the souls in Purgatory it is not. It is immensely prolonged by the desire and hope of seeing God; and much more, because a soul suffering there has no terrene objects to divert it, nor other affections. It is entirely turned to God, and it has no desire but to enjoy him. This desire ungratified, it lives in a most tormenting martyrdom. God would wish to have the soul with him in

Heaven; but he is obliged by his justice to purge it by fire. If a king, after concluding a marriage with a beautiful young lady, should order her, on entering the kingdom, to be chained and cast into prison for some fault, who would say that her fault was light? God keeps just souls, who are his spouses and destined to reign in Paradise, not only prisoners, but also in torments. For what? For venial sins. Yet, blind man dares call venial sins light and of little moment. O folly! The saints, enlightened by God, did not so esteem them. They performed the greatest penances for them. St. Maurice, for not having given immediate notice for the baptism of a child that died soon, renounced the bishopric, and condemned himself to live always as a pilgrim.

St. Eusebius, for a distraction at prayer not well chased away, condemned himself to close his eyes during life to all earthly things. The priest Evagrius, in punishment of a slight detraction, remained forty days and nights without covering. St. Jerome writes of St. Paula, in his epitaph, that "he so mourned the smallest fault, that he seemed the greatest criminal" (*ap. Fabri Do. 5 post Pent., con.* 3.)

How can I have so little sense, after committing innumerable venial faults, as to wait to expiate them all in the great fire of Purgatory, being able to expiate them so much more easily in this world? Being able easily to remedy past venial sins by tears and penance, and by caution to prevent them for the future, should I have so little judgment not to do so?

It is wonderful what every day happens in this world. If there is question of any bodily ailment, how small soever, it is held in great account, as if it were a great evil. On the contrary, if mention is made of the evil of the soul, it is held for nothing. If a man have a little mole on his face, he cannot suffer that small deformity: he takes advice, and procures every means to be freed from the stain. Should he have a toothache, a cold, a slight fever, doctors are immediately called in, medicines are taken, a rigorous diet is observed. Should any one say: These are not mortal maladies; there is no danger of losing life: why then use so many remedies? the answer is: These are sicknesses which require attention: they are small evils, but are tiresome, and may degenerate into great evils if not speedily cured.

Holy faith, enlighten the mind. So much is said and done for the small evils of the body; and what is said and done for the slight faults of the soul? But there is no mortal sin; we do not for this go to Hell: it is a matter of little consequence! If it is not a grievous fault, it is a grievous evil. "No matter." But you will have to satisfy for it in Purgatory in a frightful fire. "It is no matter." O folly! O deplorable blindness! My poor soul, how little are you divested of human feelings! with how little respect to your great dignity are you postponed to the vile body!

COLLOQUY.

Beloved Spouse of my soul, now that I am enlightened by thy divine light to know venial sin, I am as they who look at the stars through a telescope, and find those planets immeasurable which at first seem small.

How have I been deceived and blinded by the Devil, to esteem as nothing what was so grievous? So solicitous for the health of the body, that I make much of a slight illness, and am negligent for the soul! I have despised the great evil of venial sin, solely because it was not the greatest of evils, such as mortal sin! Ah! unfortunate me! What fears will be mine at the moment of death, if I have not done penance! I shall be forced to weep with holy David.

Ah! those faults which I contemned and trampled under my feet as nothing, will inspire me with terror. What greater horror shall I feel after death, when I shall be obliged to satisfy in the terrible pains of Purgatory, one by one, for all my innumerable defects?

My crucified Jesus! I embrace thy most sacred wounds, and I protest to wish now to do penance for my sins: now I wish to weep for them most bitterly; and now humble, contrite, and with tearful eyes, I beg pardon a thousand times. I have certainly done thee a great injury by displeasing thy infinite goodness; but a much greater offence have I been guilty of in thinking little of thy displeasure. Blind and ungrateful that I have been! Know, however, that in future it shall not be so. I will fly from sin more than from serpents and dragons; not only from mortal sins, but also from venial, and the very slightest faults; for I have not courage to embitter any longer thy most loving heart, my God, my Creator, my Redeemer, my Father, and my all. As I am so miserable and frail, do not permit me to be separated from thee. Strengthen me with thy grace.

MEDITATION VII.

On Purgatory.

INTRODUCTION.

WHOEVER wishes to purchase a house, goes first to see it, and observes attentively whether it be commodious, pleasant, well furnished, and tastefully decorated. If otherwise, the contract is not concluded.

There are many who, unwilling to do penance for sin in this life, are contented to remain hereafter in Purgatory, not for months, but for years; even, if necessary, till the day of judgment. Provided they avoid Hell, they make little account of Purgatory. Miserably blind! I beseech you, before you thus resolve, look into that horrid prison, in which you seem satisfied to dwell. Consider the pains of the suffering souls. Their lamentations will be a great lesson for you. Their sighs will be your best sermon. While you compassionate their sufferings, they will teach you the manner of satisfying the debt due to your sins.

As Cain, chastised by God, served as a sign to impress on others a horror of sin—(St. Basil of Seleucia (*or.* 6) says, his sufferings were silent lessons for others)—so souls punished by God in Purgatory will afford much learning at their own cost. Let us act with them as Job did with his friends. Scarcely had they seen him covered with sores, pallid, having lost his children and goods, and obliged to lie on a dunghill, than struck with horror, they threw themselves on the ground; and for seven days and nights they did nothing but consider him with astonishment, without uttering one word (*Job*, ii. 13). "How uncivil was this silence!" says Origen (*book* III. *in Job*). Why deny a wretched man the comfort of a sweet word? He answers: "Be not surprised at it, for the profound silence of the friends was not only compassion for Job, but also fear for themselves." They discoursed thus: "If Job, who is so just and holy, was tried by God with these strange calamities, what should we fear who are guilty of so many more faults?" We should use the same language; considering with dread the torments of the suffering souls. If these, for slighter faults than mine, weep inconsolably tears of fire, what shall become of me, who am full of faults, and do not think of penance? Not only in this holy time of the exercises, shall I provide for the principal affair of avoiding Hell, but for the important one of avoiding Purgatory, as far as I possibly can.

To this end the present meditation is directed. In it we shall consider—1. The intensity of the pains of Purgatory; 2. The great difficulty of avoiding them; 3. The importance of avoiding them.

FIRST PRELUDE.

Imagine that you see, near Hell, a horrible place, full of black and sulphureous flames; and therein innumerable souls, not in despair, like the damned, but devout, and full of most tormenting desire of seeing God. They weep and lament without consolation, and extend their hands to implore our help.

SECOND PRELUDE.

Let us pray ardently for light and grace to efface our sins in this life, that after death we may be freed as much as possible from those flames, and let us repeat with all our heart: "Be pleased, O Lord, to deliver me; look down, O Lord, to help me." (*Pslm.* xxxix.)

FIRST POINT.

The intensity of the pains in Purgatory. St. Augustine hearing some persons say, that, provided they escaped the fire of Hell, they cared very little for that of Purgatory, was excited by a just zeal. He said to them: "Be silent, and do not in future utter such folly; for if all the torments were united which tyrants have inflicted on holy martyrs—all the sufferings which executioners have given malefactors—and all the pains of the world, they would bear no comparison to the pains of Purgatory."

The fire which torments suffering souls is precisely the same as that which torments the damned, except in the eternity of its duration. The holy Church calls the pains of Purgatory the same as those of Hell. The fire of Purgatory is enkindled with an infernal heat, and hence is so active that it is not simply called ardent, but the spirit of ardor (*Isa.*, iv. 4). It would dissolve a mountain of bronze far more easily than a furnace on Earth would consume a straw. Besides its natural activity, it has a superior power, given by God, who makes use of it as an instrument of his wrath. God himself says, by Zacharias, that he, much more than the fire, shall burn and purge elect souls, and with his breath will blow the mantle of their flames (*Zach.*, xiii. 9).

O most terrific fire! Herein are tormented for months and for years, not the bodies, but the souls of the elect. The torment will be excessive, because 1. The soul being more noble than the body, it is far more capable of feeling in a lively manner what is pleasing, as well as what gives pain.

2. While the soul is united to the body, its suffering is much lessened by the body, which being gross and heavy, serves as a shield and rampart; but in Purgatory, being free from the body, it receives the impression of pain directly.

3. While the soul animates the body, if a pain be in the foot, or if the hand be wounded, the head does not suffer, nor the members that are entire. In Purgatory, the soul separated from the body, is entirely martyred with every torment.

Besides, the suffering soul is tormented with more than fire. 1. By reflecting that for such slight things, atrocious pains must be endured. 2. Considering the folly of having neglected during life to redeem its faults by meritorious actions. 3. Seeing the monstrous ingratitude of children and heirs, on whose account the soul is in those places. They live in forgetfulness of its necessities, and while able with a few suffrages to free it from torments, they omit this duty. Shedding torrents of tears, the soul will grow angry with itself, exclaiming: "How foolish and blind I was. I might have expiated my sin by giving in alms what I had acquired by my labors; I preferred favoring ungrateful heirs, who spend my substance, and are unmindful of my pains. Wretch that I am!" "I am forgotten as one dead from the heart." (*Pslm.*, xxx.)

Beyond all the pains in Purgatory, is the privation of the beatific vision. This indeed is the excessive pain. St. John Chrysostom said (*Ho.* 24, *in c.* vii. *Matth.*), that the Hell of Hells is to be *always* deprived of God. We can also say, that the Purgatory of Purgatories is to be *long* deprived of God.

Thus every suffering soul is martyred by desire and love. Every soul disengaged from the body, knows clearly the goodness of God. It desires him with ardor, and amidst continual sighs and groans, appears unceasingly to repeat the prayer of the blind man in the Gospel: " O Lord, let me see." (*Luc.*, xviii.)

When will that fortunate day come on which the Sovereign Goodness will be unveiled? The soul would wish for the pain of fire to be redoubled, provided the pain of desire should be removed; like Rutilia, of whom the Moralist writes (*ad Helvid., cap.* xviii.) that he preferred suffering with an exiled son, rather than endure alone the desire of seeing him.

The soul, however, will be much more crucified by love than by desire, and in three manners. 1. A natural love, by which it is carried to God, as its beginning and its end, with greater force than a stone descends to its centre, or the flame ascends to its sphere. 2. Supernatural love, by which in the most lively manner it attaches itself to God, as to its sovereign, only, and eternal good. 3. Most ardent charity, well knowing that it is to be " espoused to the Divine Lamb"—(*Apoc.* xix. 7)—knowing that as spouse it is destined to an eternal kingdom. It sees that its most beloved spouse closes the gates of Paradise against it. Its love thus deluded, suffers great torment. How long is this great suffering to last? O God! who can say it without horror? For months, for years, sometimes even until the day of judgment.

How horrified and tremulous is the malefactor who is consigned to an obscure prison or to the galleys for three years? How a sick person laments if the surgeon inform him that he shall have to suffer a most painful operation during a quarter of an hour? Shall not the blood freeze in our veins, when we reflect that for many sins we must suffer inexpressible pains, not for hours or days, but for months and years?

St. Augustine says (*in Ps.*, xxxvii.): "In Purgatory one day shall be as a thousand years." The desire and hope of seeing God, and of passing from excessive torment to excessive joy, will cause one hour to appear longer than a century. This has been attested by many souls from Purgatory.

St. Antoninus relates, that a sick person was bedridden for a long time, and could scarcely survive his tortures. An angel appeared to him, and in the name of God begged of him to choose either to suffer those tortures for another year, or to stay one half hour in Purgatory. "One half hour in Purgatory," said he: "then my sufferings will soon end." Having said this, he expired a short time afterwards. Scarcely had he expired, when the angel went to visit him in Purgatory. No sooner did the unfortunate man see him, than he said with loud and inconsolable sobs: "Ah! angel, you deceived me—you assured me I should only remain one half hour in Purgatory, and I am now burning here for twenty years." "What?" replied the angel—"What twenty years! Only a few minutes have passed since your death, and your body is still warm in the bed." So true is it that the pains of Purgatory, in a manner, torment, by the force of imagination, so that every hour appears a century to the suffering soul.

Beloved, let us here pause, and thus discourse. Is it true that Purgatory is such as I have depicted, or not? If it be infallibly certain, how then can you make so little account of it? Can you err more strangely than by not believing it? Richeomo relates of a lame man in Arles, that seeing the room on fire, where he lay immovable, unable to assist himself, or to receive assistance from others, he made so great an effort that he put his whole body in motion. In escaping from the burning, all his ailments ceased. Will not you, in view of the terrible fire of Purgatory, which you have so well deserved for your sins, arouse yourself, and forsake your evil habits? It was certainly great folly in the relatives of Lot, when their grandfather told them, in the name of the angel, to fly from Sodom, to avoid the dreadful deluge of fire (*Gen.*, xix. 20), that they made no account of it; thought it silly—that the holy patriarch was joking or mad. What then shall be said of the foolishness of those who, admonished by faith and the ministers of the Gospel to flee from the pains of Purgatory, hear the summons without profit, as if it were but a jest?

Ah! my God, it is but too true what Osee said weeping: "There is not in the world the true knowledge of God" and the soul. What then follows? "Cursing, and lying, and killing, and theft, and adultery have overflowed; and blood hath touched blood"—(*Osee*, iv.)

SECOND POINT.

The great difficulty of escaping the pains of Purgatory. How great soever an evil may be, if it can be easily avoided, it is much alleviated. But if the evil be great in itself, and if there be great difficulty in avoiding it, then it is certainly immense. This is precisely the evil of Purgatory, as Cardinal Bellarmine attests (*de Annis Grat.*, c. xiii.)

Amongst perfect and holy men, very few have succeeded in going straight to Paradise. Bellarmine being near his death, heard from the general of the Society of Jesus, Muzio Vitelleschi, that his most holy and exemplary life gave every one hope that after death he would go straight to Heaven. "No," replied the humble cardinal, "I have no such hope."

St. Teresa relates, that, having known the state of many virtuous souls in the other life, she only recognized three who went to Heaven without passing through Purgatory. This should not occasion surprise, for the reason St. Bernard offers, namely, that as there is no good which is not sovereignly remunerated by God, so there is no evil, however trifling, which remains unpunished.

2. The most holy souls are subject to slight imperfections. They must satisfy for them in Purgatory. God will not allow any soul to enter Heaven which is not entirely free from every stain. How acute is the eye of God, to know those slight stains which we cannot discern. Of him it is said, he finds something to reprehend even in the purity of angels. "Even the Heavens are not pure in his sight." In good works is

found much to amend and judge; so that holy Job feared that even his holiest actions were not entirely pleasing to God. How terrible are the judgments of God, and how different from those of men! Man sees the exterior: God sees the heart.

Father Balthazar Alvarez, of the Society of Jesus, confessor of St. Teresa, was, from the testimony of his sainted penitent, one of the most holy men who flourished in his time. He prayed to God to reveal to him how his good works appeared before him, and God granted his request, and showed them to him, under the symbol of a bunch of grapes, the greater part of which was decayed, bad, and immature: two or three only were whole, and these were covered with mud. Our Lord said to him: "Such are your actions. Two or three only are good; and if I examine even these rigorously, they will not fail to be reprehensible."

O God! how rigorous are thy judgments in discerning the faults of men! Who can die so pure that he can have nothing to account for in Purgatory?

In the history of the Church many apparitions are related of souls from Purgatory, who revealed the pains they suffered for apparently very slight faults. Surius mentions, in the *Life of St. Severino*, on the 23d of October, that as a cleric was fording a river, one appeared before him, and seizing his hand, burnt it, saying: "I suffer this pain for having recited certain prayers with little devotion."

Gregory of Tours, tells of St. Martin, that, while at prayer by the tomb of his sister, rather recommending himself to her as a saint than praying for her, she suddenly appeared before him with a dark habit and downcast pallid countenance, saying that she was in Purgatory for no other defect than for having washed her hair on Friday, without reflecting on the passion of our Lord.

The sister of St. Peter Damian revealed to a holy soul, that she was condemned to Purgatory for eighteen days, for having, through mere curiosity, remained in a room to listen to the songs which were being chanted under her windows.

St. Severino, Archbishop of Cologne, was condemned to a most severe Purgatory for having recited the canonical hours without due regard to the distinction of time; and yet, this was occasioned by great affairs at court, for which he esteemed himself sufficiently excused. We read many similar examples in ecclesiastical history.

Let us enter into ourselves, and draw for our instruction that conclusion of St. Antonine, after he had related similar examples to his religious: "Fear then every venial sin committed, and every committed sin not fully atoned." If God is so rigorous in punishing the slightest faults in Purgatory; if even the most virtuous and holy persons have not succeeded in avoiding Purgatory; what will become of me, who for so many years have committed innumerable venial sins, and have not done any penance? I am so delicate, that I cannot bear the prick of a needle. How can I suffer to be scorched in a most atrocious fire? Why have I so little sense? Why do I not conceive a sovereign horror for the slightest fault? Why do I omit doing penance for faults already committed? "Walk in the light o. your fire, and in the flames, which you have kindled"—(*Isaiah*, l.) Let us avail ourselves of the flames of Purgatory, to know the purpose of Christian penance.

THIRD POINT.

The great importance of avoiding the pains of Purgatory. It is most certain that a soul cannot enter Heaven, unless entirely free from every stain, and with every debt fully satisfied. This being premised, we are either to punish our sins during life, or God will punish them after death. "This cannot be avoided," says St. Augustine. During life, sins are purged by the waters of tears and penance; after death they are purged in the burning furnace of Purgatory. Is it not better to efface sin with water than with fire? During life, one day of penance, even an hour, can satisfy that which could not be remitted with a year's Purgatory. Ludolphus re-echoed the sentence of Ezechiel: "A day for a year have I given thee" (iv. 6.) Is it not infinitely better now to suffer a little instead of suffering much in the next life? The penance performed during life satisfies for sin. The pain of Purgatory is only suffering for sin. The satisfaction during life includes merit; suffering after death does not merit anything. One thousand years of suffering in Purgatory could not acquire the slightest degree of grace, nor any new degree of glory in Heaven. Which are we to choose, if we have any sense? Suffering here a little, for a short time, with merit; or suffering there much for a long period without merit?

Finally, divine justice is much more satisfied with the penance done in life, though small, than with the pain, though great, which is endured in Purgatory. The former is spontaneously inflicted or willingly accepted; whereas the latter is a forced sacrifice, a pain of necessity.

For all these reasons, it is easy to know how much it imports us to satisfy for sin now, and to avoid the awful pains of Purgatory. Yet there are so many who, well aware of their numerous sins, have not the slightest idea of satisfying for them. They eat, sleep, enjoy themselves, and mind every other affair but this. Blindness! Folly!

Augustus heard of the death of a Roman, who, oppressed with grievous debts, had lived most joyfully, and without solicitude. So too he died. "Purchase for me," said the emperor "at any price the bed of this gentleman; for it must be very soft, since its master slept on it with so many debts, and so quietly." How much softer must be the bed of those who, having contracted the greatest debts with the divine justice, yet sleep without care; never considering that they have to atone for all in Purgatory, with the most severe torments! Boundless stupidity! Mournful folly!

Let us now come to the practical fruit of this meditation; let us resolve to avoid Purgatory, by adopting all the means calculated to avoid it as much as possible. The first is to do penance for our sins, and to perform all the good works we can; and not to place our hope in the suffrages of those who shall outlive us; and let us act promptly before a mortal accident befall us.

The Disciple relates that a lady was recalled to life to accomplish penance for her faults. She invented the most strange cruelties to torture herself; she inhabited tombs, rolled herself in the snow, threw herself on burning coals, tore her flesh with horrible instruments. She would say to those who expressed their astonishment: "Ah! this is nothing in comparison to those pains I suffered in Purgatory."

The second is, to use every diligence to gain holy indulgences, by which our sins are satisfied for, in union with the merits of Jesus Christ. The servants of God have always performed these devotions, when they wished to prepare themselves more particularly for the hour of death. What is requisite to gain indulgences? Being able with little effort to avoid inexpressible pain, why do we not avail ourselves of these easy means?

The third is, to be merciful now to the suffering souls, by giving them copious suffrages. God will so dispose persons that the charity we exercise to others will hereafter be exercised by others towards us. The souls which have entered Heaven will be most grateful to us. Blessed is the person who has sent even one soul to Paradise. Who can doubt of the efficacious intercession before the throne of God for the deliverance of the benefactor who freed him from Purgatory? Unfortunate are they who have not satisfied the pious duties enjoined by their ancestors. The just will cry for vengeance before the tribunal of divine justice against the rapacious usurpers of their labors, who therefore cannot expect to enter Heaven. From Purgatory itself they will curse the substance of their ungrateful heirs. In proof of which Bernardine de Bustis relates, that a father died, who, by his great acquisitions, left his son very wealthy. But the ungrateful man soon forgot his benefactor. He never thought of praying for his deceased father, who was burning in Purgatory. Although his funds were most ample, he came to the greatest poverty. All misfortunes appeared to conspire against him. Continual tempests desolated his gardens; sudden disasters destroyed his cattle; conflagrations ruined his houses; law-suits or enemies obliged him to spend all the money he had collected. Driven to despair, he discovered his state to a servant of God, and begged him to pray for him. He did so; and it was immediately revealed to him that the ungrateful son could not enjoy the goods he had inherited; for his father, to whom he gave no suffrage, cursed him every day in Purgatory. His maledictions were executed by divine justice in punishment of the shameful ingratitude of the son.

Let us *now* do good to our deceased friends: we shall thus insure it to ourselves. Let us imagine that Jesus Christ says to us, for each of the deceased, what he said to Lazarus: "Loose him and let him go." (*Jo.*, xi. 44.) Satisfy the legacies of your ancestors for the discharge of their consciences, and cause them to enter Heaven; and do so promptly. The most benign theologians allow a short space of time. But should not delays be considered inhuman if we reflect on what St. Augustine says on *Psalm* lvii., that every hour in Purgatory is equivalent to a thousand years of pain.

It is written of Father James Rem, of the Society of Jesus, that every time he passed by a cemetery which was near his college, he heard arise from those mouldering bones these lamentable voices: "Have pity on us, O Father James, have pity on us!" Let us also imagine that the souls in Purgatory cry out to us in a similar manner: "Son, Brother, Friend, have pity on us."

COLLOQUY.

O God! what a great thought is this which now astounds me! How frightful are the pains of Purgatory! How difficult even for the saints to avoid them; and I do not think of it? I do not try to extinguish by penance the inexorable flames which await me; on the contrary, I add continually new fuel with repeated and greater sins. If I foresee I have to suffer some evil, although light in this world, I strive by every art to avoid it. Yet knowing by faith that a most severe Purgatory awaits me, I do not make the slightest effort to avoid it. Miserable that I am; How shall I ever endure so cruel a fire, who cannot bear the slightest inconvenience for my soul?

St. Bernard shed torrents of tears (*Ser de Quadr. debiti,*) and says: "My past sins demand fruits of penance. My sins are more numerous than the sands of the sea-shore, and my evils are beyond number. How then shall I count them? How shall I satisfy to the last farthing?" If a saint most innocent, most virtuous, buried alive in a cloister, nourished by fasting, weeps and trembles from head to foot, and thinks he cannot satisfy God for his omissions, what then can I say? I who am guilty of innumerable misdeeds, and have not done penance and do not any penance for them? Saint Gregory had reason to exclaim: "What shall the rod of the desert suffer, when even the cedar of Paradise falls?"

I am negligent in atoning for my sins here,

hoping afterwards that others will draw me from Purgatory. How foolish! Have I lost my senses, to expect that others will do for me what I do not for myself? Others will act towards me as I do to my deceased friends, that is, forget them in a few days. What a cross will it be for me in Purgatory to reflect that I could very easily have atoned for my sins, and that I did not do so because most imprudently I wished to confide in those heirs whom I well knew to be often thoughtless and ungrateful! My God! now by thy mercy thou givest me light to know this truth, give me also the grace to profit by it. I am resolved to make up my accounts better in future; and from this moment I will begin to do penance for my sins by weeping over them most bitterly. Pardon, my God, pardon my having offended thee so often. Mercy, my God, for a poor blind person who has acted without reason! From this day, with thy grace, I wish to wash my sins with the water of my tears, and not to wait until I purge them in the fire of Purgatory.

MEDITATION VIII.

On Death.

INTRODUCTION.

ONE of the most pernicious effects of sin is death. Adam sinned, and for this expressly he was condemned to die, with all his descendants. According to the reflection of St. Augustine, although death be the offspring of sin, yet nothing so much prevents and destroys sin, as meditation on death. What a great point is this! It strikes the mind with amazement more than any other truth.

By faith we believe the other grand truths—judgment, Hell, Paradise; but we do not see them. A lively thought of death works a thousand conversions and changes of life; and daily fills cloisters and deserts with persons, who, reflecting on the brevity of life, and the vanity of terrestrial things, turn from the world, the better to dispose themselves for a happy death. "Death worketh in us," says the Apostle (II. *Cor.*, iv. 12).

Painters representing saints and servants of God, usually draw them with a skull in their hands. Why so? Because almost all who become saints, did so by reflecting that all the world holds in esteem—as honors, riches, pleasures—must end in a few years. All ends in the grave.

The famous Gerard, a Dominican, having read in the fifth chapter of *Genesis*, of the first men who lived on Earth, he observed that the life of each of them terminated with this epitome: "And he died." Thus Adam lived 930 years, and died. Seth lived 912 years, and died. Enos lived 905 years, and died. And longer than all, Mathusela, who lived 969 years, finally died. Here he closed the book quite anxious and pensive. He thus discoursed with himself: "So the life of nearly ten centuries ends: now it is as if it had never been. What now remains of their ways and riches? Nothing at all. What do I hope for? what do I resolve upon?" He answered: "I am resolved." He abandoned the world, and enclosed himself in a cloister, where he died holily.

So it is but too true that death worketh in us. May it please God also to change our minds in this most important meditation on death. What death shall we meditate on? There are various ways of dying—suddenly of apoplexy: by earthquakes; by shipwrecks. Let us meditate on the most placid kind of death, on a death gradual and expected; that by seeing how terrible this is, we may conclude how much more frightful the other deaths must be. We shall consider—1. what precedes death; 2. what accompanies it; 3. what follows it.

FIRST PRELUDE.

Let us imagine that we enter a cemetery. O! what horror; here, broken skulls thrown on the ground; there, piles of bones heaped up; all around, ashes and bones. Then say: These were men like myself; and I, one day, (and perhaps sooner than I imagine) shall be as they now are. Here is the end of all their show and credit—thus will mine also end. Each of these skulls appears to say: "Remember my judgment; for thine shall be such also: yesterday for me; to-day for thee."—(*Eccl.*, xxxviii.)

SECOND PRELUDE.

Say to God, weeping with holy David : " Lord, enlighten my eyes, that I may not sleep in death, lest my enemies say they have prevailed against me." (*Ps.*, xii.) Give me, now, light to know, and grace to execute, what I shall wish to have done at the hour of death.

FIRST POINT.

What precedes death. Many terrific things precede death. First—a certainty that we must all die; this being an irrevocable decree made by Heaven: " It is appointed unto all men once to die." In other human things something may arise to gain a law-suit—to be cured of a disease; but with regard to death, no one can say : Perhaps I shall not die. Jesus Christ died, the blessed Virgin, the saints, popes, kings, all died. We also shall die.

Cæsar Augustus having taken Perugia by force of arms, the citizens who had rebelled against him, with sighs and groans, begged pardon and life. Oh! no, said Cæsar, shaking his head, and stamping his feet on the ground, Oh! no, you must all die, without a single exception.

After the sin of Adam, we were all condemned to die; and we shall all die. Guard yourself with the most vigorous diet—have the most expert physician—adopt the most precious antidotes—finally you must die. That day is to arrive for all, in which you will be alive in the morning and dead in the evening, or alive in the evening and dead in morning. The time will come, when I who am speaking, and you who listen, will have it said of each of us, "Oh! do you not know such a person has passed to another life?" This period will come to every individual.

Mark a game of chess! There are on the chess board several pieces of wood, each making a different appearance, kings, queens, noblemen; but when the play is ended, all these pieces of wood are thrown in confusion into a small box, and without any distinction, all are mixed together. Men, whilst in existence, make different appearances; some noble, others plebeians; rich, poor; finally, all die; all are thrown into a fœtid burial place, where their bones and ashes are alike and undistinguished.

All must die! O God! what a thought! what terror! If among mankind, one only should die, certainly all ought to be solicitous and well disposed; how much greater is the necessity of preparing, knowing that we must all die?

If all men were gifted with immortality, except one, and he should live recklessly, what would be said of him? The same will be said of me, and of every person, who, knowing for certain that he shall die, seldom or never thinks of it.

2. Death is preceded by the greatest uncertainty, as to how, where, and when we are to die. 1. We know not *how;* of fever or wounds; a foreseen death, or a sudden apoplexy; a shipwreck, a misfortune which frequently occurs; whether of an illness during which our intellect will be unimpaired, or our senses disordered; when the soul is in the state of grace and well disposed, or in the state of sin; of all this we know nothing. "A man knows not his end."

2. We know not *where;* at home or abroad; in

a place where we shall be assisted by a priest, or not; after placing all domestic affairs in order, or when all hope is destroyed; in the midst of great enjoyments like Ladislas, king of Hungary and Bohemia, who married Magdalen, daughter of the king of France, and died precisely at the moment he sent the most pompous embassy to accompany his queen: the intelligence of his death reached France while ladies and gentlemen superbly adorned, were entering the royal chamber.

3. We know not *when*. " You know not the day or hour:" rather, we know that death will come when we least think of it. How many weep and despair in Hell, for having thought that they should live long, and for that reason deferred their conversion to old age: they were suddenly overtaken by death in the bloom of youth, and in the midst of their wickedness. What folly then, securely to promise ourselves a long life, when it does not depend on us, but on God, who has declared that he would "shorten the years of the wicked."—(*Prov.*, x. 21.) You say: " Doubtless I shall attain old age; then I will arrange the affairs of my soul." Will you risk your eternity on a *perhaps?* rest the most important affair of man on a doubt? I will advance farther and assert, that not only *perhaps*, but *most probably*, you will not attain old age; because experience teaches, that the greater part of mankind die in youth. In a great crowd of persons, how many aged men are there? Very few. Very few attain old age. This truth God wished to teach us from the beginning of the world. The first time death came, there were only four persons in the world: Adam, the oldest: Eve, the most delicate: Cain, the most

robust: Abel, the youngest. Which of these did death first assail? The youthful Abel: according to the saying of Nissen, "The first of premature death." What folly, not knowing the time of our death, fully aware that we may die any moment, and yet not to be always well prepared for death!

Finally. The last mortal sickness which precedes death. This is often occult and malignant; in the beginning it is not considered fatal, but mortality is discovered during the last days of life. Friends, to keep up the spirits of the sick person, persuade him not to fear; even physicians have not courage to speak clearly until the case is totally despaired of; then, in a few hours, entire provision is to be made for the great affair of salvation, for eternity, and for all the interests of the family.

A general cry ensues: " Haste, haste, send for a confessor, lawyers, heirs, friends, quickly; the sick person will soon be no more, and there is great danger of his losing his senses, and thus be incapable of doing anything." The confessor arrives. The invalid, deceived by the hope of his friends and relatives, does not yet know that but a few hours of life remain to him. The confessor, with holy zeal and charity, endeavors to gild as well as he can the most bitter pill of announcing his death, with the sweetest words. "Sir," he says, " by the fidelity I owe you, I tell you, your sickness increases; should the fever of yesterday return to-day, which I hope not, to-morrow you will be in the other world: you have ever been so wise for all other affairs, that you will certainly be much more so for this last affair of your salvation. Have courage then; I am here to assist you; here are the wounds of Christ open for you." This is to say in plain language: "Prepare thy house; to-morrow thou shalt die." What an admonition! O God! what a thunderbolt to the wretched dying person! When Saul heard from Samuel, already dead, that on the twentieth day he should die: " To-morrow, thou and thy sons shall be with me"—(I. *Reg.* xxviii.) he fell prostrate, stunned out of himself, nor would he taste any food.

King Ezekiel being admonished of his death by the prophet, he cried in despair: " How can that be possible? Must I die in the midst of my years?"—(*Is.*, xxviii. 10.) Who could have told him that he was in the middle, and not at the end of his days, if not his false imagination? But he is admonished to die in the best years of his life, when he was on the point of gaining his post, about to settle his son, to increase his revenue; when of all other things, death, precisely, was the least in his thoughts. " In the hour, you least expect." He felt his conscience most entangled and ill disposed. O God! what trials!

A gentleman, in this manner, being admonished of his death: " Wretch that I am," he answered, " I cannot, I cannot." He turned on the other side, and repeating continually, " I cannot, I cannot," he died in despair. " Unfortunate me!" will the dying person say: " how can I in a few moments, with the head bewildered by fever, make in a hurry the confession of many years, replete with bad habits and scandal? How shall I make, as I ought, an act of supernatural sorrow?"

He will then be undeceived about that which the Devil gave him to understand, that he could do at the hour of death what he would not do during life.

The testament precedes death. The confessor having quitted the sick person, the notary immediately enters with his witnesses, at the entreaties of heirs and interested persons. Having advanced to the patient, he will thus commence his interrogations: "Sir, to what burial-place do you leave your body?" Ah! what a harsh request! Into what place do you wish your body to go and putrefy, which has been so caressed for many years." The dying person has to answer: "In the cemetery of such a church." The notary proceeds: "Who do you constitute heirs of your property? how will you dispose of your goods?" Against his inclination, the dying person begins to utter, with tremulous lips, these dolorous words: "I bequeath:" while pronouncing them, he will say within himself: "Thus end all my labors—all the acquisitions I have made in so many years, with so much prejudice to my conscience. How much better would it have been for me, had I left with merit, in the hands of the poor, what I now leave through necessity, to ungrateful heirs. I bequeath my goods to that son, who, I well know, has but little sense, whose morals are not of the best, and who, in a short time, will dissipate all the fruits of my labors. I bequeath palace, gardens, money, rents, furniture, interests: I leave all things." Thus he is despoiled. Having entered naked into the world, naked he must leave it. (*Ps.*, xiv. 18.) The same happens to him as to a merchant, who, overtaken by a great storm, throws himself into the sea, and with much labor saves his life, laying hold of a deserted rock, where he has nothing, sees nothing, hopes for nothing. In this state St. Augustine approaches the bed of a dying person, and thus interrogates him: "Where is what thou hast loved?" Tell me, are you undeceived as to the vanities of this world? What have become of all your labors and acquisitions? Do you not see clearly now that there is nothing good in this world, but this holy crucifix, which you bear in your hands, and which never abandons you? How much better would it have been for you, to have served him, and not the world—to have labored more to acquire merits than temporal goods!

Now that God gives you light, learn to profit by it: learn at the expense of others to make in time a good testament for eternity. We read of two testaments in the divine Scripture; one which (in *Eccl.*, xiv. 19) is called " the Testament of the World"—the other David calls the " Eternal Testament." (*Ps.*, civ. 10.)

Let us reflect on the testament for eternity, of which St. Augustine asks: " What do you leave to Christ;—what for eternity?" What good works do you bequeath for the good of your soul? How important is this matter! There are not a few who, at the moment of death, bequeathing many things, and making agreements for the benefit of relatives, friends, and servants, only omit making a pious arrangement for their own souls. Let us think in time of making our will for eternity.

SECOND POINT.

What accompanies death. The dying person made his arrangements as well as he could. God alone knows how his spiritual affairs were settled with the confessor, and his temporal affairs adjusted with the notary. The sickness begins to increase; the symptoms return; the fever is at its height; a few hours only are expected of life. The sick person feeling his spirits decline and his agony approach, extends himself supinely on the bed, stunned and astounded. Of what does he think? The unfortunate Absalom died hanging from an oak tree, transfixed by Joab with three cruel lances.

Three fatal thoughts shall also wound the dying person, namely, the thought of the past. the present, and the future. He will consider all his past years, all the pleasures he enjoyed, all the honors he courted; and in that "day of knowledge"—as was said in *Ecclesiasticus*, xxvii. 9—" Oh !" he will exclaim, "how they have passed like a shadow, smoke, wind! All that has happened to me in so many years, appears to me a dream." In his dream he imagines he is conducted to a dark grotto by a magician, who, with a magical wand having made many circles on the ground, many treasures present themselves before him. Occupied in collecting with both hands, jewels, money, and riches, he awakes, and turning his eyes around, he no longer sees jewels or riches, and knows his hands are empty. Ah! this happens often to the dying!

Job (xxvii. 19) makes this fine comparison: "The rich man when he shall sleep, shall take away nothing with him; he shall open his eyes and find nothing." All that he has enjoyed in forty or sixty years of existence,—all will appear to him as nothing. He will say to himself: "Had I abstained from those unlawful pleasures, from these unjust gains, the pain would be already passed. Oh! how happy I should now feel!" He will run over in thought his past sins, which will surround his bed like a countless army.

The impious king Antiochus, after committing many excesses in Jerusalem, without making any account of their enormity, was at the point of death. He heaved most profound sighs, which appeared to be the utterance of despair. "Now I recall the evils I did in Jerusalem."—(*Mach.*, vi. 12.) Now I know well the wickedness, of which I was ignorant during life. "Wretch that I am," will each dying person say: "by the last gleam of light, things appear so different from what they did previously. Passion made me consider as innocent sympathy what was profane love, and as just contracts, those which were hidden usury. In confession I explained my own sins, but not those which I caused in others by my scandal and evil counsel."

Thus the past will be a most acute sword, to pierce the mind and heart of the dying person. The thought of the present will be much more so. The day of death which Job called (xxi. 30,) "a day on which we lose everything." The wretched dying person has to make many most bitter and final preparations. He has to detach himself forever from all his goods, which henceforth can no longer be his, but belong to others. He will cast a glance around his apartment; seeing the desks, looking-glasses, tapestry, it will appear to him that all this furniture repeats to him, in the lan-

14*

guage of St. Augustine: "You shall see us no more." You will no longer see us, nor will you be our master. What anguish will this cause in a selfish soul! With much more pain he will see his bed surrounded by afflicted and weeping children, wife, friends, and faithful servants. Reflecting he has to leave them all, never to see them again in this world, he will feel his heart rent asunder.

The Ephesians hearing that the apostle St. Paul was on the point of departing from them, never more to meet them in this world, wept most bitterly, and embracing him in the most affectionate manner, they endeavored to retain him as long as possible.

What then will be the sentiments of a dying person when, turning to his own, he says: "My children and friends, I shall no longer see you, and you will no longer see me."

Finally, he has to separate from his own body, with which he has lived for so many years in such strict union that they have been but one and the same being, nourished with care and delight. "Ah! my body," he will say, "until the day of judgment we shall no longer be together; you in the interim will go and decay and moulder in the dust." O God! what sorrows of death are these!

These pains are increased by the snares and temptations of the demons, who in that last hour will arouse the passions, to drive the wretched person to despair. The Devil seeing but little of life remaining, and knowing that on this short time the eternity of the dying person depends, tries by all means to overcome him. He acts like a creditor who, so long as his debtor is in the city, leaves him unmolested; but if he ascertain he is to depart, he arrests him, cites him to the tribunal, and obliges him to surrender by hostile means. The Devil does not annoy the sinner much who is in health; but when he is about to depart for the other world, oh! then, indeed, he tempts him by the fiercest suggestions. Well knowing the weakest part of his heart, and the temptations with which he has induced him to fall easily and frequently, with these he assails, and combats him with greatest facility.

In a letter which St. Cyril wrote to St. Augustine, he mentions having spoken to a man resuscitated through the merits of St. Jerome; and having heard from him that being near death, so many horrible devils surrounded him, that it appeared as if they were countless. What a conflict will it be to resist so many infernal enemies, especially for those who during life were not used to overcome their temptations, but rather to be overcome by them. It is true, that while the sick person is tempted by the Devil, he is on the other hand encouraged by the assisting priest, who suggests to him fervent acts of piety, inducing him to confide in God, and to recur to the saints. But whoever did not act thus during life, will not do it at death, or will do it coldly; repeating "Yes" with the lips, and not with the heart, to the words suggested by the confessor. How could you expect a man half alive and stunned by fear, to make those supernatural acts which he seldom made in health?

Cardinal Bellarmine relates (*de Arte. Moriendi, l.* 2, *c.* vi.), that visiting a dying nobleman, and exhorting him to make an act of contrition, he responded: "What means an act of contrition?"

The cardinal then began to explain it to him. But he not caring to hear more about it, added: "I do not understand you; this is not the time for such things." Shortly after he expired.

How could it be expected that in an instant he should learn and practice the lessons of the attending priest—he who never would hear anything of his soul? One who has never learned the use of his sword, will profit little in a moment from a skilful fencing master. He will not know how to execute what is suggested to him. The same happens at death. One not accustomed to supernatural acts will hear his confessor suggest them to him. With what confidence can he then have recourse to Mary, since he had but little devotion to her? How shall he be able to invoke the saints who did not observe their feasts, but even blasphemed their names? Finally, when the holy crucifix shall be placed in his hands, O God! how shall he consider those wounds, and that blood which he so often outraged by his grievous sins?

A missioner of the Society of Jesus went to the city of Lucca, to meet an unfortunate person who was to be hanged the following day. He found him on his knees in the midst of the prison with a crucifix in his hands, weeping and sighing in so pitiful a manner, that the efforts of the zealous father to console him were ineffectual. At length the criminal interrupted his sighs, and with great ardor turning to the father, said: "You may think I weep through grief of my imminent death. I weep solely because during forty years I had no greater enemy than this. Now I find myself alone with this crucifix. For many years I left it to go after the friends, on whose account I committed those crimes for which I am to die. Now all have abandoned me. My parents have already disowned me, and blush to be related to a malefactor. My friends, for fear of being thought accomplices of my crimes, say that they do not even know me. Finally, nothing remains with me but this crucifix, which only I have offended." Thus speaking, he sobbed most sadly.

What affections and sentiments the dying person conceives while looking at the crucifix! How much more strongly is he convinced of his monstrous ingratitude towards his good God.

Finally, the dying person will be most tormented by the thought of the future—the uncertainty where he is to lodge in the other world. He knows that most probably he shall immediately be thrown into flames. Oh! what terror!

A gentleman when dying, anxiously turning to his confessor, said: "Father, where shall I be tomorrow?" "Where shall you be!—I am sorry to tell you, but I cannot betray you; you will be in fire. I hope through the mercy of God that it will be in the fire of Purgatory, but fire it will be." The gentleman began to sob and cry out: "Wretch that I am, how shall I suffer so much pain who know not how to bear the prick of a needle? I who am now covered with fine linen, to-morrow I am to burn." Oh! wretch. The dying person must think with horror that in a few hours he will find himself before the terrible tribunal of God, to render an account of his many years of continual and grievous sins.

If the Abbot Elias, after eighty years spent in most bitter penance, trembled with fear, what shall a sinner do? He will be appalled by the cruel thought, that in a short time he is to receive an irrevocable sentence, either of eternal joy or eternal torment.

Mahomet II., great lord of the Turks, glorious for the two hundred cities he acquired for the Ottoman empire, cruel and fierce beyond all belief, reserved for himself a great tract of country for a splendid hunt, prohibiting any one under pain of death to fire a shot or wound an animal there. Two of his young sons, thinking that they were not comprehended in the order, being princes of the blood royal, went a hunting there. The father no sooner heard it, than he arrested and imprisoned them, and afterwards condemned both to be hanged, in so determined and barbarous a manner, that no one durst ask him for pardon. The Mufti alone, head of the Mahometan religion, took a favorable opportunity of representing to him that these were the sole heirs of the kingdom. Although he was of an age to have another successor, this was uncertain; in the name of the whole empire he begged of him to leave a successor. The barbarian was dismayed at this appeal, and said: "To succeed to my kingdom one suffices; let the other then be hanged for a public example. But which shall this be? The eldest? I will not select him. The youngest? No: let them draw lots." Mahomet seated himself on his throne in the great divan hall. Mutes surrounded him; the heads of the government, both political and military, trembled before the king. Two tables were placed; one covered with mourning, had a scaffold on it; the other, covered with rich brocade, held a turban, necklace, and sword. Between, was a table of dice. The two miserable princes were then called to this most fatal game. They had no sooner witnessed this apparatus, than each felt faint from fear. Recovering themselves a little, and taking the dice, O God! what was their anxiety! what trembling in the act of throwing! On one point, more or less, depended such opposite destinies, either to be miserably strangled, or to be emperor of the East!

How much more anxiety must an agonizing soul feel, finding itself at the point of death, on which depends for it either eternal glory, or eternal torments! What agony! what sobs, what sighs, from the dread of such opposite destinies. The last agony of death arrives. The countenance grows pale, the eyes become dim, the organ of hearing is deafened, so that the priest labors to make his voice heard; the nose becomes pointed, the lips black, the chest swells—then the last mortal tear falls from the eyes. The priest having placed the candle in his hands, begins, according to the rites of the holy Church, to utter the "Depart." He says: "Depart, Christian soul, out of this world, which is no longer for you." Hearing this, the dying will say in his heart: "O God, after this departure whither shall I go?" "In the name of the Father, who created thee." "Yes, it is true that God created me, but I have not executed the end for which he created me." "In the name of Jesus Christ, Son of the living God, who suffered for thee." "Yes," will it be said, "but I have not well availed myself of this blood." "In the name of the Holy Ghost, who sanctified thee." "Ah! I have not corresponded to the lights of the divine Spirit." "Go forth, soul, from the body: may the splendid choir of angels receive thee." " Who knows but instead of angels, demons may meet me?" Thus continuing to say the remainder, the dying person will make horrible contortions, rolling the eyes. After long intervals of breathing, doubting whether he is dead or not, the priest exclaims: " Jesus, Jesus." He breathes his last sigh. Thus ends in one moment all the greatness, riches, nobility, beauty, and science of him who lived for many years without thinking of his soul, lived as if he were never to die. O God! what a thought is this? How is it possible that a man gifted with reason, who well knows all this, who many times has seen it, does not resolve to contemn the world, and give himself entirely to God?

THIRD POINT.

What follows death. Three things follow death: one which concerns the body, the other relates to the soul; the third regards the goods of the body. These three things holy king David implied when he said: " They shall go into the lower parts of the earth; they shall be delivered into the hands of the sword; they shall be the portion of foxes"— (*Ps.*, lxii.)

The soul having left the body, will go immediately to the tribunal of God to be judged under the sword of divine justice: " They shall be delivered into the hands of the sword." The goods of the body, " the wolves will take;" that is, the greedy and rapacious, tearing and stealing everything. Often they do not wait until the man has expired; even from the room where he is agonizing they take whatever they can. Robert Lycio writes, that while he was exhorting a dying person to confess, the man, perceiving his domestics searching every corner of the room to take whatever they could find, no longer thought of his soul, but began to weep and cry out: "Oh! my labors, my riches!" Saying this he expired. "They shall be portions for wolves."

What will be done to the body? The body shall descend into the earth. The man has just breathed his last. His eyes are closed. The frightful garment is placed upon him. Thus pale, decomposed, and ugly, he is exposed to the view of all. They consider him with astonishment and horror; even the nearest and dearest friends are afraid of remaining alone with the dead. A few hours then elapse before he commences to putrefy; he is sent away from the house; carried to the church; the sepulchre is opened; the grave is dug, the body is covered with earth; it corrupts and becomes the food of worms, which we see daily in our cemeteries. O God! what a strange change of scene! This is to happen to all, rich and poor, noble and plebeians, to me who speak, to you who listen. What a subject for meditation! How efficacious to induce us to amend and to humble our pride!

Alexander the Great, once seeing Diogenes walk round a cemetery, and being astonished, asked: "What are you doing here?" The philosopher, to humble the pride of this famous man, replied: "I am seeking amidst these bones for the head of your father." So true is it, that the deceased, thrown into the burial place and reduced to dust are intermingled. None is able to distinguish the king from the vassal, or the captain from the private soldier.

Let us consider, beloved, is it true or not, all that has been here said? Can you hope to avoid death? Certainly not; this would be the greatest folly. Is it true or not, what William Granbergi, Archbishop of Cambray, caused to be written in large characters in his cabinet. "From nothing to life; from life to death; from death to eternity." If so, how does it happen, that we think of everything else, except the most important affair of man, that is, to die well? We can die but once; if not well accomplished, the error is eternal. It is usual to fail at first, in embroidery, dancing, and similar things. Why then not accustom ourselves to die to self, to the passions, before leaving this life? Imagine that an angel from Heaven admonishes you, that you are to die three days hence. How would you employ the interim? In exact confession, in the performance of fervent and supernatural acts, in pious works. Now, you have no certainty of living for three days. Why not do for yourself, what you would wish to have done at the hour of death? Why not execute for yourself those pious works, which you wish your heirs to do for you? Let us endeavor, by the thought of death, to amend our failings, and increase our merits; to detach ourselves from all the vanities of the world, and to serve God alone. The great thought of death reformed a very noble youth of Cologne, named Lifardo. After filling the first offices in the country, he became a Cistercian monk. To humble his pride, the superior gave him charge of a little flock, which he tended for several years with much humility. The enemy, not suffering such virtue, began to suggest, that he degraded himself too much, and that in conspicuous places he could serve God better, and do more for his neighbor, without losing his time in an employment as vile as it was useless. This temptation was so strong, that Lifardo resolved to return to the world. One night, awake, and thinking how he should quit the monastery on the following morning, a majestic person suddenly appeared before him, and darted rays of glory around him, and with a resolute voice, said: "Arise, dress yourself, and follow me." Lifardo immediately arose, and followed him. Arrived at the door of the dormitory, it opened of itself, and they advanced towards the church, where the doors also opened. Having entered and arrived in view of the cemetery, the guide imperiously raised one finger. O prodigy! at this signal, all the sepulchral stones are raised in air. The person turning towards Lifardo, who trembled with fright, said, "Look, in this tomb lies the body of one deceased but a short time: see the skull, and in it those worms, which issue from the eyes, and enter the nostrils and the mouth: see that decayed and putrefied flesh exhaling a horrible odor, and know that the same will happen to you." Having taken the monk by the hand, he desired to conduct him to the other sepulchres. But the monk entreated him with tears, not to afflict him any more, as he feared it would cause his death. He was terrified and astounded. The angelic conductor then said: "I pardon you, but with an express agreement, that humbling all pride, you abandon every thought of relinquishing the religious state." Having thus spoken, the angel reconducted Lifardo to his cell.

Finally, departing, he said: "Remember, man, thou art but dust, and unto dust thou shalt return" —(*Cesarius, b.* iv. *c.* iv. *et alii.*)

Would to Heaven, that we also had a similar thought impressed on our mind. How useful it would be, when we retire to rest at night, to extend ourselves with our hands joined on the chest, and say: "In this position I shall be in my coffin, much sooner than I imagine." How advantageous it would be to keep in mind the excellent saying of Thomas à Kempis: "The day will come when you will not see the night; or, the night will come when you will not see the morning."

COLLOQUY.

My Lord Jesus Christ, in whose hands are life and death, humble and contrite, I come to thy feet, to implore thy assistance on that great and terrible day in which I must depart from this world. Ah! miserable that I am: "Sinning daily and not repenting, I fear death." I fear my death; for it is a perpetual separation from what is enjoyed in this world. Much more do I fear for my irregular life, full of faults, and void of merits, which does not give me hope to meet well that moment on which eternity depends: "Sinning daily and not repenting, I fear death." If I continue to live as I have done, thoughtless of my soul, and as if I were never to die, it will fare badly with me in my last agony. Deign, my good God, to be moved to compassion towards me. Through thy mercy thou enlightenest my mind: give me also the grace to execute well what I now propose. I am resolved to change my morals, and from this day forward to place the greatest of affairs before every other—to prepare myself well for death. I will from this moment accustom myself to those Christian acts which I should make at death, when the holy crucifix will be placed in my hands. Most sacred wounds of Jesus Christ, open and bloody for me, I now adore thee a thousand times. I embrace thee, and I beg of thee humbly to assist me to a happy passage, and a blessed life in Heaven. My God, do not abandon me in my extremity: " When my strength shall fail, do not thou forsake me"— (*Ps.*, lxx. 9.) I beg it of thee, through the merits of thy agony and death. I beg it of thee, through those sad tears which thy blessed mother, our most powerful advocate, shed at the foot of thy cross. Amen.

15*

MEDITATION IX.

On the Death of the Just.

INTRODUCTION.

It is not true that death is always so alarming and terrible as the world considers it. On the contrary, St. Chrysostom says: "It is of itself in the order of those indifferent things, which may be good or evil"—(*Ser.* 3, *Ep. Phil.*)

As water of itself is neither sweet nor bitter, but may be rendered sweet or bitter according to the different liquors which are mixed with it: so death is most terrible to the wicked, and most agreeable to the just. To explain this, St. Charles Borromeo caused a picture to be painted of death. Seen on one side, it appeared fierce and destructive, with a murderous scythe in hand. On the other side, it seemed joyful and smiling, holding a golden key to open the gates of Paradise. The death of the wicked, a torment to the impious, is the daughter of sin. "Through sin, death." It cannot be said to have been made by God. (*Sap.*, i. 13.) Inasmuch as it is a passage for penitents to eternal life, it is a reward given by God. The fire in the furnace of Babylon, was a great refreshment to the three innocent children, while it burned their perfidious executioners, according to the saying of St. Chrysostom (*Ps.*, lii.) The same thing which constitutes the punishment of the wicked, gives excessive joy to the just. Having meditated how terrible death is to the impious, let us now consider how lovely it is to the just. God has placed it in our hands, to have death as we please.

We shall divide this meditation into three points, in which we shall see, 1. What precedes the death of the just; 2. What accompanies it; 3. What follows it.

FIRST PRELUDE.

Let us imagine that we see a just man dying. Oh! what a beautiful sight; he is without fear and anxiety; with a joyful countenance, resigned to the divine will; his sighs are enkindled by his desire of seeing the face of God. How bitter soever his pains may be, he is not disturbed. He gives an example of Christian patience. Conscience is without solicitude, because he has well arranged his spiritual affairs. He exchanges sweet colloquies, with the holy crucifix, Mary and the saints.

SECOND PRELUDE.

Exclaim to God, with lively affection: "May my soul die the death of the just." Lord, I beg it of thee, through the bowels of thy tender mercy.

FIRST POINT.

What precedes the death of the just. 1. Great tranquillity of soul. Though it be true, according to Aristotle, that there is nothing so terrible as death, still the just man fears it not. He has every reason not to fear it, knowing his conscience to be in a good state; he does not apprehend the risk of evil after death. On the contrary, he has the hope of sovereign good in Heaven. Always well prepared to die, any death, how quick soever, is not unprovided to him, but anticipated by his good dispositions. In perils of tempests, earthquakes, and conflagrations, sinners grow pale and tremble. Not so with just souls. They appear well disposed, and confiding in the grace of God.

It is related of St. Aloysius Gonzaga, that diverting himself one day in a country house, he was asked by a religious, his companion: "If you were now admonished that you were to die, what would you do?" The saint answered: "I would continue to amuse myself as I am doing, for long since I prepared for death as well as I possibly could."

Nazianzen writes of St. Basil (*Orat. de S. Basil*), that threatened by the tyrannical prefect, if he refused to coincide with his wishes, he should endure privation of goods, banishment, cruel torments, and death, the saint, with a generosity worthy of himself, said: "Know that I fear none of your threats; not the privation of goods—for I esteem myself as having nothing; nor exile—for I well know the whole Earth is the Lord's; nor torments—for my body is already so attenuated, that it can endure but a little longer; finally, I do not fear death, as it will afford me the happiness of seeing God in Heaven; it will also be of very little trouble to me, having already experienced it in part by daily mortification." What great happiness—what content for the just, not only not to fear death, but to expect and desire it, like the apostle St. Paul, who said: "I desire to be dissolved, and to be with Christ"—(I. *Phil.*, xxiii.); because he lived in the world as a pilgrim, such as we all really are.

The pilgrim desires nothing more earnestly

than to arrive at his country. Thus the just man sighs to arrive at Heaven, his true country. Mercenaries who labor unceasingly all day at work, look with anxiety for the last hour of the week, to receive the reward of their labor. The just, whose days (*Job*, vii.) resemble those of servants, from continually laboring and suffering for God, await the end of life to receive the reward of their many meritorious works. The apostle asserts (*Phil.*, i. 21), "that it would be a great gain for him to die." From instinct, every one desires happiness and beatitude: this is " the accomplishment of all desires," according to the angelical doctor. As the just man ardently loves God, so he desires nothing in a more lively manner than to see and enjoy him: knowing that he cannot attain this without death, his desire of dissolution increases, and he is sometimes obliged to exclaim with St. Paul: " Who will deliver me from this body subject to death?" When shall I be free from the trouble of this body, which prevents me from seeing and enjoying God? With the same sentiment, holy David spoke: " When shall I appear before the face of God?"—(*Ps.*, xli.) St. Augustine made use of the same language, (*Soliloq.*, c. 1,) reflecting on the answer given to Moses: " No man can see me and live." Excited by holy impatience, the saint exclaimed: " O Lord, let me die to see thee. I wish not to live but to die. I long to be dissolved and to be with Christ." Finally, St. Jerome being in his last agony, with sweet words spoke of death: " Thou art dark, O death, and yet welcome: sweet and lovely, distilling honey on my lips." Hence arises the great peace of the just, when admonished of death. Confessors have not much labor, nor is it necessary to make use of artifice and studied expressions, to give them this notice. Well aware of the good disposition of their souls, they receive this annunciation with resignation and joy. Thus, good Christians do not sorrow in hearing death spoken of, but they rejoice; and thank the priest for the good news; and with entire resignation place themselves in the hands of God. It sometimes happens, that they will not even have prayers for the prolongation of life, but solely, that the divine will may be accomplished. St. Aloysius Gonzaga, being admonished to die, after thanking the person who announced it, said: " I have rejoiced in what was said to me, we shall go into the house of our Lord."

A French lady, being admonished of her approaching death, turning with a most joyful countenance to him who had told her, and taking a very rich diamond from her finger, said: "Take this, as a reward for this most agreeable news which you have given to me."

The just man, at the hour of death, is not subject to solicitude or anxiety concerning temporal interests, nor what regards the soul, having leisurely well provided for all. With a tranquil heart and serene countenance he expects death. That, apparently, happens to him, which was admired in the famous Temple of Solomon. The sacred text says, that in constructing that great edifice, no noise was heard of hammers, axes, or other instruments for building, but all was done with the greatest silence (III. *Reg.*, vi. 7). How did it happen, that in erecting so extensive a structure, and with so great a number of workmen, no noise was heard?

Abulenses says, that all the pieces of wood and marble which were to serve for the great structure, were first worked on the mount with such proportion and equality, that afterwards in the Temple, nothing more was required, than to place the pieces together. So in the agony of a just man, when there is question of adjusting all that concerns the great journey to eternity, there is no noise made with notaries and witnesses to a will; nor long conferences with confessors to set in order accounts of conscience. Why so? These things were already prepared on the mountain; that is, in the solitude of the spiritual exercises, which he usually made every year, or in the daily retirement of prayer. Then he reflected at leisure, and settled by the light of God, how he would dispose of his temporal goods: with long and frequent examinations of conscience, he disposed himself to most exact confession, as if each should be the last of his life: thus, having all things well disposed, he does not lament nor disquiet himself nor others: it appears to him that he has nothing else to do, but fly to Heaven after death.

O God! what an easy, what a sweet manner of dying! Ecclesiasticus had reason to say (i. 13), that "men who fear God passed very well the extremity of their lives." Why do you not resolve at once to do that which, at the hour of death, you will wish you had accomplished? For a long period, perhaps, you purposed doing so, but deferred it from day to day, deceiving yourself with the hope of doing it later. At length open your eyes; delay no longer; perhaps this is the last light which the Lord will give you. Life is uncertain; mortal accidents are frequent; our years are advancing. For what are you still waiting? "Whilst we have time, let us work good."

SECOND POINT.

What accompanies the death of the just. Two things principally accompany the death of the just: 1. Exemption from the most grievous evils of death; 2. An anticipation of future beatitude.

1. The just man does not feel the torments of death. (*Sap.*, iii. 1.) His dissolution may, in truth, be called the shadow, or appearance of death; for, one of the greatest evils of death is, the severe separation which is made from all that is created; from friends, relatives, even from self. He who has lived unceasingly detached from the world and from himself, actually, or in affection by means of Christian mortification, has not at death to make such a separation from necessity, having already spontaneously made it, and for some period. Frequently, well disposed persons in their agony, do not wish to hear their families spoken of, or other interests, as if they never had any: their sole wish is, to prepare their souls for eternity.

Another great evil is, the memory of former sins. The impious Antiochus, when dying, said with a sigh: "Now I recall the evils I did in Jerusalem." If the just man remember his former sins, he also recollects the contrite confessions with which he cancelled them, and the numerous penances by which he satisfied the pains due to them. Thus, he is rather consoled than grieved.

The snares and temptations of the Devil at that time are great evils; for they are most fierce and troublesome at death. The just man does not fear them, being accustomed to overcome them; and having well practised the method of resisting the Devil, he then finds facility in doing so.

God specially assists whoever was faithful to him during life, and defends him from infernal lions, as he defended the innocent Daniel in the lions' den. (*Dan.*, vi. 22.)

Finally, a great evil is the loss of life, which of itself is most precious and most dear to man. This loss the just man does not mind; he knows that death does not deprive him of life, but only changes it into a much better existence in Heaven. St. Bernard exclaims: "O good death, not taking life, but changing it to better!" Consider the person who dies holily, in the grace of God, and he is exempt from the most grievous evils of death; for he can truly say with holy David: "If I should walk in the shadow of death, I would not fear, for thou art with me."—(*Ps.*, xxii. 1.)

Is not this a great advantage for the just not to have any evil at death, which is itself considered the greatest of all evils. He who has lived well, enjoys at death unspeakable delight, and may exclaim: "Lord, in despoiling me of this mortal body thou investest me with the liveliest joy." Solomon, praising the valiant woman in the Proverbs, says: "She shall laugh in the latter day." —(*Prov.*, xxxi.) This happens to all just souls, for several reasons. We read in the lives of the holy fathers of a monk of Scizia. This holy man was dying as he had lived, a saint. While many monks surrounded his bed, bitterly lamenting the loss they were going to sustain of their dear friend and beloved master, he suddenly began to laugh. What is still more strange, looking around him, and seeing them continuing to weep, he laughed louder a second and a third time. The servants of God being astonished, said: "What means this laugh? Is this a time for laughing? we weep so much for you, and you laugh. What does this mean?" The saint, with a most joyful countenance, said: "Know that I laugh for three reasons. 1. I laugh *at* you for having so great a fear of death. 2. I laugh *for* you, knowing some among you are so negligent as not to have prepared for death. 3. I laugh *for* myself; after the labors of this miserable world, I go at last to eternal repose." For these motives and for others, every just man rejoices at the end of his life.

St. Bernard discoursing on these motives, reduces them principally to three. 1. He who dies well enjoys departing from this world, wherein sin is so easily committed. He appears to say within himself: "Blessed be God that I am departing for another world, in which I can never displease that God I so much love, and who so well merits to be loved." 2. He enjoys departing from this valley of tears, in which there are so many misfortunes, so many perils for soul and body: he consoles himself, saying: "May God be blessed, I shall no longer see so many vanities, scandals, and imperfections as there are now amongst men. Blessed be God, that I have no longer to endure so many risks of failure, shipwrecks, plagues, earthquakes, conflagrations." Finally, he rejoices because he knows he is to pass from labor to reward; from exile to his home; from prison to the liberty of the children of God; from tempests to the port; from combat to the crown. He appears to say joyfully within himself: "Oh! how happy I now am to have mortified my body and suffered for

God! Blessed fasts, blessed austerities, blessed alms, blessed steps I took to the church and oratories. Pains and sorrows have passed, I now find a good provision of merits for the other world. If I had spent my life in delights, all should have now passed without fruit for me, and I should not now feel this great happiness. May God be a thousand times blessed, who gave me light and grace to be able to accomplish what I have done." Amidst these internal enjoyments the happy dying man is not only without anxiety and fear, but with a joyful countenance, with sparkling eyes, and a soul resigned to God. He will not speak nor hear of any subject but God and Paradise. As he had always been humble, pious, and patient, he shows still more clearly at that last moment examples of all these virtues.

The soldiers of Gideon combating against the Madianites, with lighted torches hidden under earthen vessels, having afterwards broken these vases in view of the enemy, suddenly showed these lights, which with unheard of terror glistened before the foe, and humbled their pride. (*Jud.*, vii. 20.) So, at the dissolution of the bodies of the just, they will appear luminous examples of every virtue, wonderfully edifying the spectators, and causing great confusion to the demons. How painful soever his distemper and bitter his medicines, the just man offers all to God, and blesses him for thus effacing his Purgatory in part. He is not angry with any person, but always composed, and grateful for any assistance. Being in the habit of invoking with tenderest devotion, Jesus, Mary, and the saints, oh! with what confidence he does the same at death! Frequently turning towards his advocate St. Joseph, he begs his special assistance, particularly after receiving from the hands of his confessor the holy crucifix. O God, with what fervor of spirit he considers and embraces it, protesting that all his love and hope repose in those precious wounds. He also seems to say: "The greatest comfort I have at this time is derived from the mystical rod, Mary, and from the adorable wood of the Holy Cross. If any temptation occur, he feels that the same crucifix is for him an impregnable buckler which defends his heart. Is not this inexpressible happiness for the just man; a foretaste of his approaching, eternal beatitude?

Who does not weep with tenderness, when hearing what happened to St. Gertrude in her last agony? With the holy crucifix in her hands, shedding most sweet tears, she opened her heart to her Redeemer: collecting on her dying lips the little strength that remained to her, she spoke to Jesus with the warmest affection, insomuch that our Lord would from that moment reward her. Detaching his nailed hands from the cross, with them he opened his side, and approached it to the lips of Gertrude, that she might expire within it, as she happily gave up her last sigh to God. Was not this an anticipated Paradise for that holy soul?

We read of several saints having died laden with these extraordinary favors. St. Paul, the first hermit, died on his knees, with his hands joined on his breast, his eyes turned towards Heaven, and praising God. St. John of God being in his agony, left his bed, and on his knees revered the cross, and amidst devout embraces surrendered his soul into the side of Jesus: being dead, he remained on his knees, still embracing the cross.

The venerable Abbot Robert, at the death of one of his Cistercian monks, who was much given to prayer, saw angels descend from Heaven, who from a precious little basket strewed lilies and roses on the dying person, then took his soul in their hands to carry it to Heaven. (*M. Spec., dist.* iii. *ex* 22.)

The invincible Cardinal Roffense, who was condemned by Henry VIII. to be beheaded, for not signing his name to a divorce from the queen consort, left prison worn out, emaciated, scarcely able to take a step with the gout, which obliged him to use a stick to walk. At the view of the block on which he was to be beheaded, he was so filled with transports of joy, that he cast away his stick, saying: "Come, feet, take these last steps, by which the body goes to a glorious death, and the soul to Paradise."

St. Francis of Paul, knowing by revelation the hour of his translation, extended himself on a cross, and caused the history of the passion to be read aloud; then embracing tenderly and pressing the crucifix to his heart, repeating several times: "Into thy hands, O Lord, I commend my spirit," he expired on Good Friday, precisely at three o'clock, not only without signs of pain, but showing extreme joy.

Is it not well to die the death of the just? Is it not a noble commencement of those enjoyments which are to be theirs in Paradise? If there were no other reward for a good life, but such a death, would it not be a great recompense? It now de-

16*

pends on us to have it, if we wish? Death answers, like the echo, and corresponds to our life. (II. *Cor.* xix.) Shall we be so inconsiderate; being able, with a little labor, to attain a most happy death, and yet neglect it? St. Paul says: "If we sow during life the thorns of sin, we cannot at death reap great merit."—(*Gal.*, vi. 8.)

THIRD POINT.

What follows the death of the just. Two things happen to the just after their death, each of them most happy and glorious: one concerns the body amongst men; the other, the soul amongst the blessed. God often so disposes of the body, that it remains either odoriferous or flexible, at least with a serene and beautiful countenance, as if asleep: far from infusing fear, it gives pleasure to those who surround it. Some devoutly kiss the hands and feet; all wish, through devotion, to have something belonging to the deceased, and implore his intercession with God. Others continually repeat: "He is blessed." Each relates some particular virtue most conspicuous in him. Some praise his patience, his devotion, his charity to the poor. With all, his memory remains in benediction. Finally, the wisest certify that his death should not be lamented, but emulated: to this his dearest relatives and most intimate friends agree: of which we have a clear testimony in holy David. Two of his sons died, one an innocent child, the other an impious rebel, namely, Absalom. For the death of the innocent he did not shed a tear, after having shown great signs of grief for his sickness (II. *Reg.*, xii. 13): he no sooner died, than he adorned himself, and returned to his usual manner of living. On the contrary, for the death of his wicked son Absalom, he did nothing but sigh and sob, saying: "Absalom, my son Absalom."

How strange! David weeps so much for the death of a wicked wretch, who caused the crown on his head to totter; and he does not weep for the death of an innocent son, who might have become the support of his old age and of his kingdom.

What does this mean? St. Ambrose says: "Be not astonished. David had reason: he weeps for the death of the impious Absalom; for, from temporal death, he passes to that which is eternal. He does not lament the death of the innocent, because it is for him the beginning of a blessed immortality. Whatever follows the death of the just as to the body, is glorious and precious; much more glorious is that which follows the soul in Heaven."

St. Henry, the worthy spouse of St. Cunegunda, once praying at the sepulchre of St. Wolfgang, saw in a vision a hand, which wrote on the wall these words: "Post sex." "After six." He said within himself: "This is a clear admonition which God gives me, that in six days I shall die." Consequently he began with great fervor to prepare for death. But after six days he had better health than ever. He then said: "My death will happen after six weeks;" during this interval he prayed, and did continual penance; at the termination of this period, he was exempted from the shadow of sickness. He then said: "I cannot but think it signifies after six years." During all this time he practised so many virtues, that he acquired the name of a saint. At the end of six years he was elected emperor. The preparation for death during six years served to acquire for him the imperial crown.

A thousand times happy is the just man, who not only for six years, but during his entire life, unceasingly disposes himself for death; this lengthened preparation will serve to acquire for him an eternal crown. Happy he, who after leading a short life in the world, amidst the flames of divine love arises, by death, like a phœnix, to an immortal life among the blessed. Holy Job therefore consoled himself: "As the phœnix I will multiply my days." He does not enter the sepulchre, despoiled like the rest of mankind, but loaded with virtues, with the merit of the riches he dispensed to the poor for the love of Jesus Christ. "Thou shalt enter into the grave in abundance." (*Job*, v. 26.) The just man's body goes to the grave, his soul goes to a crown in Heaven.

Thus St. Cyprian encouraged the martyrs to die willingly for Christ. What jubilee, what inexpressible joy shall the soul, that is saved, experience, seeing itself suddenly in the enjoyment of eternal felicity amongst the blessed! It will say with St. Peter of Alcantara, who appeared to St. Teresa: "O happy penance! which merited for me so much glory. Happy fasts, alms, that acquired for me so beautiful a Paradise; I bless you a thousand times."

Let us, *now*, enter into ourselves, and thus discourse. If the death of the just be as sweet, as we have learned—so much so, that Father Francis Suarez, a celebrated doctor of the Society of Jesus, pronounced these words on his death-bed: "I did not think it was so sweet to die,"—who would not desire this beautiful death? who would not repeat: "May my soul die the death of the just?"—(*Num.*, xxiii.)

These words, however, were pronounced by the impious Balaam, who desired to die well, while he lived badly, and without intention of amendment. What folly! Am I less foolish? Knowing clearly how precious the death of the just is, I desire and sigh after it, yet I walk in the paths of iniquity. How can I expect to have peace at death, if I now spend months and years for the interests of the body, without spending one day to settle the affairs of the soul by an exact general confession? How can I pretend to have special assistance from God, from Mary, and the saints, in my last moment, if I do not now think of gaining their patronage by devout homage? With what merits can I go to the other world, if I am now negligent of performing good works? If I wish not to fear, but to rejoice at death, I must deeply impress on my mind the great sentiment of St. Ambrose: "There is nothing to fear in death except the fearful things we have done in life." St. Augustine says the same. (*Ser.* 27, *de Verb. Dom.*) If you live well, you will not die badly.

Death should be *moderately* feared; as much as is necessary to regulate our lives well, says St. Ambrose. We should sovereignly dread, not temporal, but eternal death. We should not act like Cain, who, as St. Ambrose reflects (*Cain and Abel*, II. ix.), guilty of fratricide, solely feared temporal death; but he did not fear dying miserably for eternity; consequently, he did not think of doing penance for his sin.

A person who lives in a Christian manner, and

who believes and hopes in eternal happiness, should not have such great fear of death, as infidels, who do not believe in Paradise. (I. *Thess.*, iv.) The separation of the soul from the body, is but a shadow, an appearance of death. (*Ps.*, xliii.) The division of the soul from God—this is true death.

It is natural for children to fear shadows; but it would be pusillanimous in a Christian to excessively fear temporal death. It shows but little love for God, to have too great a fear of death, by means of which we go to God; and little gratitude to God, who often takes persons early out of this world, to unite them to himself. (*Sap.*, iv. 17.)

I should then purpose to be ever resigned to the Divine Will. When it shall please the Lord to call me to himself, let me accept with courage and thanksgiving the admonition of death. If this appear hard, reflect that Jesus Christ purposely wished to suffer agony and death, to take off its bitterness.

Should it seem difficult to do for God what God has done for me? When the Redeemer commanded St. Peter to come to him on the waters, he gave him assistance to walk on the waves as if on dry land. So the same Lord who commands us to approach him by the sea of agony and death, will give us grace to overcome all the trials which accompany death. St. Augustine (in *Ps.* xxxix.) says: "He does not let him perish whom he told to walk."

COLLOQUY.

My good God, in whose hands are the life and death of man, prostrate on the Earth, I adore thee. Whilst in thy presence, I reflect on the happy death of thy faithful servants, I am forced to exclaim with a holy envy: "Happy are they—a hundred thousand times happy."—(*Apoc.*, xiv. 13.) Blessed are the dead who die in the Lord. Oh! how much do I desire to share their happy fate.

I well know that I do not possess their merit; for this I feel an inexpressible displeasure. My God, if in the past I have not lived justly, but as a wicked sinner, know, that in future it shall be no longer so. I detest, at thy feet, all the evil I have done, and I resolve to commence a new life. "I have said: Now I will begin." Deign to assist me, I beg of thee, with thy grace, so that thou mayest reform and sanctify my manners in such a way, that I may enjoy at death an anticipation of the happiness which thy servants experience; "that I may be refreshed forever with thy vision," according to St. Cyprian. Deign to console me in that dread moment, and grant me benignantly that last final grace which I cannot merit, but can obtain from thee. Humbled at thy feet, with tearful eyes, with most humble prayers, I implore thy infinite clemency. Give me, Lord, this final grace, not through my merits, (for I do not possess them,) but through the bowels of thy infinite mercy, and grant it to me through the intercession of thy most holy and sorrowful mother, and through the assistance she gave at thy agony and death. Amen.

MEDITATION X.

On the Particular Judgment.

INTRODUCTION.

Seneca writes, in his *Questions on Nature*, that every kind of venomous animal—toads, vipers, even dragons—if struck by lightning, lose their poison, and are innocent thereafter. If, then, we desire that a sinner should lay aside the venom of his vices and perverse customs, he must be wounded as it were by the thunder of the holy fear of God; especially by the thought of that terrible and irrevocable sentence which he is to receive at the divine tribunal. The judgment made of the wicked in human judicature, is called in law, the most terrible employment of human power. How much more tremendous the judgment of sinners by the majesty of an offended God!

When the Chaldean soldiers dragged the unfortunate Sedecias to the tribunal of Nebuchadnezzar (IV. *Reg.*, 25), he judged him in this manner. First with a severe and stern countenance he reproached him for his felony; he then caused all his children to be murdered before him; then he had his eyes removed by main force; finally, loading him with chains from head to foot, he condemned him to perpetual imprisonment in Babylon. What a terrible judgment! How severe the condemnation! More terrible, beyond comparison, is that which takes place at the tribunal of God, to the soul, the instant it leaves the body: much more minutely will the process of sins be examined. The sentence will not decree temporal pains, but eternal torments. Let us then meditate in earnest; and act so that the particular judgment after death may assist us to live well, and dispose us not to fear at that terrible tribunal. Thus acted holy David when he said: "Thy judgment aids me." Thus should we also act.

We shall divide this meditation into three points, and consider: 1. The soul appearing at the particular judgment. 2. The examen. 3. The sentence.

FIRST PRELUDE.

Imagine that you see in the other world a most obscure place; in it a large black bench, on which is raised a tribunal: there behold Christ seated, his eyes dazzling; in his mouth a sword; his right hand wields a group of thunderbolts, and in his left is a balance of most tremendous justice. Before him is placed a poor guilty soul, between her angel-guardian and the demon. The latter accuses, with great violence, and the angel-guardian tries to defend, while the soul is in panic.

SECOND PRELUDE.

Humbled before God, and with a contrite heart, say: "When thou shalt come to judge, condemn me not." Lord, remember thou hast created me to save me: thou hast shed the last drop of thy blood to save me. Condemn me not on that terrible day.

FIRST POINT.

The soul appearing at the particular judgment. No sooner shall the soul leave the body, than instantly it is cited before the tribunal of God, to be severely judged. On every account, this judgment will be most terrible.

1. For the *time*. All is to be completed in one moment. At tribunals on Earth, wretched culprits have time to breathe. Until the fact be proved, witnesses examined, reasons debated, the case summed up, there is cause to hope and fear in turn. At the judgment of God, time is not wanting to decide the question. The judge was witness of all crimes; "I am judge and witness;" to decide on the punishment, and to form a just decree. God being infinite wisdom, immediately knows what is to be decreed by justice, so that judgment is accomplished in a moment. If the sentence be unfavorable, it will be like a thunderbolt, which will suddenly astound the miserable sinner.

2. It will be terrible, as to the *locality*. For in the place where the person dies, a tribunal is there erected, and the soul is judged in view of the corpse, which is deformed and ugly. O God! what sentiments of anger will the soul conceive against that body, which it will curse! It will think: "To please thee, I find myself in these fears and perils. How much better it would have been for me, had I mortified thee as thou deservedst, for the love of Jesus Christ. For this putrid carcase, which decays in a grave, I am about to be condemned to eternal torments."

3. It will be terrible for want of company. The soul will find itself alone at the tribunal of God, without friends, relatives, or intercessors. David (in *Ps.*, xxi.) calls his soul, his only one, because it is to appear before the tribunal of God, with only the angel-guardian on the right hand, and on the

left the demon. The Devil, that befriended the sinner whilst alive, now accuses him in a hostile manner. Exaggerating his wickedness, he exclaims before God, and cries out to condemn him. St. Basil says: "The co-operator becomes the accuser." He will say: "Lord, he has been a dissolute, interested, scandalous person; he has a thousand times transgressed every precept of the Decalogue and of the Church; he *then* should go to Hell." The holy angel-guardian will answer: "Silence, infernal beast; if he did evil, he also did good; so many communions, so many mental and vocal prayers, so many times he assisted at the church." "Oh! what good was this?" the Devil will say triumphantly, "confessions without contrition or amendment; communions without preparation or fervor; mental prayer, one continual distraction; vocal prayers recited negligently and half asleep. In the church what irreverence, discourse, even immodesty? Is not this evil rather than good? But let it pass for good. How little it was, and incomparably less than the evil. Let it be seen in the scales of the sanctuary; in one balance let his innumerable sins be placed. How they outweigh his good. At this view, the unhappy soul, knowing itself to be guilty and convicted, trembles. The angel-guardian considers it with a melancholy countenance.

Above all, at this judgment, the presence of Christ, seated on his tribunal, will be terrible. It will be an insupportable torment for the soul to consider the countenance of Christ. 1. Because he appears as a great and angry judge. 2. As a great benefactor betrayed.

As an angry judge, he will show himself with a

severe and fiery countenance. With what horror he will be viewed, may be conjectured by the following recital. As some religious were once reciting their office in choir, with little reverence, a holy crucifix in the midst of them, opening its eyes, cast a severe look towards them. It sufficed: for in a short time each of them, one after the other, died from the great terror experienced. If then, a severe look from the merciful crucified Jesus, was sufficient to cause death, what will the awful look of Jesus, as an angry judge, effect? 3. He appears; *he*, a great benefactor betrayed! Merely to see him is to that soul a great punishment for its ingratitude. What horror for a son to appear before his father after having plotted his death? Or, for a wife to come before her husband after having dishonored the nuptial bed? Or, for a favorite to be conducted into the presence of his monarch after having conspired against him?

Peter Tultuman relates (*b.* IV., *c.* ii., *s.* 10), and Lobezio (in the *Way of Life and Death*, *b.* I., *c.* iii., *s.* 6), that a king of Asia, named Elenahan, greatly inclined to mercy, went once to hunt, and found by chance a little leprous child abandoned to the wild beasts. He takes her by the hand, conducts her to the palace, and hears from the physicians, that to cure her, a bath of human blood is necessary. He causes a vein to be opened in the arm of his eldest son. The emission of blood exceeded the strength of his own son, who dies. She, however, is perfectly cured. Becoming afterwards extraordinarily beautiful, she was adopted by the king as his daughter, made heiress of the kingdom, and espoused to a prince of the royal blood. What greater kindness can be imagined? She, however, proved ungrateful and perfidious. After having betrayed the fidelity she owed her consort, she took refuge with another king, an enemy, and waged war against her benefactor. Providence so disposed of matters, that she was overcome in battle, and brought prisoner to court, where the council assembled to decide on the kind of death she should undergo. Some decreed fire, others the axe, or the sword. The oldest of the counsellors said: "Let her present herself at the feet of the king. Let his majesty be enthroned, and let her be constrained to have her eyes fixed on the king's countenance." His majesty was pleased with this sentence; and that rebellious creature came before him; she had scarcely raised her eyes to look at him, than struck with terror, she grew pale, trembled, fell on the ground, and died.

The soul presented before the tribunal of God, was once infected with the leprosy of original sin, and destined to eternal death. She was revived by the King of kings, in a bath of divine blood, shed on the cross. She was likewise adopted for daughter, by sanctifying grace, and made heiress of Paradise. She too rebelled against God, waged war against him by her sins; and now at the particular judgment, she is obliged to look on her great benefactor and her judge. What terror then will be hers? "They shall behold me, whom they pierced," says *Zachary*, xii.

From all these we may learn how wretched will be the state of a soul at the tribunal of God, even before the beginning of the judgment. St. Augustine says, apparently weeping, *Tract* lviii.: "Ah!

17*

miserable sinner, what wilt thou do at that time; for wheresoever thou shalt cast thine eyes, thou shalt see objects of terror. On high, God stands as an irritated judge; beneath, the chaos of Hell, which awaits thee; on the right, innumerable sins; on the left, countless demons; and within thee, conscience, which torments and condemns thee. What wilt thou do?" Reflect that at this tribunal, and in this terror, you will certainly be. This is of faith. (II. *Cor.* v. 10.) You will there find yourself much sooner than you imagine. We may say of the particular judgment, what Jesus Christ said of the general one, in *Luke*, xvii., namely, that it would come like the universal deluge: that is, suddenly, and when men thought of nothing but of banquets and espousa's. As death usually comes when least expected, and when men amuse themselves; so, immediately after death, follows the particular judgment. Knowing all this, you do not reflect upon it; you act as if it were not to happen, or as if you did not believe it. You live without resolving to settle the affairs of your conscience. O blindness! O lamentable negligence!

SECOND POINT.

Examen at the particular judgment. James of Paradise, a Carthusian, tells in his book on Mortal Sin, that a religious of this order appeared after death to a companion and great friend while at prayer, and showed himself under a melancholy countenance, and invested with deep mourning. The religious asking him why he was so downcast and melancholy, he heaved a deep sigh, and answered: " No one believes it." The astonished religious again interrogated him: " What is it that no one believes?" The deceased answered: "It is this: how strictly God judges and how severely he punishes." He then disappeared, leaving the religious half dead with fright. No one can believe, and no one can imagine, how rigorously God judges and punishes the sins of men. It cannot be otherwise; for if man who has but feeble knowledge of evil, judges others so severely, and appears to find a defect in everything, how much more rigorously will God judge, who is infinite in wisdom, and has perfect knowledge? If even in the angels, who are most pure and holy spirits, he finds something to amend, how many deficiencies will he see in man, who is an imperfect and vile creature?

It is written of St. Matilda, that once in a vision she was conducted to Heaven to be judged by the angels. They reprehended her for so many failings that she almost died with terror. What then shall become of a man not holy, but wicked, when he shall be judged by God, who has so much more knowledge than the angels?

What fear and dismay would an ignorant person feel if he were minutely examined by a great theologian, or a great legislator? What confusion for an ignorant soul to be examined by a God of infinite wisdom, who knows and can convict him of every fault? O God! how terrible is judgment!

The Devil has strongly accused that soul, and the angel-guardian has tried by all possible means to defend it. Christ as judge then speaks: "Come, render an account of so many years of life so badly spent. Give an account of every thought, word, and action." Come to be examined. This examen, said David, is made by the very eyes of God.

(*Ps.*, x. 14.) Why the eyes? God who sees all, even to the bottom of the heart, has no need of tongue or speech. He not only sees all failings, but makes the soul, too, see them most clearly, as in a looking-glass. (*Ps.*, lxxxvi. 8.) God will say: Consider how many sins you committed; in childhood, how sad and disobedient to your parents; in youth, how many lies and frailties—how scandalous and unconstrained in speech; in manhood, how irregular in conduct—how many frauds and injustices; even in old age, you did not think of doing penance for your sins; on the contrary, you were then more avaricious, passionate, and vindictive. " Render an account." Of the precepts of the Decalogue and of the Church, there is not one but which you transgressed several times. Render an account of your employments, exercised with so much negligence and infidelity: of your children and family, of which you have so little care; of the good you omitted; of the good so ill done. Render an account of the sins which others committed by your bad example, or evil counsels, or want of vigilance. Render an account of the many graces, and benefits which you abused. What could I do more for your salvation, or for your sanctification? " What could I have done for my vineyard, and have not done it." I provided you with so many sacraments, priests, sermons, holy books; and so many means of increasing merit. Ungrateful soul, you have rendered them useless. Miserable sinner! At this most just research he will remain confused! Oh! how well will he then know, what he never wished to comprehend during life. Then, indeed, will he understand both the grievousness and multitude of his sins. A beam thrown into the sea cannot be entirely seen, immersed as it is in water. It appears so light that any child might move it with the hand. But when drawn to the shore it cannot be moved even by a strong man. Thus sin is not entirely known, in this world, as to its malice; hence it is committed by all with great facility. When seen on the shore of eternity, all its malice will be known—its weight and its ingratitude.

The multitude of sins will also be known. As in the rays of the sun innumerable atoms are discovered floating in the air, which were not observed in the shade; so in the light of the countenance of Christ, man will discover the innumerable sins he has committed, and of which he had never thought, or counted them only as trifles. Oh! what dismay for a sinner, to discover a countless array of transgressions committed and forgotten.

An apothecary was one night asleep in his room, where he kept enclosed, in a vase of porphyry, a great number of vipers for medicinal purposes. These reptiles, grouping together, about midnight, forced open the wooden cover that enclosed them, and escaped to all parts of the chamber, and even on the bed of the terrified apothecary. He sees himself surrounded by a numerous collection of poisonous vipers, creeping on him, to bite and kill him. The unfortunate man knew not how to flee or defend himself. At every step, and in every place, he appeared to encounter death. While he defended himself from some, he was assailed by many others.

How much greater will be the terror of a soul at the tribunal of God, seeing himself surrounded by the multitude of his sins; the wretched man will not know how to defend himself. For example: while he seeks to excuse the time he spent at play, his irregularities will reproach him; and palliating these, scandals, interests, hatreds, and sacrileges will reprove him. What terror? what dismay will seize him? The most awful thing will be to hear from God the demand which God himself made to Eve, after she had committed sin: "Why hast thou done this?" Tell me, why so many evil deeds? What induced you to offend so grievously your God, Father, Redeemer, who even died for you on a cross? "Why hast thou done this?" Why did you turn away from me, to follow the world, which is so great a traitor, even to follow the Devil, that is your sworn enemy? What answer shall the sinner give in his defence? "What shall I do, when the Lord shall arise in judgment." (*Job*, iii.) He will say: "Lord, it is but too true, I have sinned, but I did not know thy law." "What," God will reply, "after so many masters have exhausted themselves teaching you—so many confessors and preachers! You were so wise for every other affair; you were ignorant only of the manner of serving me." "Lord, I knew it; but, to speak clearly, I could not live well in so sad a world and with so many irregular passions." "You would be in the right," God will say, "had you been obliged to observe my law by the sole strength of nature; but why could you not do so with the assistance of my grace, which I was ever ready to bestow on you? Why could you not do what so many others have accomplished, who were more noble, younger, more delicate, than you, and in the same places and occasions as those in which you failed? Could you not even live like a good

Christian, where so many others have become saints?" "Lord, all this is true; but the evil is already done. I can do nothing now but repent and implore thy mercy." "My mercy! this is the time solely for my justice. 'I will not have mercy.' To obtain my mercy by penance, you should have thought of it sooner; when you were excited to it by divine inspirations and interior remorse of conscience. 'Time shall be no more.'" At these words the sinner, full of the greatest confusion, is obliged to confess: "I am guilty!" In this judgment, says St. Bernard, " there is no pardon, no delay, and no refuge."—(*Ser.* 54, *in Cant.*)

To the charges of Christ shall be added those of the angels and of all those who shall be present at that awful tribunal.

There was a rich and noble youth who, knowing the vanity of the world, resolved to retire to a monastery, and attend solely to the salvation of his soul. His parents and friends tried to dissuade him; but he firmly answered: "I will save my soul." His widowed mother tried by every means and artifice to dissuade him: he continued to say: "I will save my soul." Finally, with great generosity, he became a religious in a hermitage, where he lived with great fervor for many months. By degrees he grew tepid; and his mother having died, he began to think of the inheritance he might have enjoyed in the world, and to waver in his vocation. At this period, he one night thought he was before the throne of God, where many devils accused him, and his afflicted angel-guardian could not find means to defend him. His mother then appearing before him, thus reproached him: "Where are those words you used to repeat—'I wish to save my soul?' How can you wish to arrive at Paradise, while you walk with rapid strides on the road to Hell?" At this bitter reprehension, even though asleep, he fainted; and he awoke more dead than alive. He began to say within himself: "If the judgment of which I have dreamt struck me with so much terror, what will the reality be? If I cannot bear the severe countenance of my mother, how shall I suffer that of an irritated God?" He resumed his first fervor; and at the hour of his death his mother again appeared before him, saying: "Now indeed, son, you have truly saved your soul."

The holy angel-guardian, no longer as advocate, but as minister of God, will confirm the divine words, saying: "Wretch! after so many inspirations, you promised God and your confessor to change your life and become a saint. These promises were all false. You changed your life, becoming more wicked: or, if you formed the resolution to despoil yourself of one vice, it was to adopt another more scandalous. Begone; you are unworthy of pardon or of pity."

Dearly beloved, seriously reflect on this point. Is not the judgment of God most minute and severe? Who can deny it? Why, then, do you not think of settling the affairs of your soul? You labor so much for temporal interests, in making up accounts, and you do not spend a thought on spiritual interests. What blindness! Now open your eyes. If you wish for a happy passage, examine and judge yourself. "If we judge ourselves, we shall not be judged."—(I. *Cor.*, i.,) says the apostle. St. Bernard gives the reason (*Ser. Sup. Ps. qui habit*): God will not judge twice. The good thief, because he judged and condemned himself, (*Luc.*, xxiii. 41,) was immediately absolved by divine mercy. Calculate, now, the grievousness and the number of your sins, and calculate also the quality and number of your good works: if it appear to you that they are not in proportion, resolve to lead a more penitent and holy life, and say, from your heart, to God : " Lord, as thou givest me light to know this most important truth, give me also grace to practise it."

THIRD POINT.

Sentence of the particular judgment. This sentence will be most terrible, on every account.

1. Because a sovereign interest is concerned. In human tribunals the sentence of a law-suit for many thousands is anxiously expected. In a criminal case, when the offence is capital, what fear, what beating of the heart, what anxiety in him who awaits it! Yet, only temporal goods are treated of or the life of the body. What alarm then shall be felt at this judgment, in which the decision is made of eternal goods or evils, not for the body alone, but also for the soul?

2. It is a sentence either of extreme happiness, or extreme torment; there is no medium. Human tribunals frequently award sentences, without entirely deciding in favor of one party to the total ruin of the other; and by half measures succeed in partially consoling both partïes. In the judgment of God, the decree is to be passed either for Paradise or for Hell, without any medium. Oh! how terrible.

St. Lewis Bertrand once preaching on this subject to a great audience, burst into tears. No longer able to speak, he broke off the sermon, and fled to his apartment, where his religious found him, pressing his head against the ground, exclaiming: "Unfortunate that I am; I know not what sentence awaits me; either Paradise or Hell, without medium."

3. The sentence cannot be repealed. As no superior tribunal exists to that of Almighty God, the award of divine justice cannot be recalled. Besides, as justice teaches, an appeal is given on account of reason, or of fact. No such appeal can occur with God, whose mind is most perspicuous, and his laws most clear: he does not stand in need of witnesses, being at the same time, judge and witness of our actions. "I am the judge and the witness."--(*Jer.*, xxix.)

4. Finally, it is a sentence of pure justice. In this world, compassion frequently prevails in condemning the guilty, in regard to the substance or the manner of punishment, on account of nobility, or other prerogative, or from powerful intercession. At the judgment of God, pure justice will be executed; without any mixture of mercy; equally to all; whether noble or ignoble, great or little, without exception of persons. During life, God in chastising sinners, used the greatest clemency, and punished them much less than they merited.

What terror will pervade the soul, in receiving its last sentence. When king Balthazar, in the midst of his banquet, saw three mortal fingers writing on the wall the sentence of ruin, the sacred text says: "He suddenly grew pale, trembled, and was troubled in thought; his strength failed, from the great fear he was in, and his knees knocked against each other."—(*Daniel*, v. 6.) Those who were invited, the courtiers, the queen, the ladies, all were in confusion; and the joy of the great banquet was changed into mourning and horror. The same night, Babylon was surprised by Cyrus: the wretched Chaldean king was cruelly murdered. If, then, a sentence of death, written in mute characters, and not pronounced by a terrific voice—expressed by a simple hand, and not by the mouth of an angry God—caused so much fear in Babylon, what will the awful sentence be, when pronounced by God, at the particular judgment, on the eternal destiny of man?

The divine Judge hears the contradictory accusations of the Devil and the defence of the angel-guardian. If he find the soul by its works worthy of mercy and reward, turning with a pleasing countenance, he will joyfully say: " Come to Heaven, which I have merited for thee." At these words, the angel-guardian, full of joy, will conduct the soul to the eternal joys of Paradise. " Well done, good and faithful servant." On the contrary, if the soul is convicted of being guilty of innumerable sins, without having performed penance, and thus merited eternal pains, then God, full of fury, will say: " Begone, far from me, I no longer recognize thee as mine." " I know thee not." Turning to the demons, he will say: " Take him away with you to Hell, cast him into exterior darkness." His angel-guardian will also be obliged to say the same.

Ven. Bede (*English History*) relates, that an English soldier finding himself grievously infirm, was visited by king Corrado, who exhorted him to confess; but he answered, that he would do it later, as by confessing at that period, he should be considered a coward and too fearful of death. Shortly after, the illness increased; the king returned to the charge and more earnestly begged of him to confess. The soldier with a terrific howl answered, that already he was in despair, and condemned; for, two devils had read all his sins to him from a large book; two angels then appearing before him, took out the small book of his good works. The devils exclaiming, that soul belonged to them, the angels consented, saying: "Take it, for it is yours." Ven. Bede weeping over this sad case, concludes: "He shall do fruitlessly eternal penance, because he avoided timely repentance." Christ, the judge, having passed the sentence, and the angel-guardian approved, the wicked soul will be immediately put into chains by the Devil, and dragged down into the abyss.

When Joshua had vanquished in battle, five Amorrhite kings, who were extricated from a cave, whither they, fearing, fled and enclosed themselves, he caused them to be extended on the ground, in view of the whole army, and to humble their pride, he commanded the soldiers to tread them under foot. He then caused them to be suspended on gibbets. (*Joshua*, x. 24.)

The soul condemned by divine justice, will be given up to be trodden on, and to be the sport of Devils, for endless ages. Reflect that you are to receive your eternal sentence at this judgment; you know not whether for Heaven or Hell. If you wish to learn it from your manner of life, perhaps your hope of joy is not well grounded. If the Lord has declared he will condemn at judgment whoever has not given food to the hungry, or clothed the naked, what will become of you, says St. Austin (*Ser.* 31, *ad Frat.*), who, perhaps, have taken the bread of the poor to maintain vanity and luxury, who have despoiled widows and orphans of their substance? St. Bruno, though penitent and holy, trembled from head to foot, and confessed that he was dwelling in fear and terror. What, then, will become of you? This thought, which made the saints tremble, should it not cause the blood to freeze in your veins? "Every man trembles" at grievous perils. (*Ps.*, lxiii.) Do you not fear to risk a sentence that involves your eternity? If so, says St. Augustine, you are not a man, but a stone. My God! "Fix thy fear in my flesh."

COLLOQUY.

What shall I do, my God, in thy terrible judgment? What shall I do? How shall I appear in thy presence after having so frequently offended thee? "O Lord, when thou shalt come to judge the earth, where shall I hide myself from the countenance of thy wrath? for I have greatly sinned in my life." When I reflect on the years of my past life, I do not find anything which is blameless. "I have done nothing worthy in thy sight." On the contrary, I find innumerable sins and ingratitude. How then shall I render an account of myself? If those have a more rigorous one to give who have received greater benefits, what shall I do, and what shall I say, after having been more specially beloved by thee, and favored, than others? The sole thought of it "fills me with immense shame and confusion." One thing, however, consoles me—namely, to know that thou art now a father and not a judge. I have yet time to settle the affairs of my soul. Therefore, humble and contrite I cast myself at thy feet: " I implore thy majesty to blot out my iniquity." Efface, I beg of thee, with thy most precious blood, the stains of my sins: forgive. O Lord, forgive. Weigh now by the standard of thy cross my failings. Judge me now, and absolve me; so that, being benignantly absolved by thee now, I need not fear after death thy terrible tribunal. Amen.

MEDITATION XI.

On the General Judgment.

INTRODUCTION.

GOD is not content with judging man privately and in secret at the particular judgment; he will judge him at the last day publicly, and with all the dreadful pomp of tremendous justice. In presence of the whole world he will justify the dispensations of his providence, which were not clearly understood by mankind. He will manifest the grievousness of man's sins, even the most hidden. He will show the equitable reasons which move him to award to each one a proportionate sentence either of punishment or reward. How terrible this judgment will be!

Henry the Great, fourth of the name, of the line of Bourbon, King of France, having ordered some bronze cannons, of great size, he had this terrible motto inscribed on them: "The last argument of kings." No power can here resist. All must yield.

The ultimate proof of God's indignation, is his final judgment. "The last argument." Heretofore the Lord chastised sinners from time to time, but his chastisements not being universal, or being mitigated by some sign of mercy, were only the small effects of his indignation. These chastisements were only grains of divine wrath, and God lessened their weight, sometimes in one way, and sometimes in another: at one time on Pentapolis, by burning it; or on Samaria, desolating it by famine; and thus of other cities and kingdoms. At the final judgment, he will inundate on the wicked of the Earth, all the divine fury, without any sign of clemency: " The last argument." This last day, then, is called by Joel (ii. 2), God's own day of vengeance : " The day of the Lord ;" and by Sophonias (i. 15), " The day of wrath." It is, in fine, a day, in which the justice of God will show itself more terrible than Hell itself. What more can be said? This is clearly seen from St. Peter, (II. ii.), where he says, speaking of the rebellious angels, that God having condemned them to Hell, he kept prepared for them, as the last and greatest pain, the horror of universal judgment. Upon which A. Lapide says: " There remains still for them the final judgment." Oh! then, what a great judgment! Let us meditate on it, with all the application of our mind.

We shall consider: 1. The citation of men. 2. The trial of their evil deeds. 3. The last definitive sentence of eternity.

FIRST PRELUDE.

Let us imagine that we see Christ, our Judge, seated on a luminous cloud, with a fiery countenance and wrathful eyes, coming to pass sentence, either of life or death, on the whole world gathered in the Valley of Josaphat. Let us imagine our angel-guardians crying out to us: " Arise, ye dead, and come to judgment." Oh! you, who by sin are dead to grace, or you who are dead to your first piety and fervor, come and meditate seriously on the general judgment.

SECOND PRELUDE.

Let us say with all our hearts to God: "Free me, O Lord, from eternal death on that tremendous day, when thou shalt come to judge: condemn me not."

FIRST POINT.

The citation of mankind at the final judgment. Men will be called in two ways to the universal judgment: 1. They will be cited by the elements, and by all creatures, which being put in great commotion, will give clear indications that the last day is approaching, God saying by the prophet: " I will give wonders in the Heaven and on the Earth, before the great day of the Lord shall come." (*Joel,* ii. 50.) Afterwards they will be cited expressly and at the sound of trumpet by the angels. All those signs predicted by the prophets in the ancient Testament shall be verified, and all that our Redeemer foretold with his own lips. Cities and kingdoms will revolt, and be in tumult by rebellious and sanguinary wars; seasons will change, and all the order observed until then in the planets and elements shall cease. The sun will be eclipsed; the moon will be streaked with blood; the Heavens will be filled with mournful phenomena; fiery exhalations will descend on the Earth like falling stars; terrific plagues will desolate kingdoms; prolonged famines will make countries desolate; the sea rising beyond its boundaries, will swallow up entire provinces; while unfortunate man, astounded and appalled with great fear, will not know whither to fly to save his life; as the prophet Amos says, (v. 19,) like one who fleeing from a lion, will meet with a bear, and to flee both, taking shelter within, is bitten by an asp. Thus miserable men, to fly from the inundations of the sea, will hasten to cities; chased thence by plagues and wars, they will run to the open country; being there persecuted by wild beasts from the forests and thunder from Heaven, they will hide in the caves of mountains. Here again, they will be assailed by horrible earthquakes, which, dividing huge stones, will open before them a profound chaos. Oh! what terror! What confusion! What mourning! Above all, that immense fire will be horrible, which, arising from the four parts of the world, and spreading itself extensively, in a very short time will burn everything—kingdoms, provinces, cities, villages, men, beasts, birds, cattle, plants—the most ancient archives, obelisks, pyramids, of which it was thought, they should last forever—all that was magnificent, rich, or great in the world, will become ashes. "The earth and its labors shall be burned."—(II. *Pet.*, iii. 10.) All this shall happen, because God wishes to act with sinners, as men do with those infected with plague, whose house, apparel, and whatever is contaminated by their pestiferous breath, is consumed.

As a great captain, having defeated the enemy, sets fire to the tents, where the troops lay encamped; or as a spouse who, finding his consort in fault, throws habits and jewels on the ground, which were the cause of her infidelity; thus, all the creatures of the world.—Heaven, Earth, and the elements, having served man either for shelter, or for incentives to sin, and the entire world being contaminated by man's wickedness, God will therefore purge this same world by fire. Before

GENERAL JUDGMENT.   215

punishing sinners, he will punish other creatures, as guilty of having concurred and served as instruments to all the sins of the world. Who can depict the horror of seeing a world entirely consumed by flames, and innumerable victims burned alive without redress?

After this conflagration, nothing being in the world but ashes, the voice of man no longer heard, nor the song of birds, time at an end, and eternity commencing, all mankind, from the beginning to the end of the world, will be expressly cited to appear at the general judgment, in the valley of Josaphat. The angels flying in the air, and blowing their dread trumpets, will exclaim: "Arise ye dead, and come to judgment." At this astounding citation, all the dead obey. Then will be seen arising from the earth and sea innumerable bodies and dislocated bones, which reuniting, will form the figures of their ancient persons: then the souls coming, the bodies will revive, but with what diversity! The just, those who are saved, joyful and serene, will take up their members, saying to each of them: "Come, my body, let us reunite; it is but just, you who have been my companion in suffering, should also be my companion in enjoyment." On the contrary, the wicked, the damned, with what anger and suffering will they assume their ugly, horrible, and putrid bodies! If the soul of a man who had been but a few days dead, should be replaced in his body, just as it is in the grave, decayed, black, and full of vermin, how shocked would it be at this disgusting and horrible object! What torment will it be to a damned soul to be reunited to its putrid body. "Ah! cursed body!" will it utter, "for the love of you, I find myself in so many torments: now come also and suffer the same pains."

Thus resuscitated, all men will assemble from every quarter of the Earth, in the great valley of Josaphat. They will go in crowds, without any distinction of kings, of ploughmen, nobles, or plebeians, rich or poor. Scarcely have they arrived at the place destined for judgment, when the angels of Heaven appear to separate and collect, in different places, the just and the wicked. What a sad separation: those who are saved—the saints—will be placed at the right; the reprobate, the damned, will be chased to the left; there the selfish, robbers, swearers, and the sacrilegious will be ranged. Oh! what a torment, and how opprobrious for those to whom the angel says: "Go hence, go with the wicked, your companions!" What great confusion when the angels say to the prince, to the nobleman, to the advocate: "Go there, among robbers!" They answering: "What! I with robbers?" "Yes," will the angel say, "why did you oppress your vassals, rob the poor of their due, and the orphans of clothing? You are to go with robbers." What confusion for a matron, or a young person, who held a good reputation: "Go there with the accomplices of your sin: you could hide your irregularities from the eyes of men, but not from those of God." "The angels shall go and separate them."

Beloved, reflect if the citation be so terrible and all that precedes judgment, what will the judgment itself be? Reflect, you by necessity are to be present at this great extremity: this is of faith. What then shall be your lot? When resuscitated, you will again resume your flesh and bones; you will do so with joy if saved, or with despair if a reprobate; you will go to the valley of Josaphat with a certainty of being blessed or cursed. What place then do you think will be assigned to you by the angels—at the right or the left—amongst the chaste, humble, and devout, or the scandalous, the selfish, and dishonest? O God! what a great subject is this (!) In such peril, can you thoughtlessly live and smile; and on the contrary not tremble from head to foot?

Rupert Holkot writes, (*book Sap.*, *c. i. p.* 31,) that three travellers once walking by the valley of Josaphat, one of them sitting on a stone, said, smiling: "As this is the place of the last judgment, by anticipation I will choose my place, to be at my ease and listen. Then raising his eyes to Heaven, he saw the Son of God in the air, with a terrible countenance, in the act of judging. The wretched man was so struck with terror, that he fell in a faint on the earth. Having come to himself he was struck with terror, and never after smiled. Even if the word *judgment*, were pronounced in his presence, he burst into tears, grew pale, fainted, and appeared more dead than alive. If then, a shadow only of judgment sufficed to cause a swoon, how is it, that a man believing and meditating seriously on the same judgment, does not conceive a holy fear which may serve to detach him from every human pleasure, and improve his morals?

SECOND POINT.

The trial of the misdeeds of men in the general judgment. All mankind being gathered and properly distributed by the angels in the valley of

Josaphat, Christ as judge, will descend from Heaven: all beholding him will be terrified. "All the tribes of the earth shall mourn." Why so? They will see their God, not as formerly, compassionate and amiable, but angry and severe. As David, before going out to battle against the Philistines, deposed his royal robes, and dressed himself like a warrior, and put on a helmet instead of a crown, armor instead of a mantle, and the sword instead of a sceptre. (III. *Kings*, ii. 2.) Our Redeemer, having laid aside the thorns and nails, and all appearance of a loving father, will be invested as a most severe judge. (*Isa.*, lix. 16.) He will be seated on a dark cloud, "armed with zeal." (*Sap.*, v.) He will have for breastplate, incorruptible justice; for sceptre, rectitude of mind; for shield, unchangeable equity; for lance, his wrath. (*Sap.*, v. 21.) Before him will be fire; around him whirlwinds and tempests; all the creatures of the world armed against sinners. What more? He will have standing by him his cross, to serve as a reproof to the ingratitude of those who did not profit by the passion and the blood of the Redeemer, and by which they could have easily been saved. (*Num.*, xvii.) For the same reason, he has chosen for the theatre of his great judgment, the valley of Josaphat, situated opposite to the mountains of Olivet, where the redemption of man commenced, and Calvary, where it terminated. The wicked considering these two places, will be convinced of their own perversity; and the remembrance of Christ crucified will confuse and be a reproach to them; he would have been their salvation and their glory. Oh! what terror. If only to meditate on these things makes one shudder, what will it be to experience them? No sooner shall Christ crucified appear in this terrible manner as judge, than he will act on souls in the same way, as the sun does on material creatures: before the dawn of day a most obscure night envelopes the universe, white cannot be distinguished from black, what is soiled from what is clean, what is precious from what is vile: scarcely has the sun appeared on the horizon, than instantly is discovered all that is plain, soiled or black.

The same will happen in souls. Before the Sun of Justice shall appear in judgment, their failings will not be seen; nor will it be known who was honest or dishonest, who was selfish or who just, who was good or who impious. So soon as the Divine Sun appears, all the good will be discovered, and all the evil, in each soul. St. Bernard said with reason, "that the punishment of the most enormous sins will be God," since he, being light, will discover them to the whole world. What confusion will it be for the sinner, when, in the light of the divine countenance, he will clearly know all his most hidden sins, and he will see them discovered to the eyes of the whole world.

Xifilino and Dion write of Nero, that he was not less extravagant than cruel. Once, having summoned senators most conspicuous from their age and employments, he desired them to go instantly to the public square, and dance in the costume of comedians. They protested it would be contrary to decorum and to the dignity of their rank as senators, and that they would thereby become a fable to the vulgar. Nero replied: "It must be done; for I so wish it." They complied, wearing masks and dresses to disguise themselves; but in the midst of the most ridiculous part of the dance, guards raised the masks, and the unhappy senators were exposed to the hisses and taunts of the populace. Their confusion was so great, that many of them, according to Dion, were struck dead. What, then, will it be for sinners, at the general judgment, when the mask of their wickedness shall be removed, and they known for what they really were, not as they once seemed. Parents, friends, and companions will say: "See him who was thought a good man—a saint; he was nothing but a hypocrite. See her who was esteemed chaste, into what a precipice she has fallen! Who could have believed it! See him whom we believed a mirror of honor, an oracle in council; how many treasons did he commit? how many deceits? how many thefts?"

O God! what confusion will this be! The most humble St. Bernard used to say of himself: "What confusion for me, when it shall be said: 'Behold the man, and his works.'" This will be the greatest of all pains, of those with which, as St. Thomas of Villanova says (*Conc.* 1 *Advent*), man is chastised as natural man; for the other natural pains of the damned might be endured by beasts, which can be wounded, burnt, and tormented, but cannot be afflicted with shame and confusion.

How much more this manifestation of sins and this confusion of sinners must become tormenting to the reprobate, when Christ, as Judge, will publicly denounce each one! God says by the mouth of the prophet Joel, (iii. 2), that he will in a manner argue, to convince the wicked of their misdeeds. O impious man! come and defend yourself, if you can, from your evil ways. The culprit will, doubtless, say: "Ah! Lord, you well know how feeble I was, and badly inclined." Christ will answer: "Did I not strengthen you with my grace?" The sinner will allege, "I was noble, young, and in the midst of a thousand occasions of sinning." "Were not Lewis of France and Casimir of Poland noble, young, and in the midst of the delights of a kingdom; yet, they were not only good, but saints? Why did you not do as they did? You waited for old age to live well. What rashness! Did you not know that life is short and uncertain?" "I confided much in your clemency." "Perfidious creature! you confided in my clemency to continue your impiety." "The Devil strongly instigated me by the incentives of the seven capital sins." "Did not your angel-guardian strongly defend you with his counsels? Had you not the seven sacraments as preservatives against the seven capital sins? Answer then. 'Thou wilt contend with me in judgment.'" (*Jer.* ii.) Could the sinner even deny his actual guilt? No. God, as witness of his evil deeds, and those of his accomplices, would immediately convict him. When king Saul, (contrary to the command of God, who ordered him to put to fire and sword all the booty he had taken from the Amalekites), reserved the best cattle and the most precious furniture, he was immediately reprehended by the prophet Samuel. Then the king overcome with shame, denied his faults. (II. *Reg.*, xiv.) The prophet replied: "Tell me what means the bleating of those sheep? Do you not hear many voices crying out against you? The cattle even accuse you of falsehood." In the same manner God will say to the sinner: "Do you not hear the voice of the poor saying, you were our tyrant; we were hungry, you did not feed us; naked, you did not clothe us. Laborers will exclaim, you did not pay our wages: Clients and widows will utter, you robbed us of our substance. Companions will allege, that you scandalized them by your irregularities." When the apostle of the Indies, St. Francis Xavier, saw his passage to China frustrated by the cupidity of the Prefect of Malacca, he threatened to accuse him in the Valley of Josaphat.

Miserable sinners thus convicted by God, accused by creatures, disgraced before Heaven and Earth, unable longer to support their shame, " will cry out to the mountains to fall and bury them," to hide them from the face of God and man. Meditate, beloved, seriously on this point. Reflect, if you continue to live irregularly, what must be your confusion at the last day? What excuse can you give to Christ, as judge, after being benefited by him, enlightened by celestial illustrations, and provided with spiritual means to be saved? The Gentiles or the Turks might in some degree excuse themselves, by saying, they did not know the divine law, and that they were born among pagans. But, says Villanova, what will you answer? If in the retirement of these spiritual exercises, you do not settle the accounts of your soul, or prepare to answer the interrogations of Christ, your judge; how can you do so in the midst of a thousand distractions and a thousand occupations? Let us settle the affairs of our conscience with God, now while he is a father; let us not wait for the time when he will be our judge.

My most amiable and merciful Redeemer, here I am humbled, and weeping at thy feet.

THIRD POINT.

The last definitive sentence. After God shall have justified his providence to the world; after he shall have convicted and confounded sinners, he will finally pronounce the last definitive sentence. Oh! what a terrible sound will this be? God already said, by the mouth of Isaiah: " I have always been silent, and my patience appears to have exceeded; now, indeed, I will speak; and desolate the world." How can this be, O Lord? says St. Augustine. (*Hom. de Tribul.*, iii.) Have you not spoken by many prophets, threats, and chastisements? Did you not speak, by the plagues of Egypt, by the deluge of fire which descended on the unfortunate Pentapolis, and by the deluge of water in which the universe was drowned? He again supposes Christ answering, that all he said before was as if he were mute, as compared to the terrible words which he will pronounce in giving the final sentence on the eternity of each one. Oh! this indeed will be the terrific speaking of God— every word will be a thunderbolt, which will strike terror into every mind, and consume all hearts.

In preceding centuries God had often spoken "with words of thunder." (*Ps.*, xvii. 14): yet this may be considered "his time of silence." (*Esther*, xiv. 16.) The period of the last judgment may be called the time of his majesty and show. (*Esther*, xvi.) God, then, in person; with his own mouth,—not committing to others the publication of his eternal and irrevocable decrees,—

turning first to the right, towards his elect, with a joyful and most amiable countenance, will say, "Come to the eternal kingdom, destined as a reward for your virtues and your merits. Come, O humble brethren, devout women, penitent sinners; come, for you are blessed by me, and by my eternal Father. Blessed a thousand times the sufferings you endured for my love. Blessed the alms with which you nourished me, in the person of my poor—relieved my thirst, and clothed my poverty. 'Come, O ye blessed of my Father, come and possess the kingdom prepared for you from the beginning of the world.'" After this, these noble souls, full of light and glory, will be seen ascending with the angels to Heaven.

We should reflect, with St. Bernard, that it is not without great purpose that God sends the blessed to Heaven, before the cursed descend into Hell; for he wishes that, viewing the beatitude of the elect, the reprobate may always know the great good they have lost by their sins. While the reprobate, on the left hand, will be foaming with rage and envy—a brother seeing brother going with joy, to Heaven; a husband, his consort; a friend, another friend—Christ, the judge, will turn towards them " in the wrath of his countenance," (*Ps*., xx. 20.) as David says, full of fire and anger, and pronounce that decree, which in a few words, contains a group of horrors. " Go," he will say, " ye cursed, into eternal fire; go, depart from me, for I will no longer see you—Depart." Ah! what a bitter separation. From whom have they to depart? From just men; from angels: from Mary; but above all, from God. Oh! what anguish! Far, then, from God, who is all, they are to be deprived of every good. "Ye cursed." Had they received the blessing of God before they departed from him, then going away, they might be consoled. No, says God, before they suffer, I curse them as enemies, and as rebels. Into fire! Departing from God, whither are they to go? Into a fire which devours them, but does not enlighten them—torments, but does not kill them: "Eternal fire!" For how long? Always, without ever being extinguished, either for hours, or for years, or for millions of centuries. Never!—never!—never! Miserable, unfortunate, disgraced, they are to depart. From whom? From God. How? Cursed. Whither? To fire. For how long? For all eternity. Oh! what a condemnation. O God! what punishment. O God! what an eternity.

This most terrible sentence being pronounced by God, it will be approved as most just by all the angels, saints, and just souls, who will come to judge even sinners, according to the words of the Holy Ghost, (*Wisdom*, iii. 8.) as the angelic doctor St. Thomas explains. (*Opusc.* ii.) So great then will be the horror, confusion, and pain of the unfortunate and impious, that unable any longer to support the countenance of an irritated God, who thus condemns them, in union with his whole Heavenly court, they will not wait to be dragged by the devils into Hell; they will descend there of their own accord. "They shall go into eternal punishment:" thinking it a less evil to be in Hell, than at that tremendous judgment. This is testified by Theodoret, Theophilact, and Boccade, after Silvera in *Apoc.*, *qu.* xv. *num.* 137.

Beloved, enter into yourself, and thus discourse: It is of faith, that one day I must appear at this great judgment. I am to be there strictly examined and irrevocably judged, and I know not what sentence shall be mine, whether of life or of death. Oh! what a risk. How can I entertain this great thought, and live with such irregularity, and not tremble? The primitive saints of the Church, gathered so much fear from this reflection, as to cause the blood to freeze in their veins. St. Bernard was not ashamed to acknowledge himself amongst them. I, a miserable sinner, wish to be in peace and security, while the most innocent and penitent saints have trembled.

The famous Pelagia, having heard a sermon preached by St. Nonnus, on the general judgment, was not only converted, but to practise more severe penance for her sins, she built a small cell on Mount Olivet, whence might be seen the whole valley of Josaphat. When the Devil tormented her with some thought of former faults, opening her window, she said, "Consider, O miserable Pelagia, this theatre of your future judgment; you will here find yourself, and know not whether at the right or the left. Come then, afflict yourself, and chase away this diabolical temptation." You also, when assailed by some temptation or danger of offending God, turn, at least in thought, to the valley of Josaphat. How much will your mind be there strengthened? St. Jerome even, that great saint and doctor of the Church, to tame his passions, imagined that he always heard the sound of the deadly trumpet, which is to call the dead from their tombs. Why not use the remedy, he found salutary?

It is related that a great king when travelling, met two poor, discalced holy hermits. While viewing them, he thought—" Oh! how much better these shall fare at the day of judgment than myself." Alighting from his horse, he placed himself on his knees before them, and kissed their hands. The courtiers were offended, thinking it beneath his majesty, and induced the prince his brother to expostulate with him. The king was silent, but the following night he had a trumpet sounded before his brother's palace, to that fatal air usually played when malefactors are condemned to death. The wretched prince sprung from his couch, and threw himself at the king's feet to know the cause of that sound and of his condemnation. The king thus answered: " You, though innocent, fear much the anger of a brother; yet you are surprised that I should honor those hermits, who, by their sanctity, remind me, a culprit, of the great judgment of God."

How much would it import you to reflect often on the terror of the last trumpet? How much would it avail you to conceive a holy fear of God, and to make good use of the time, which you have now, to pacify God by prayer? In that last day no one could or dare do it. Say then to God: "My most sweet Saviour, I embrace thy most holy wounds, and I most humbly beg of thee, through the merits of thy divine blood, shed for me, to forgive me my sins, that I may not have reason to fear at the day of judgment."

COLLOQUY.

Great God of terrible majesty, eternal Judge of the living and the dead, here I am at thy feet, confused and astounded before thy terrible judgment. I am ashamed to appear at thy tribunal, guilty of my many sins. Thy prophet Jeremias consoles me, however, (ix. 24,) with these words: "I am the Lord, doing mercy and judgment." Thou, who one day will act as my judge, be now my merciful Father: indulge me now; then weigh in the balance of thy cross the sins I have committed. As for myself, I confess I am guilty of meriting the most grievous chastisements, and I protest I am the most wicked creature in the world. Thou art my good Father, and I have disobeyed thee; thou art my Lord, and I have despised thee. Thou art my Redeemer, whom I have crucified; thou art my God, against whom I have sinned. I deserve, certainly, that thou shouldst chase me away with this sentence: "Depart, accursed;" but those feet which have been wounded for me, will never admit it, nor will thy loving heart ever consent to it. What dost thou say then? Here is the sentence: "I will not the death of a sinner." No, I do not wish that the sinner should die, how many faults soever he may have committed. O infinite goodness! O love without comparison! But what dost thou wish, Lord? "I only will that he be converted and lead the life of grace. Let the sinner return to me, and I forgive him: let the enemy come, and I embrace him; let even Judas come, and I embrace him." O mercy, benignity, and charity of God! How worthy of thee! My God, thou wishest that I should live. I should rather die of contrition, and die of pure love for thee; but as thou wishest that I should live, I will lead a new life; I will live dead to the world, and to my passions, and live solely to thee, who art the way, the truth, and the life. Amen.

MEDITATION XII.

On Hell.

INTRODUCTION.

THE great patriarch St. Ignatius used to say: "Whoever warms himself often at the fire of Hell, will not fall into it." And with good reason; for, to bridle the strongest passions and overcome the greatest temptations, there is no more powerful thought than that of eternal flames. The greatest saints have often renewed the memory of them for their advantage. St. John Chrysostom, in the room where he dwelt, always had Hell painted in glaring colors. At every glance and in every action he wished to recall to mind this salutary thought.

St. Jerome, writing to Eustochium, admits that the true cause which excited him to leave Rome and bury himself in a cave, was the fear of Hell. St. Augustine, reasoning on Hell, affrighted his hearers by his palpitations more than by his words; for, trembling from head to foot, he did not blush to acknowledge that he feared Hell. St. Bernard having once meditated on Hell, made a resolution never to laugh again during his life.

If the saints have so much feared Hell, how much more should sinners, who are ruled by their passions and frail on every occasion! How much more should you be terrified, who doubtless should long since have gone to Hell! And you are not there now, because God in his infinite goodness did not inflict death on you while committing mortal sin, as he has done on so many others.

St. Augustine, weeping, said to God: "A million of times thou couldst have damned me, if thou hadst wished it."

Imagine that God should send this message by an angel to a damned soul: "Come, God in his infinite mercy grants thee to return to life for eight days, so that, making the spiritual exercises, thou canst do penance for thy sins." What would he not do in those few days of life? Understand well, then, beloved! God has conferred on you a much greater benefit in not sending you to Hell when you deserved it, and in giving you all this time for penance, than if he had first sent you to Hell, and afterwards permitted you to return to life to satisfy for your sins; consequently, you ought, in gratitude to God, apply with greater fervor to the amendment of your life. Act so that the fire of Hell may extinguish the fire of your passions.

We shall divide this meditation into three points, and consider: 1. How great the pains of Hell are. 2. What are in Hell the pains of the body. 3. What are the pains in Hell of the powers of the soul.

FIRST PRELUDE.

Let us fancy that we see Hell, and imagine whatever is horrible to behold. A cavern, full of black flames, sulphur, devils, dragons, fire, swords, arrows, and innumerable damned, who roar in despair. Imagine the worst you can; then say: "All this is nothing if compared to Hell."

SECOND PRELUDE.

Say: "Ah! my God, thou who 'hast the keys

of death and Hell'—(*Apoc.*, i. 18,) I beg of thee, through the bowels of thy mercy, that thou keep constantly shut the gates of Hell, and act so ' that Hell may engender in my heart thy holy fear,' as thy Chrysostom says."

FIRST POINT.

How great the pains of Hell must be. In order that what is related of Hell in the sacred Scriptures and the holy Fathers, and in whatever is said by preachers, may not appear exaggerated, we should consider it as it certainly is—as nothing compared to the reality. The reason is clearly deduced—that the pains of the damned must be enormous and inexplicable.

The first reason is, because in Hell the honor of an outraged God is to be restored. To understand this, imagine that a great king, whilst asleep, is bitten by a venomous scorpion. From the pain of the wound, he rises and calls the surgeons, who, having well examined it, say : " Sacred majesty, you are to die : the poison has already insinuated itself into the veins : art has no means to extract it: you are dead." " I dead!" replies the king: " and murdered by a vile worm ! I declare that I will revenge myself on this worm, and cause it to be punished for the death of a murdered king. Let the scorpion be found."

The entire apartment is then searched for the guilty worm. What punishment can be given sufficient to satisfy for death inflicted on a king? He is cut, crushed, trampled, burnt to ashes; all is nothing, and insufficient to satisfy for that great injury.

The sinner is a most vile worm. By sinning he

crucified anew the King of kings—the Redeemer. (*Heb.*, vi. 6.) If not in effect, at least in thought and deed, he acted in a hostile manner against God. What punishment then shall be given him in Hell, to atone the great outrage offered to God? Flames, swords, devils? All is little—all is nothing.

He who gave a mortal wound to William, Prince of Orange, was fastened on high by the extremities of his two thumbs, with a hundred pounds of lead attached to his toes. Then he was beaten with iron rods. When loosened, very long needles were threaded, and passed through his nails and skin. The following day his hairs were plucked out one by one, and he was exposed to a slow fire. Finally he was impaled: and, during his agony, the hand that inflicted the wound was burnt with plates of heated iron.

If such pain was adjudged to him who presumed to wound a prince, what torments should be inflicted in Hell on him who outraged a crucified God?

The second reason is, that not only the outrage offered to God is to be expiated on a wretched damned soul, but the glory of divine justice is to be exalted by making known to all the blessed in Heaven, " what God can do when he wishes to take revenge" on his rebels. (*Ezech.*, vii. 9.) Discourse then thus: " When God wished to show forth his omnipotence, he created this beautiful world. His mercy went so far, that he became man in a stable, and was crucified on Calvary. Now that he intends to show forth his justice in Hell by the severity of torments, what will he do?"

Add another reflection: " When God chastised

sinners on Earth, he always combined mercy with justice, and he did not punish them with the extent of his rigor. (*Job*, xxxv. 15.) Wishing to chastise in this gentle manner, what has he done? He drowned the world with a deluge of water? He consumed Pentapolis with a deluge of fire, and he depopulated kingdoms by the plague. What then will he do, when he shall show forth in Hell the whole extent of his rigor ?"

God afflicted holy Job, by taking from him his children, goods, health—everything. It is said this was a slight stroke of the divine hand: " The hand of the Lord hath *touched* me." (*Job*, xix. 21.) God threatened Jerusalem, by Ezechiel, with most fatal ruin, with fire and sword ; and this is called a " drop of his fury." (*Ezech.*, xx. 76.) He punished the same Jerusalem with imprisonment of its citizens, and the slaughter of one hundred and sixty thousand of them: and it is written: " This was but a small effect of divine wrath." (II. *Macc.*, v. 17.) What then shall it be when the whole weight of divine anger shall descend on the damned, to torment them inexorably ? " The wrath of the Lord shall be upon them."

Finally, when God proposed to make some trial of his friends on Earth, how much sickness and persecution did he send them? Job proceeded so far as to say: " Lord, you show yourself. too severe towards me." (*Job*, xxx. 31.) What did God permit to fall on his favorites, the martyrs ? That cruel tyrants and fierce executioners should torment them, and murder them in a thousand ways by racks, and boiling cauldrons, and famished wild beasts. If to try his friends, God made them suffer such dreadful pains, what will he do hereafter to torment his enemies in Hell, and by their sufferings to exalt his own glory?

Third reason: God knows sin clearly, and hates the sinner with a sovereign hatred. He has infinite power to chastise him, and he purposes to chastise him most severely. He has therefore formed Hell as the centre of all evils: "A place of torments," on which he sheds every pain and calamity. (*Job*, xx. 24.) As he has united every good in Heaven—(*Deut.*, xxxii. 23)—so he has united every evil in Hell. God wishes to try sinners as much by his justice, as he had previously shown mercy to them: "Pouring forth wrath according to his mercy." (*Eccl.*, xvi. 12.) Was not the mercy shown by God to sinners infinite? Who can deny it? He went so far as to shed all the blood of his veins to save them! If then the rigor of his justice is to be as great in punishing them, what will it be? With what inexplicable torments will this rigor show itself? "in the time of his wrath." God, in a certain manner, will exert his power in chastising the impious. Why? They abused his goodness to the extreme by sinning. This is the reflection of Cardinal Hugo. "Hence the Lord, too, will be extreme in their punishment."

Beloved, are not these reasons most clear? Can they be denied? Who, possessed of common sense, can deny that the pains of Hell are beyond our understanding? All that can be said of them, so far from exaggerating, falls far short of the truth. Now let us meditate particularly on the torments of Hell.

SECOND POINT.

What are the pains of the senses of the body in Hell. Consider the entrance of a damned soul into Hell. Imagine that a delicate man, who has had all the conveniences and pleasures of the world, placed on a bed of down, under splendid drapery, and dying in enmity with God. He dies, and is buried in Hell. On first feeling the tortures and scorching of that insufferable and devouring fire, on first seeing the crowding demons, what does he say? "Wretched and unhappy man that I am, whither have I come?" He repeats the words of St. Bernard: "How is it possible to remain here? These torments are not for me, who am used to delights!" "I can bear no more: I cannot remain here!" Whether he wills it or not, in spite of himself, he must remain there to roar in despair for all eternity. The miserable emperor Zeno was buried alive in a tomb, by Arianna his consort, while he was overcome with wine, and in profound stupor. When he awoke in darkness, and felt nothing but bones; oppressed with the fetid odor of dead bodies, he began to sob and roar, "Have mercy! open, open to me!" "Where am I? Courtiers, chamberlains, friends, for pity sake, open to me. O my vassals! have pity on me." Finding that he is not heard by any one, he gives way to the greatest fury and despair; he tears his flesh with his own teeth, and striking his head violently against the wall of his tomb shatters his brains and kills himself. *(Cedronus.)* Unhappy damned soul! On first finding himself in Hell, he sobs and roars and wishes to find pity, and then despairs, and tears his flesh with his teeth. (*Isa.*, ix. 20.) Death is a thousand fold removed from him.

Consider then, in detail, the pains of Hell.

1. *The place.* This is a horrible and terrific cavern, situated, perhaps, in the centre of the Earth. In the divine Scripture, it is called " a place of torments," " the well of the abyss," a lake or river of fire, in which the damned are immersed like fishes in the sea: frequently it is called " a plain of fire." Why so? Gehenna is an extentive valley situated beyond the walls of Jerusalem, in which the impious Manasses had erected a great column of bronze, in honor of the idol Moloch. Mothers often sacrificed their children to it, burning them alive, so that king Josias, heir of the kingdom, " condemned this abominable valley of Gehenna" (IV. *Kings*, xciii.): and having overthrown that infamous symbol, he ordered all the filth of Jerusalem, and all the dead bodies to be thrown there. Hell then is called Gehenna; for in that voracious cavern, all the filth of the world is collected and enclosed without exhalation or air, and thus producing a fetid pestilence. Hell is also a most obscure prison and very narrow, considering the innumerable damned souls. They have to remain immovable, one over the other. " As sheep they are crowded in Hell." (*Ps.*, xlviii. 15.)

The heretics of Maestricht girded the arms and legs of three fathers of the Society of Jesus with circles studded with points of needles, so that they could not move without feeling the pricking of the needles. They then enkindled a slow fire around the fathers. What torture! How much greater is that of the damned, who being in a place full of flames and tortures, wherever they move encounter new torments!

2. *The companions.* What a torture it would be if two capital enemies remained chained together for life? What will it be, to remain in company with innumerable enemies for all eternity! These are, first, the devils, declared enemies of man, who in Hell have power from God to tear and torment the damned as much as they will. Second, the accomplices in sin; these wicked companions will curse and tear one another. The scandalous mother will curse the daughter, and the vain daughter will curse the mother who taught her vanity and scandal. Third, those who were guilty of the same faults; for they will be placed together to burn like so many logs of wood: the selfish with the selfish; the dishonest with the dishonest; gamblers with gamblers. A wicked wretch said: "If I am damned, I shall not be alone, I shall have many companions with me." Fool! do you not know that every companion will be a new torment and tormentor! You have not courage to live in a cloister of strict observance, where you would have many companions, good and holy. How will you remain in Hell with a crowd of damned, each one of whom will be a new sword to wound and afflict you? Finally, the wild beasts, dragons, and horrible monsters, torment and slaughter. The people of Japan used to fill a ditch with serpents, and then placed the martyrs there, with their head downwards to the waist. What barbarity! The ancients enclosed parricides in a leather sack with a dog, a viper, and an ape, and then threw them into the sea. What a martyrdom! How much greater will be

the torments of the damned, obliged to remain with innumerable monsters!

3. *The sight.* It is tormented by frightful devils. A holy religious saw at death two such monstrous and ugly devils, that he cried out, saying, that rather than see them again, he would walk till the day of judgment on fire of sulphur and dissolved metal. By great darkness, much worse than that of the Egyptians; by a dense and black smoke which has no exit, and which will prevent the miserable damned from breathing. (I. *Kings,* ii.) Then the inconsolable and unceasing tears of fire! and the sight of those whom they counselled or induced to commit sin, and of those who were the cause of their sinning and their eternal damnation.

St. Bridget (*b.* VI. *Revel.,* lii.) said that she saw a woman coming out of a lake of fire, without any heart in her chest, without lips on her countenance, with eyes dissolved on her cheeks, with asps on her bosom, who cried out to her daughter, who was still alive, " My daughter! no longer a child, but a venomous serpent! Wretch that I am for having brought you forth, but much more so for having taught you to commit sin. As often as you return to the commission of sin, from the bad example I gave you, my pains are renewed with vigor."

6. *The hearing* is continually tormented with ferocious howling, inconsolable sobs, rage, blasphemies, from the despair of those in that horrible abyss. O what punishment is this!

Plutarch writes of Scylla, that one day he imprisoned six thousand persons; and as he closed his speech in the senate, he caused them all to be murdered. O God! what cries, what weeping, what rage did they feel and utter! How much worse is that which is heard in Hell?

7. *The scent* is tormented by the odor of sulphur, and by the noisomeness of all the sewers of the world, which crumble into that abyss, and by the bad odor of the damned, which is much worse than that of the most putrid bodies. One damned soul alone, says St. Bonaventure, if he came into the world, would suffice to infect it all. What odor, then, will exhale from innumerable damned souls, shut up in one enclosure?

It is related in the life of St. Walburga, that a murderer, having killed a pilgrim, took him in his arms to bury him in a remote place. The murdered body clasped him so strongly, that the wretched assassin could not by any means detach himself from it, even with the sword; so that the mangled body caused him to die by its intolerable scent. (*Bolland.*, 23 *Jan.*)

8. *The taste*, in punishment of gluttony and intemperance, murmuring and dishonest words, is tormented by ravenous hunger. Such hunger that each one will tear his own flesh with his teeth. (*Isa.*, ix. 20.) Tormented by insupportable thirst, Dives, from Hell, asked nothing of Abraham but a drop of water: while he was tormented with gall, wormwood, and disgusting liquids.

The Roman tyrants forced several martyrs to drink boiling resin and liquefied metals. How much worse will the devils torment the damned!

The feeling, for crimes of excessive delights taken in the world, is tormented by swords, pincers, bites, tearing of vipers and dragons, horrible blows given by the devils. (*Job*, xx. 25.) Above all, the damned are tormented by so active a fire, that it appears to be the very spirit and essence of fire: such a fire, that a mountain of bronze thrown into it, would dissolve in one instant: a fire which possesses the evil of burning and tormenting, but has not the good of enlightening and consuming; a fire which combines all torments, and the pains of all sickness, wounds, and frost and snow. "By the word fire," says the angelic doctor, "every suffering is meant."— (*App.*, *q.* xcvii.) This fire intimately penetrates and devours the damned. (*Joel*, xxiii.) As food devoured by a wild beast becomes the same substance as the animal; so the damned, devoured by fire, become burning coals. Elsewhere it is said, that they shall be salted with fire. (*Deut.*, xxix. 23.) Salt, when rubbed on flesh, profoundly penetrates it. Fire acts in a similar manner on the bodies of those miserable creatures. The damned, then, no longer appear as men; but as moving coals, in a sea of fire; they even seem as animated Hells. The brains will boil as in a vessel, the blood in the veins, the intestines in the body. O God! what terror! What horror! Otho, king of Bohemia, caused one of his pages to be wrapped in an oiled sheet, then burned alive like a lighted torch, merely for not being attentive to awaken him from sleep.

King Wenceslaus caused one of his servants, who had not prepared his food well, to be placed on a spit, and turned on a slow fire. (*In magno Chronic Belgico*, p. 273.) How much more horrible is the fire of Hell! What is still worse, the damned have to suffer all evils together. In this life one person cannot suffer every sickness at the same time; he cannot suffer every torment, nor for a long period; for weak nature, unable to bear it, avoids them by death. If in summer he suffers from heat, he cannot at the same time be exposed to the frost of winter; and so of the rest. In Hell it is not so. Heat and cold, hunger and torture—every evil is there. God said it in *Deuteronomy*, i. 18. O Hell! Hell! how terrible—how frightful thou art! Beloved, let us discourse seriously on this point. Do you believe or disbelieve these things? Are these fables, or enigmas, or are they evangelical truths? They cannot be discredited. Jesus Christ has said them, faith teaches them, the Scriptures and theologians attest them. What folly then to wish to purchase by a momentary pleasure, great and eternal torments.

If a person said to you—" If you throw yourself into a burning furnace, I will give you a kingdom;" who would be so thoughtless as to do it? The Devil says: " If you throw yourself into Hell, I will give you a little pleasure, in yielding to your passion;" and will you be so void of reason as to do it? " You cannot bear," says the Carthusian, in astonishment, (*Sup.*, *art.* 7,) " to hold your finger in the flame of a lighted candle, yet you show very little fear to dwell in the horrible flames of Hell." Is not this the greatest blindness and folly? Well did the three noble, religious youths answer their wicked companions, who, as the Carthusian relates, strongly tempted them to abandon religious life, by saying: " Your pride is too severe, you are too delicate, this kind of life is not fit for you." The youths thus repulsed their wicked suggestions. One answered:

"If I cannot now bear with religious observance, how shall I suffer hereafter the pains of Hell?" The second responded: "Because I am delicate and cannot bear much, I prefer this little severity for the love of God, rather than eternal suffering, with the hatred and disgrace of God." Finally, the third said: "I can suffer in this world, for I have God to assist me with his grace, but in Hell the wretched damned souls are entirely abandoned by God." What beautiful sentiments, which each one should repeat to himself: "I am delicate; I can suffer only a little for God; and how shall I suffer in Hell all evils, and the hatred of God?"

Let us not add by our sins fuel to the fire of Hell. On the contrary, let us extinguish that fire by fervent penance. Let us avail ourselves of the light of those eternal flames; and make them guides to walk well in the divine precepts. (*Isa.* l.)

THIRD POINT.

What are the punishments of the soul in Hell. The angelic doctor teaches, (12, *q.* xiii. *art.* 4,) that there is no creature so miserable and unhappy, that he has not some participation of the divine goodness. Of the goods communicated by God, some belong to the essence and some to the perfection of nature. Those goods which belong to perfection are lost by sin; and those which relate to the essence are left for greater chastisement. In the damned there is the good of existence, which being always unhappy, is always tormenting; there is life, but it serves as a greater torment, being always miserable, without hope of terminating misery by death: there is the use of the three powers of the soul, the memory, understanding, and will, which cause the greatest affliction.

1. *The memory* will be Hell in miniature for the damned; for he will remember his past pleasures. Although on Earth the recollection of former good often recreates the fancy, to the damned it is a continual cause for martyrdom. He will say within himself: "Who would believe it, that after so many delights, I should find myself in so many torments? Pleasures have passed like a dream, and these torments are never to finish. I was once courted, having been rich and noble, now I am the object of all ignominies and sorrows." What inexpressible pain! Abraham reminded Dives of the delights he had enjoyed in the world: "Remember the good things thou didst receive in life."

2. He will remember for how little he was damned; for a momentary pleasure, for giving way to a passion which passed like lightning; and "for so little," he will say, "I have to suffer so much." When unfortunate Esau found he had forfeited his birthright for nothing, he howled like a person in despair, and roared like a lion. (*Gen.*, xxvii. 34.)

When miserable Jonathan saw himself condemned to death, solely for having tasted some drops of honey against the orders of his father, king Saul, he could not contain himself, he said, with sobs, "What! must I die? For what reason? For tasting a few drops of honey. Oh! this is a subject of grief beyond expression."— (I. *Kings*, xiv. 19.)

What then will be the agony and rage of a

damned soul, remembering the slight cause, and the short pleasures for which he finds himself in so horrible a Hell?

Once, a damned soul, covered with a black mantle, appeared to Blessed Humbert. Heaving a profound sigh, he said, that the Hell of Hells to him, was the remembrance of having been damned for a fault of short duration.

The lost soul will remember with how little trouble he might have avoided Hell, and yet did not do it. He will repeat to himself: "Nothing was necessary to escape being damned, but to make a good confession. What great labor would this have been? For a little shame, I did not do it. How foolish I was. How often did I clearly hear it in sermons? Did I not frequently meditate on it in the spiritual exercises? Alas! without fruit. How many have committed much greater sins than I have? As they were wise enough to confess them and do penance, they are in Paradise. I alone have been a fool; I cannot complain of any one but myself." With unavailing repentance his lamentations will be greater than those of *Job* (xvii. 11.)

The intellect of the damned will also be tormented in several ways, by the most fatal reflections, which he makes concerning his sufferings. The first reflection will be, "what a gross mistake have I made? What a most solemn and irreparable error is mine? What false ideas did I entertain on Earth? I thought myself very wise when I knew many natural sciences, when I knew how to become rich and powerful. I made no account whatever of those devout faithful persons, who, though illiterate and deprived of every other prerogative, knew how to be saved."

A doctor of the university of Paris appearing to the bishop of that place, told him with a sad voice, that he was damned. The bishop asked him if there was any knowledge in Hell. The miserable man answered, that he only knew three things: 1. That he was eternally damned. 2. That his sentence was irrevocable. 3. That he was eternally condemned for the pleasures of the world and the body. Then he asked the bishop "If the world still existed?" "Why?" interrogated the bishop. "Because," said he, "during these days so many souls have fallen into Hell, that I thought there could not be many more remaining."

The second reflection will be, "I merit this pain, because I offended an infinite majesty. I was often admonished by priests of what has happened to me, and I could easily have foreseen it. God has given me every assistance to be saved, and I abused it all; thus the fault is mine. God became man that I might be saved; he was crucified for me. For a short pleasure I rendered the blood of a God vain and useless for me." These thoughts are so many nails, so many shafts which transfix the damned soul. Above all, the intellect will be afflicted by the privation of the beatific vision, and by the experimental knowledge it has of the effects of divine justice. The saying of Isaias is verified. How is it that the damned do not see God, yet for their confusion, feel his justice?

The angelic doctor distinguishes (*App. qu.* 92, *ar.* 2) between the intuitive vision by which the blessed alone see without veil the goodness of God;

which vision constitutes their happiness; and the abstractive vision, by means of enigmas, by which they perceive in a twofold degree some of the divine attributes. This is also the portion of the damned, so that knowing the effects of divine justice, this knowledge will serve for their greater punishment. What a torment this will be to the understanding of the damned. God, who has been my creator, my father, and who ought to have been the object of my happiness, I now recognize as the author of all my torments. What punishment, what anguish! Finally, they will by a thousand different emotions be tormented: by contempt, rage, sadness, disgust. Souls will envy those who are in the enjoyment of Heaven, and of whom they made so little account during life. The master who is damned will not bear to see his servant saved: the beggar envy him of whom he was an enemy. The sinner will enclose a thousand hatreds in his heart, without once experiencing any sentiment of love. He will hate God, as the author of his punishment: he will hate the saints, for approving of his torments: he will hate himself as the cause of his own ruin. He will be a maddened victim in that fire which exalts the infinite justice of God. (*Apcc.* xiv. 11.) He will despair, for he never can obtain aught he wishes. He must always suffer against his will. He would wish to die and terminate his tortures, but he cannot. He desires a drop of refreshment or a moment of quiet, and will never have it. He wishes not to see fierce devils before him, and yet must always see them. What torments are these! The greatest of all pains is that of the will. Even the most excruciating punishment of Hell is called the pain of damnation,—the privation of God our sovereign good and last end. The bitter necessity of never seeing God and of never loving him, is a torment which may be called infinite, because separation becomes sad in proportion to the loss.

Hard is the exile by which native country is lost. More painful still the confiscation of goods by which property is lost; more heart-rending is the perpetual separation from parents and friends; but the keenest loss is that of life. How agonizing then must be to the damned the loss of God, who is an infinite good? It must be an infinite torture. A soul separated from the body flies more ardently to God, its last end, than the flame to its sphere. What noise a volcano enclosed in the earth makes to ascend to the Heavens! It goes so far into mines as to crumble and precipitate rocks, and with its earthquakes even kingdoms totter. Let us hence infer with what force a soul, separated from the body, is impelled towards God, and with what pain it is repulsed, and obliged to remain in Hell! The wretch weeping with tears of fire, is ever repeating; "This amiable God, who created me, who loved me so much that he died for me, I am never to see! This beautiful Paradise, made purposely for me, and for which I was created, I am never to enjoy. I can never see Mary, the angels, or the saints!"

Absalom was exiled, for the murder of his brother. At length, at the request of Joab the general, he returned home, but on condition that he should never appear before his father. (II. *Reg.*, xiv. 24.) He felt this punishment so much, that not being able to bear it longer, he sent to entreat the king to admit him into his presence, or to kill him; esteeming it a less evil to die than to live in such torment. What anguish then, never to see that God who had been the most loving father! Always to recognize him as an enemy! to see that it is he himself who with his breath blows the mantle of flames! "The Lord shall deride them."

Beloved, meditate on this, and weep bitterly. This is the Hell you have so long deserved. Hell is more than all that can be said of it. Go to the mouth of this horrible furnace, and exclaim: " Here I should be, if after having committed that mortal sin, God had not preserved me from sudden death." Infinite mercy of God, how much do I owe thee! I shall say with St. Augustine: " A thousand times thou mightest have damned me, hadst thou wished it." "Wretch that I am, I can be damned; innumerable souls like me were damned; many also who have committed less sins than I have. Judas was damned, and he was an apostle. One who had been a saint, and had wrought miracles, was damned. I at great risk live, and do not tremble from head to foot, and all my blood does not freeze in my veins."

3. Reflect that it is not difficult to be damned. On the contrary, according to the general opinion of doctors, the number of those who are damned exceeds that of those who are saved. How terrible! The learned Bellarmine says: " If, of all mankind, one alone should be damned, this would be a just reason to induce every one to fear for himself, and to live well."

Arnulph, Count of Flanders, suffered from a certain malady. The physicians recommended him to undergo an operation. He, however, would not expose himself to the danger until an experiment should be tried upon some other person. He caused all in his states who were similarly afflicted to submit to the surgeon's knife. Among twenty cases, nineteen succeeded, only one died; yet the death of this individual so frightened the count, that he refused to be operated upon.

What should be our fear in the great affair of salvation, knowing that not one alone, but many are damned? "This is so tremendous a sentence," says St. Augustine, "that he who is not aroused at its voice, and does not amend his vices, does not sleep, but is already dead."

In the last place, reflect how hideous a Christian must appear in Hell in the midst of a crowd of Pagans, Turks, schismatics; and what is still worse, to behold there Christians of every grade. To understand this, know that a soul, on entering Hell, is immediately despoiled of all supernatural gifts, graces, and infused habits. There remains only the sign of those sacraments, which impress a character, and cause confusion and torment. Infidels, seeing in reprobate Christians characters of baptism and confirmation, will exclaim: "Wicked wretches, you indeed have no excuse for perdition; you were regenerated to grace by baptism; you were strengthened by confirmation, yet you are damned: you are perfidious and ungrateful." In a similar manner, God will permit that persons should know each other. They will be pointed out, and it will be said: "Here are those who made profession of sanctity, who were more favored and enlightened than others by God. Who would believe it, they also committed many irregularities, and are now under the feet of devils, and blended with the wicked of the Earth." St. Augustine with tears, bitterly lamented the misfortune of such souls.

COLLOQUY.

O great, omnipotent God, who hast in thy hands the keys of death and Hell, how terrible thou art to thy enemies! how severe in thy chastisements! I admire and exalt thy infinite justice; at the same time I do not cease being astonished at myself; how I durst offend a God who can destroy both my soul and body in Hell. Blind and foolish that I was; for my audacity one Hell is too little, I merit a thousand. I am the person, and I say it with tears in my eyes, who have little feared thy justice, who have outraged thy majesty, and who have abused thy beneficence. I am he who, as many times as I have sinned, have merited Hell, and as many times I should have been precipitated into those flames, if thy infinite mercy had not waited for my penance. My good God! as through thy goodness, thou hast so many times delivered me from damnation, deign to deliver me from it forever. I cannot bear to think that I shall not love nor be loved by thee for all eternity: all the other pains of Hell would afflict me much, but this pain of not seeing thee, of not loving thee, O my God! my Creator, my Redeemer, my All! This pain indeed is insupportable. If thou wishest to chastise me as I merit for my sins, chastise me here with sickness and persecutions, but deliver me from Hell. Here burn, here cut, provided thou sparest me in eternity. I beg of thee, through the bowels of thy mercy, grant that the eternal fire may serve alone for Lucifer and his followers, for whom it was made; but for me and for all thy faithful, extinguish those flames.

MEDITATION XIII.

On the Eternity of the Damned.

INTRODUCTION.

One of the greatest mistakes committed by worldlings is, that in affairs of very short duration, they employ all their solicitude: while of those which are eternal, they seldom or ever think. If there be question of honor or interest, which disappears like smoke, or of avoiding temporal evil, then every exertion is made: fatigue and expense are not spared; but to acquire an eternal kingdom, or to avoid an eternal Hell, men are usually as dilatory as if it did not concern them. What folly! what blindness! The saints who were enlightened by God, did not act thus. Holy David acknowledged that he tried in vain for repose; that fatal thoughts clouded his mind; and that he sometimes passed days in sad and profound silence. (*Ps.*, vii. 5.) If you ask the reason, his answer is, because he often meditated on eternity. (*Ps.*, lxxvii.) "Oh! what a grand thought!" says St. Augustine (on *Ps.*, xxix). So powerful and efficacious a thought, that it caused the blood to freeze in the veins of the greatest saints in the Church, and produced in them the pains of martyrdom. The angel of the Apocalypse after having said that Babylon, that is, perverse people, should be thrown into a sea of torments without hope of ever leaving it, adds that this thought was the patience of the saints, (*Apoc.*, xiv. 12,) which St. Thomas the angelic doctor explains: "The consideration of eternal punishment impresses the lesson of patience in this world." Happy we, if this great thought be deeply imprinted in our minds. We would then willingly suffer every temporal misery to avoid the eternal. In this meditation we shall consider three properties, which accompany the eternity of the damned. 1. It is interminable. 2. Invariable. 3. Indivisible.

FIRST PRELUDE.

Imagine that God offers you two circles, without beginning or end; one, of massive gold, ornamented with palms and laurels; the other, of red hot iron, and armed with swords and terrible scourges. He says to you: "Choose which you please; but you must have one of these circles, either eternal happiness or eternal misery."

SECOND PRELUDE.

Say to God with your whole heart: "Lord, if thou wilt have satisfaction for my sins, punish me in time, but not throughout eternity." "Here burn, here cut; spare me not here; but spare me in eternity."

FIRST POINT.

The eternity of the damned is interminable. We should consider many reasons why the pains of the damned are to be without end. 1. Because the decree passed by God is irrevocable. The blood of Jesus Christ will never satisfy for those miserable souls. 2. Tertullian (*in Apel.*) says that the matter of their torments will be eternal; the devils being eternal, and the fire eternal, because preserved and provoked by the breath of a God, who is eternal. Besides, the soul which is to suffer is also eternal; and sin, which is the cause of suffering, never being remitted in Hell, is also eternal. The third reason is from the angelic St. Thomas, (1, 2, *qu.* 87, *art.* 3,) because the grievousness of the sin increases according to the quality of the person offended. The sinner, having offended an infinite and eternal God, has consequently deserved an infinite chastisement, and an eternal torment. St. Augustine speaks similarly.

Finally, St. Thomas says (*loc. cit.*), that amongst the blessed and the reprobate there should be found an apposite contradiction. Of each it is said: "He shall reign forever and ever" (*Apoc.* xi.); and of the latter: "He shall also drink of the wine of the wrath of God, which is mingled with pure wine, in the cup of his wrath; and he shall be tormented with fire and brimstone in the sight of the holy angels, and in the sight of the Lamb. And the smoke of their torments shall go up forever and ever; neither have they rest day nor night." (*Apoc.* xiv.) As the blessed have ever to exalt the eternal goodness of God, so the damned in their punishment have always to show the eternal justice of God. "Their fire shall not be extinguished." (*Isa.*, lxvi. 24.) Thus the miserable damned have to suffer torments, which will never end. Never will God place the sword of his justice in its sheath. (*Ezech.*, xxi. 5.) Never will God show mercy to them. St. Bonaventure says: "He will close the bowels of mercy." On the contrary, there is always to be in that abyss, a death that never terminates, a succession of innumerable centuries which never end. "Death without death"—" End without end," says St. Gregory (*l.* 9, *Mor.* *c.* 25.) For ever and ever those inexorable doors are closed, without hope of their ever being opened for all eternity.

Great was the terror of Hugh of Pisa, Count of Gheradesca, when he was shut up in a high tower with his children, and the keys of the prison thrown into the Arno. How much greater will be the horror of a damned soul thrown into Hell, when those iron doors shall be closed upon him, and he shall lose all hope of quitting it for all eternity! Oh! always. Oh! never. Oh! most terrible words, capable of consuming every heart! The pain was certainly very great which the prophet Ezechiel sustained, when by order of God, to satisfy for the sins of Israel, he had to sleep on the left side for three hundred and ninety days. (*Ezech.*, iv.) How incomparably greater is the pain of the damned, who has not to sleep but to suffer exquisite torture, not on a soft bed, but on burning coals; not for three or four hundred days, or years, or centuries, or millions of centuries, but for all centuries, always, eternally!

It belongs to eternity, that where there is not union with the sovereign good and sovereign pleasure, it becomes most unhappy. Thus, if music were eternal, it would become an insupportable nuisance; if sleep were eternal, it would no longer be a restorative, but death. If then eternity be united with a slight evil, it becomes an infinite one. Thus, an eternal tooth-ache or suffering is an infinite pain; a wise man should prefer to suffer for a thousand years all the torments of Hell, rather than suffer a simple tooth-ache for all eternity. What then will eternity be in Hell, where it is not united with a simple pleasure, not with a slight pain, but with most atrocious and inexplicable torments? What will it be?

The most miserable in this world console themselves, whatever misfortune occurs to them, by saying: "At least it will terminate with death." This harsh comfort the damned will never have, for their death will never end, of which St. Augustine said: "The worst death is where death does not die." (*l. v. di. Dio. c.* 81.) Millions and millions of years will pass away, but eternity will still continue.

Father Baldigiani, a fervent missioner of the Society of Jesus, exorcising a possessed person in Rome, asked the Devil how long he had been in Hell. He answered: Six thousand years. "Then console yourself," said the father, "that so many years have passed." "Wo to me," added the Devil, "I should be consoled if these years were passed and were taken away; but what are years in eternity!"

Eternity cannot be fully understood. It can only in a certain degree be explained, says the angelic doctor St. Thomas (1 *p. q.* 10, *art.* 1), by using comparisons. Imagine that God should send an angel to the damned with this embassy: "Listen, miserable and wretched creatures: God, moved with compassion for you, has resolved to take you out of the fire of Hell, after each of you has formed with his tears a collection of water more vast than the ocean, and after there shall have passed as many millions of years as there are grains of sand in the sea, leaves on the trees, and atoms in the air." What a terrible announcement! How incomprehensible the number of years to fulfil these conditions! Yet if the damned received this notice, they would abound in joy, and consider it all as nothing. As St. Augustine says (in *Ps.*, lx.): "Every thing which has an end, is short." They would all rejoice, saying: It is true that in this case the years prescribed to suffer appear innumerable, but they will end, and that suffices. Such embassy and joy the unfortunate damned will never have. On the contrary, they are to be incessantly stunned with thunder, and oppressed with an interminable eternity. "The voice of thy thunder is on the wheel."

Here meditate, beloved. Let us confidently discourse together. Do you believe or disbelieve this eternity? You answer: "I certainly believe it." I respond: You believe it, and sin with so much boldness; what could you do worse if you did not believe it? "If," says St. Augustine, "you believe it and sin, you must have lost your reason. or stupefied your affections." O eternity! Who knows what eternity means, and continues to commit sin, has either lost faith or reason. I beg of you to think a little, says holy David. (*Ps.*, xlix. 22.) O miserable worldlings, who live forgetful of God and your souls; you walk by long strides to perdition, and while you are running towards Hell, you do not consider that when once arrived there, there is no road to return. Every man goes spontaneously with his feet to the house of his eternity. (*Eccl.*, xii.) Having once arrived there, he never can depart from it. The house in which a person dwells in the world is not properly his own. A day will come when his dearest friends will have to carry him away to be buried. Man's house is of eternity. Be careful then not to have one day to say, "Miserable me! Hell is my dwelling." Act as a wise merchant, and make up your accounts. Is it good traffic, to enjoy the pleasures of a very short life, and afterwards to suffer most excruciating torments for all eternity? Thus spoke the great Chancellor of England, Sir Thomas Moore, to Louisa his wife. He was in prison and condemned to the axe for the glorious cause of not consenting to the unlawful marriage of Henry VIII. Louisa his consort appeared before him with her little children dressed in mourning, her hair dishevelled, sobbing, clapping her hands with all that energy which love, grief, interest, and jealousy gave her, and exclaimed: "Thomas, you could live long at the height of honor; and yet you prefer losing your head on a block, and leaving us heirs of your misfortune. Do you not remember my love? Have compassion at least on these poor children." Tears and fainting prevented her saying more. Sir Thomas was moved to compassion; but animating himself, he said: "Louisa, how many years do you think I should survive my honors?" "How many years," said she, "you are of a vigorous constitution, regular in your manner of living; I think you may certainly promise yourself twenty years of life." Moore assuming a stern countenance: "Go, go," said he, "you are a very silly negotiator. Does this appear good traffic—for twenty years of life, and these uncertain, to have afterwards to suffer an eternity of torments?" Every man should thus balance his accounts. How many years can I possibly live in this world? Twenty, fifty, one hundred years? Do not these pass like lightning, as a dream; and then eternity! Eternity! How foolish a bargain! for very brief enjoyments, to deserve eternal torments, which never end;—never, never, never!

SECOND POINT.

The eternity of the damned is invariable. All the evils of life, especially if they are tedious, have some alleviation or interruption. Even the habit of suffering accustoms, and, in a manner, deadens souls to suffering. Fevers have their decline; spasms and wounds are mitigated by sleep, and lulled by unctions. The miseries of Job were alleviated by the compassion of his friends. Usually God so disposes of events in this world, that pains which are insufferable, such as death, are short; and pains that are tedious admit of mitigation. The evils and pains of Hell, however, are not so, being excessive and eternal, without alleviation or interruption.

1. The painful eternity of the damned will be without alleviation, for from whom can these unfortunate creatures have relief? From God? On the contrary, he will increase their torments. (*Sap.*, iv. 18.) "The Lord shall laugh at them." (*Ps.*, ii. 4.) From the saints? No; they will enjoy seeing these victims burn to exalt the infinite justice of God. (*Ps.*, lvii. 11.) From Heaven? No; for St. Chrysologus says that the miserable creatures will be more afflicted by the sight of Heaven, which they lost, than by the view of their present Hell. Shall they have relief from companions? As one thorn splits another, and one coal enkindles another, so the damned will tear and burn each other. The father will not forgive his son, nor the consort her spouse, nor

the sister her brother, nor the companion or friend his other friend. (*Isa.*, ix. 19.) Shall they have any relief from themselves? Even this will not be; for the damned soul resembles a tempestuous sea, agitated by a thousand irregular passions and a thousand contrary wills (*Isa.*, lvii. 20), so that the eternity of these unfortunate creatures will always be deprived of every alleviation.

2. It will be without interruption. The rich man could not obtain one moment of relief from his great thirst by a single drop of water. Add that the devils watch night and day to torment the damned (*Job*, xxx. 15); and dragons and monsters, whose talons are such, that there is not any enchantment to restrain their fury. (*Jer.*, viii.) Finally, the fire is most active and devouring.

Let us now discourse together. If even pleasures and the most agreeable walks, if not varied, become intolerable, how tormenting will the pains of Hell be, which for all eternity will not have one moment's interruption? This great thought caused a most pious king to excite one of his courtiers, whose conduct was irregular, to lead a more Christian life. This king, after having several times attempted to recall him, finally adopted this plan. One morning, at a very early hour, he invited him to a most showy but fatiguing hunt. After the chase he wished him to play for several hours. After play a comedy followed. The courtier began respectfully to complain to the king that his favors were most acceptable, but too continual. The king pretended not to hear, and immediately invited him to dance; after the dance, to a cavalcade; after the cavalcade, to a musical entertainment. The youth unable to accept of so many invitations, and finding his strength fail, threw himself at the feet of the king, saying: "Sire, I am overpowered; I can no longer stand upright. I beg of you to give me a little rest. We have been walking for eighteen hours without one moment's relief." The king then assuming a majestic air, said: "You cannot bear a walk of eighteen hours; and after a depraved life, how can you sustain continual and uninterrupted torments during the whole length of eternity?" At this severe reprimand the courtier entered into himself, reformed his manners, and led a holy life. If we also thought of this, how advantageous it would be for us in the reformation of our manners!

Finally, the eternity of the damned will be invariable. For their wounds there shall be no remedy, (*Sap.*, xi.) neither shall they have that bitter resource of those in despair; namely, that of death. "They shall seek death and shall not find it."—(*Apoc.*, ix. 6.) Besides, they cannot have any diminution in suffering by habit—as it were accustoming themselves to those sufferings; for these will always be most excruciating, and appear ever new. They cannot change the place of their torments, as on Earth. If a sick person is agitated by pains, change of position may occasion some relief, even though the patient suffers in every place. Thus, alternately he walks, runs, and reclines on his bed, placing himself now on one side, then on the other. Not so with the damned. Ever immovable in his excruciating torture, he can never move from his situation. He can never stir from that place in which he falls for the first time. What terror! What dismay! O eternity, who can think of it without trembling? My soul, what do you say; think, and resolve?

St. John Climacus relates, that a profligate youth named Toribisco, after long fixing his thoughts on eternity, said to himself: "Toribisco, we have no more to do. I must be a fool or a saint. Either you do not believe or understand these things, and then you are going to an asylum of madmen; or you believe and understand them, and are going to a hermitage to become a saint." Each should say to himself: "I do not reflect on this frightful eternity which faith teaches me; I am consequently the most foolish man in the world; or I do not reflect on it as I ought. What more then have I to do, than to change my life and become a saint?" My God, my most merciful Father, deign to have pity on my soul. By thy sole goodness thou art pleased to give me light to know eternity: give me also efficacious graces to lead such a life that I may hereafter enjoy the eternity of the blessed, and not undergo the torments of the reprobate.

THIRD POINT.

The eternity of the damned is without division. The better to understand this point it is necessary to suppose the definition which Boezio (*lib.* III.) gives of eternity: "It is a duration ever present; a perpetual to-day, without past or future." In this world evils are suffered successively. The evils of eternity appear to be all evils in union; for, the miserable reprobate, knowing that his torments are always to last, and hopeless of any termination, is continually tormented by a whole eternity which overwhelms him with horror. This can be easily explained by a similitude. Imagine a great ball of bronze, perfectly round, placed on a flat surface. The ball does not touch the surface, except at one point, yet its entire weight presses it. Thus eternity, though it presses on the damned at one point alone, in the present moment; yet it combines in its great weight the past, present, and future; uniting all for torment! The damned says unceasingly to himself: "All the years past, how numerous soever they have been, have not in the least diminished eternity. The present moment is excruciating; and future pains are never, never to end." What agonizing torture, what a terrible torture to the mind of a damned soul—"Throughout eternity, I cannot be saved! Never can I escape from this most horrible prison!"

The prophet Jonas, swallowed by a whale, for his disobedience to God, finding himself enclosed in that fish, as in a living prison, and not knowing that in three days he was to be cast on the sea shore, began to sob inconsolably, saying: "Wretch that I am, always to live and die in this dungeon."—(*Jon.*, ii. 3.) What Jonas said, while uncertain of obtaining his liberty, every damned soul can say with truth. "Ever and never are two keys of bronze which have enclosed me in this Hell. Here I am to suffer these flames eternally, those devils for eternity, this rage forever." O eternity! most terrible eternity! Yet I have said little, for it will be not only one sole eternity which will afflict the damned, but so many tormenting eternities as there are moments of his Hell; for at every instant he feels himself newly oppressed by the whole length of eternity, says the Psalmist. Hence will arise in the damned that pain, which St. Cyprian says is "worse than every other torment," namely, despair. The damned having lost all hope of obtaining mercy from God, or of having an end to his torments, will, with contemptuous rage turn against God, and with cruelty towards himself will tear his own flesh. "Here on Earth," says Vegezio (*lib.* III.), "here despair gives courage; and even cowardice is brave when hope has fled." What will it be in Hell?

Some enemies of the Israelites retired into a large cavern, where they were shut up. When Joshua knew of it, he commanded the entrance of the cavern to be sealed with large stones; and he posted there a squadron of brave soldiers to prevent the besieged from escaping. (*Joshua*, x. 18.) What despair! what dismay, for those miserable creatures, under the fatal necessity of dying of hunger, if they did not give themselves up to their enemies; or of being cruelly massacred if they surrendered! How much more miserable is the state of the damned, who cannot be freed from pain, even by death. On the contrary, they must suffer in that eternal imprisonment. What howling, what sobbing, what despair will be theirs! My soul, here meditate and weep. Can a greater pain be imagined than theirs?

The infinite justice of God cannot threaten a more terrible chastisement than the eternity of the damned! How does it happen, that many do not fear it? If human justice threaten imprisonment for a month, or the galleys for a year, terror is excited and the most wicked men restrained. Divine justice threatens an eternal prison of flames, and there is no fear, no account made of it. "As for me," says St. Augustine (in *Ps.*, xlix.), "I am out of myself when I think of it. I cannot attribute it to anything else than a want of faith."

The sinner most certainly knows, that dying suddenly in mortal sin, he shall be immediately condemned to an eternity of torments; notwithstanding, for weeks and months he keeps away from confession; he even laughs, amuses himself, and sleeps tranquilly. O madness! Some have been found so blind, that even at the point of death they did not amend: and to leave a rich inheritance to ungrateful heirs, they would not make the necessary restitution: in order to acquire a comfortable livelihood for their children, with their eyes open, they have chosen to precipitate themselves into eternal fire: certainly such folly appears incredible; yet it has often been seen in the world.

A father of the Society of Jesus was called to assist a dying person, who though of low condition, had, notwithstanding, amassed immense wealth by means of usury and other unjust gains. The father, with all the ardor of his zeal, exhorted him in the liveliest manner to make restitution, but all in vain; for the dying man never ceased to repeat, that he had not the heart to leave his wife and children poor. Not knowing what to do, the father left his room, and meeting the doctor, begged of him instantly to adopt a holy stratagem. Agreeing to the request, the physician entered the sick person's apartment, and said, as the father had recommended: "Sir, your case is despaired of, neither can our remedies avail; but one expedient remains, which depends entirely on your wife and children." The patient raised his head and began to breathe freely; and at once sent for his wife and children. The doctor then caused a lighted torch to be brought, and turning to the wife, said: "Come, put your finger into this flame, and cause a drop of grease to fall into this vase; it will be a most powerful remedy for the life of your husband." At this speech she trembled exceedingly, and retired quickly. The doctor smiled at her flight, and said: "She is a timid woman, and worthy of compassion; but you, children, will you not, for the sake of your father, consent to burn one of your fingers, until merely one drop of grease falls from it?" Scarcely had they heard the request, than following the example of their mother, they also took to flight, and with them the doctor likewise. The confessor immediately entered, and with great zeal, said: "O God! does it appear to you just, to leave your wife and children rich, who are not willing to burn one finger for you, and that you should go and burn eternally in Hell?" At these words, the dying man entered into himself, ordered the necessary restitutions to be made, and died with signs of Christian penance.

We should understand well that when there is question of eternity, no temporal thing should be considered. When Dathan and Abiron were swallowed up alive, by the earth suddenly opening under their feet, those who were present at this most fatal spectacle instantly took to flight (*Numbers*, xvi. 34), and in their flight cried out: "Let us quickly depart hence, that the earth may not also devour us." Innumerable sinners are thrown into the abyss, where they burn, and will burn eternally, in punishment of their sins. Let us learn at the expense of others; and avoid those vices, which may also precipitate us into Hell: let us fly from gambling, avarice, and all irregularities in our conduct. "Let us fly, lest the earth devour us."

COLLOQUY.

Ah! my dear and affectionate Redeemer, now indeed I throw myself at thy feet, more than ever astonished and conquered by the great thought of that eternity, with which thou punishest thy enemies in Hell. I wonder at myself, and I know not how I could have had so much blindness and rashness, knowing by faith that so cruel a chastisement was reserved for sinners. I have sinned so many times, continually relapsing into great faults, like those impious creatures of whom David says: "The wicked walk in a circle." (*Ps.*, xi. 9.) Fool that I was! I confess, O my God, that thou hast too much reason to chastise with eternal punishments him who has dared to offend thy eternal majesty. "Thou art just, O Lord; and right are thy judgments." However, the fear of thy infinite justice should not destroy in me a filial confidence in thy infinite mercy. However unworthy and wicked I may be, I am yet the work of thy hands, and a creature redeemed by thy blood. "I am thine; save me." What! Wilt thou cast into fire, and into eternal fire, a work formed by thy omnipotence! Wilt thou permit that the effusion of thy precious blood should be useless for me! No, my God, thy generous heart will never consent to it. "The Lord will not cast me off forever!" I certainly confide in thy clemency that thou wilt not do so, particularly as for this end thou givest me light to comprehend eternity in a lively manner, that with this thought I may restrain my passions and do penance for my sins. Therefore, contrite and weeping, I embrace thy sacred feet, all wounded and bleeding for love of me. I beg of thee a thousand times to forgive me, for the ingratitude I have shown towards thy infinite goodness: and I firmly resolve with the penitent David: "The Lord will not cast me off forever! I have said: Now, I begin." I will now begin a new life. I wish in future always to love and serve thee. I will never, never more offend thee. Amen.

MEDITATION XIV.

On the Prodigal Son.

INTRODUCTION.

To induce an invalid to take the most bitter medicines, and to place himself in the hands of the most cruel surgeons, nothing more is requisite than that he should know the grievousness of his sickness, and his great peril of losing life.

In order that a soul should be resolved to amend, and do penance for sin, no more is required than to know his miserable state, and the great risk in which he is of being lost for all eternity.

The lively knowledge of her miseries caused Magdalen to form the resolution to fly from the world and run to the feet of Christ.

That great sinner, Thais, after being confined for three years in a rude cave, being asked how she could endure so great a change, responded: "By always keeping before me a balance, in which I placed a cup of all my former irregularities; these I endeavored to counterpoise in another cup, by the greatest possible penance."

St. Ignatius, enlightened in a special manner to make known to him who practises these exercises what he has done wrong in the past, and the good he should do in the future, in order to attain his last end, and to avoid the punishment of wandering from it, meditates the parable of the prodigal son.

He was a profligate youth, who having abandoned his father, and given himself up to every vice, was at length reduced to the degrading condition of tending swine. Then repenting, he returned to his father, by whom he was received in the most welcome manner. All this is a symbol of what happens to a sinner in the commission of sin, and of what he should do to atone for his evil by penance.

Let us consider ourselves in this mirror. Liranus (on *Exodus*, xxx.) mentions that several Jewish women, repenting of their vanity, brought their mirrors to the temple. Moses took and enclosed them in a large shell of bronze, which was kept filled with water near the tabernacle, to cleanse the priests.

Let us consider in the lively mirror of the Prodigal Son: 1. His departure from the house of his father. 2. His return. 3. How lovingly he is welcomed by his father.

FIRST PRELUDE.

Imagine that you see in a public road, an aged sire of grave aspect; and before him on the ground and embracing his feet, a pale youth in tattered garments, who in his misery still appears to have a noble air and genteel mien. He weeps bitterly, and asks pardon of the aged man. The father is moved to compassion, and mingling his tears with those of his son, embraces and presses his child to his breast.

SECOND PRELUDE.

Say to God: my most beloved Father, at thy feet lies a prodigal, repentant son. I am too well acquainted with my faults: I have no one to have recourse to for succor but thee.

FIRST POINT.

The departure of the Prodigal Son from the house of his father. The first part of the parable relates, that a father, noble, rich, and of great credit in his country, had two children whose characters were in direct opposition. The eldest was mild, obedient, diligent in his studies, and from his wisdom gave the best hope of being one day the worthy successor of his father. The other, on the contrary, was ill-tempered, capricious, idle, fond of liberty and amusement. His father furnished him abundantly with food, dress, attendants, and every suitable diversion, yet he frequently admonished him for his greater good, and gave him suitable advice. This was so displeasing to him, that his father appeared to him an insupportable burden. He complained to other dissolute youths of the same mind, who had no prudence. Thus they would ever answer him: "I am surprised you have so much patience with that old man; you are grown up, why not manage a little for yourself? You have judgment (and truly he had); you can well be your own guide. Act as we do: beg of your father to give you that portion of inheritance belonging to you; we will show you how to manage and enjoy your fortune." Oh! what evil arises from wicked companions! what ruin from bad counsel! At these words, the foolish young man became excited, and at once throwing off the restraint of filial shame, he presented himself before his father with an arrogant look, and said: "Father, I am sorry to mention it, yet I cannot do less, for I can no longer remain at your house under my present subjection. 'I beg of you to give me my portion.' "—(*Luke*, xv.) At this request the wretched father was almost out of his mind. "Son," said he, "what a strange resolution is this? What is wanting to you in my house? If I keep you under any subjection, are you not aware it is for your good? My son, do not kill me before my time." Thus speaking, he burst into tears. The perfidious son, not being in the least moved, continued to repeat: "Give me my portion." His wretched father, not knowing what else to do, collected a quantity of money and jewels, and with tears in his eyes consigned them to his son. In great joy, he immediately went off to his friends, who highly applauded his conduct. In their company he travelled into distant countries, where, giving himself up a prey to every vice, he consumed in a very short time whatever he had. Having dissipated his fortune, a great famine ensued, and not knowing how to live, he was forced by hunger to place himself in the service of a citizen, who sent him to one of his villas to take care of a herd of swine. In recompense, he did not allow him even as much bread as would suffice for his maintenance; so that the unfortunate youth, to relieve his hunger, was obliged to share husks with the swine.

From this history we should reflect: 1. That it is a very expressive symbol of what happens to the sinner. Before his prevarication, in his first state of innocence, he was by grace the adoptive son of God, invested with supernatural gifts, and frequently nourished with the holy Eucharist. In the house of his celestial Father he enjoyed great repose of conscience, and he had a right to the inheritance of Paradise. But, with increase of years, his disordered wishes increased for a free and licentious life. To this was also added the influence of evil conversation, and the advice of perverse companions. What followed? He began to be annoyed with devotion; and a virtuous life appeared to him too difficult. He commenced to turn away from God; to receive the divine Eucharist more rarely; to avoid churches and oratories; to attend to plays and pastimes. Passing from one vice to another, he arrived at a miserable state of guilt. Considering himself in the light of God, at the holy period of spiritual exercises, he is at last forced to say: "O what a thorny wood, what a den of serpents has my soul become!"

This happened to a physician in the time of St. Ignatius. At this period, penitents left the spiritual exercises modest, retired, devout, and quite changed from what they had been. A report was circulated in Rome, that St. Ignatius gathered the people into solitary and obscure places; and there showing them ghosts and horrible monsters, so frightened them, that they remained almost stupefied. A doctor, desirous of ascertaining the truth, went through the exercises. Scarcely had he completed them, than his friends surrounded him, and thus interrogated him: "Is it true what has been said of ghosts and spectres? Have you seen any?" "Well," said the doctor, "it is but too true. I have myself seen so frightful a monster, that I shudder at the very thought of it." "What!" replied the friends, "what was this monster?" "This monster was my own soul, become so hideous and deformed on account of its sins, that it caused me to shudder."

Let us here stop to reflect. Consider yourself in the mirror of the prodigal son; see how different you are from the first years of your innocence: see how burdened your soul is, how full of sins and evil habits; see how you have become a monster, and be confounded and humbled before God, saying to him, weeping: "Spare, O Lord, spare thy people." We must consider what was principally the cause of so many evils in the prodigal son; namely, leaving the house of his father. In fancy St. Augustine goes to meet the traveller on his journey, and with words full of zeal, says to him: "What do you do? You have left your father! you are lost! In losing him, you have lost your guide, counsellor, assistance." This is the misfortune of one who withdraws from God: he loses every good, and incurs every evil: so that St. Augustine says, "What have you, if you have not God?" The good heavenly father does not desert any one; but abandons those who abandon him, so says the Council of Trent (*sess.* vi. *c.* 11). Unfortunate, however, is he who abandons God. St. Augustine mourns bitterly (*Confes., lib.* ii. *c.* 2), over the grievous evils of his youth; for he then lived far from God, and fled from the Creator to follow creatures. The misfortunes of the exiled prodigal son are reduced principally to three: 1. He dissipated all his goods. 2. He endured severe slavery. 3. He was reduced to employ himself in taking care of swine.

To these misfortunes correspond the miseries of the sinner, who abandons God. 1. By sinning, he loses in one instant the goods of the soul; sanctifying grace, the friendship of God, supernatural gifts, the right to glory, the merit of all good works previously performed. 2. He becomes the servant and slave of the Devil, who seizes on him more than on a possessed person, for the Devil only possesses the body of the latter, and the sinner is possessed in his soul. 3. That life which he should employ in the acquisition of eternal treasures for the soul, he entirely employs in satisfying his senses with the most vile pleasures of this world, by an irregular and selfish life. O misery of a sinner, who is far from God! Who can explain it; and who can lament it, as it deserves?

Open then the eyes of your soul, and if you have abandoned God, by walking in the way of iniquity, return to your heavenly father. Thus did the celebrated James, named Intercisus. Isdegerdes, king of Persia, had a special favorite, named James. He was much displeased, that he who was so dear to his heart, differed from him in religion, James being a Christian. He adopted so many means of seduction, by promises, favors, and threats, that finally the constancy of James was shaken. The king caused him to renounce his faith. Scarcely had his mother and his wife been acquainted with his fall, than these noble ladies, who were most faithful to God, wrote to him these words full of holy resentment. "James, we now abandon you, as you have abandoned God. We depart from your house, as you have departed from the faith; nor shall we ever return, until you return to the true religion." James no sooner read this letter, than floods of tears flowed from his eyes. Strongly pierced with the thorns of cruel remorse, he went with intrepidity to the king, and with great courage, said: "King, by depriving me of faith, you have taken away my God. I wish to have him again, cost what it may, even my life." The enraged barbarian loads him with bitter reproaches, and immediately condemns him to be cut in pieces. "I willingly accept your sentence," answered James. As his flesh was torn with the knife, "Cut," said he to the executioner, "cut and take away my life, with as many torments as you please: may I lose all rather than lose my God." How beautiful an example of holy and Christian courage. What will it avail me to have enjoyed all the pleasures of the world, if I have not God? Far from God there is no good which is real. If I, as the prodigal son, have departed from him I wish to return to his feet and to his love.

SECOND POINT.

Return of the prodigal son. The prodigal son, reduced to a most unhappy state of life, finally taught by his own miseries, entered into himself: for sufferings cause reflection. He began thus to reason with himself: "I am suffering for my too great wish for license. Would I had remained attached to my father! Those dissolute companions, how wickedly did they deal with me: as long as I had money about me, they all surrounded me; but when I fell into poverty they turned their backs upon me. Such are worldly friends!" He began to think of the comforts he enjoyed in his father's house, where even the domestics had as much bread as they wished. Reflecting on his own hunger, nakedness, and present misfortunes, and thinking of the best means to repair his evils, his mind was disturbed, and his thoughts confused. Considering that he could not act a better part than return to his father, he had many interior combats to sustain. "How then," said he to himself, "can you dare appear before your father, whom you have so much despised? What will he say, seeing you in this miserable condition, barefooted and in rags? At least, he must exclaim: 'Go, I do not recognize you as my son; go and seek for those friends who made you despise the tears of a father already advanced in years.' Will he not turn me out by force! or order his servants to hurl me from his presence!" These sad fancies dismay him. "But," said he, "fatal necessity obliges me; he is a father; I will go to him; if he will not admit me as a son, I will entreat him to receive me as his servant. He is a father, that suffices; I will go."

The expression "I will arise," of the prodigal son, is the practical fruit, which is principally intended to be drawn from these exercises; namely, that he who has meditated the eternal maxims, should make a strong resolution to adopt a good life, if his former life were wicked; or a better life, if his preceding were good. Without this resolution, all besides would be useless. For this, St. Ignatius did not call these weeks of spiritual meditation, but of spiritual exercises. It would avail little to meditate eternal maxims, even with compunction and fervor, if afterwards the exercitant did not proceed to the practice of what he had been meditating. This is to be done by imitating the "I will arise" of the prodigal son, and in the manner in which he executed it. A resolute act of the will is wanting; and this depends on ourselves.

If a person desire to be rich, or noble, he will not become either by merely wishing it. But, if he really wish to be a saint, he will become one, for this depends on his will, and divine grace, which is never refused, says St. Augustine. It is necessary, however, that this will should be resolute and strong; and not a simple inclination, which expresses the will by words, not by deeds. St. Augustine acknowledges this of himself. Previous to his giving himself entirely to God, it appeared that he himself willed, and willed not. It is necessary, also, that the will should be prompt to execute. As soon as the Prodigal Son had said "I will arise," without delay he went towards his own country. How many who wished to become hermits, burn now in Hell, solely from having deferred from day to day the execution of their resolutions! Among these may be ranked Otho III., of whom we read in the life of St. Romuald, as written by St. Peter Damian. Otho committed two grievous faults, namely, putting to death Crescenzio, a Roman gentleman, and his wife. St. Romuald several times urged him with great zeal to do penance in a religious cloister. Otho always answered in the affirmative; but said that he would do so hereafter; flattering himself that in the interval he would, with imperial magnificence, erect a temple in honor of St. Adelbert. Returning from Pavia to Ravenna, he there visited the saint, who urged him in a still more anxious manner not to defer his penance; and added, that death was not so far from him as he thought. Otho paused awhile, then said: "I wish to go to

Rome with my army, to subdue the pride of the Romans; returning thence victorious, I will overcome myself, and maintain the promise I made to God by changing this imperial mantle, and putting on the religious habit." Romuald smiled, saying: "If you go to Rome, you will not return to Ravenna." Having arrived at Rome, and given himself up to great irregularities, he died suddenly of poison.

How many, I repeat, who wished to become hermits, weep in Hell for having put off their conversion. St. Augustine having resolved to change his life and give himself to God, deferred its execution from day to day. Finally, he thus encouraged himself: "When shall I finish saying, to-morrow, to-morrow? This is deceiving God, and betraying my own conscience!" Where is the invalid, who, if he can be cured by taking a remedy to-day, will wait for to-morrow? Having it in my power to be disburdened of my iniquities, why wait for a later period? Beloved, meditate well on this point. Consider that God in these exercises enlightens you in a lively manner, and gives you a fervent will: if you do not now execute divine inspirations, how is it possible to do so after these exercises, when your mind will be less enlightened, and your fervor cooled? Who knows whether God, in punishment of your want of correspondence, will call you again; or calling you, will give you the efficacious grace required for a faithful correspondence? Take courage then, and say with the returning prodigal in a resolute manner: "I will arise and go to my father." Thus did St. Galgan, the hermit. When in the world, he was a famous swordsman, who thought of everything but his salvation. Once as he was walking alone out of the city walls, he heard an interior voice saying to him: " Galgan, why do you not become a saint?" Galgan stopped for a few moments, then suddenly said to himself: " I will be a saint." Without returning to his house, providing for his interests, or taking leave of his friends; as he was, he went towards the mountains, and there having chosen the darkest and severest cavern, which he thought most adapted for his sanctification, he remained. Not finding an image of Jesus Christ, before which he could pray, and not knowing what other method to adopt, he unsheathed the sword which hung by his side, and fixed it by the point in a stone. Then before the cross of his sword he commenced such prayers and penances, that though he did not survive more than a year, he became a saint, and is now venerated on our altars. In the city of Sienna in Tuscany, his head is preserved uncorrupted and perfectly entire, so much so, that it still appears alive to those who view it. His decision was a real, strong and prompt resolution; his was the true will, necessary to become a saint. We should not be dismayed, nor distrust. The prodigal son was not discouraged, but trusted to obtain his father's pardon. We should not diffide, on account of our grievous sins; for how great soever they may be, divine mercy is always infinitely greater. God is ready to grant to all the assistance of divine grace, to lead the new and holy life to which we feel ourselves inspired, and which we cannot practise by our own strength. With the divine assistance the good thief and Magdalen became saints; so can we also. Thus St. Augustine animated himself. We should not diffide with regard to God. As a physician shows his skill in curing a grievous infirmity, so God displays his power and clemency in forgiving the most wicked sinners. God graciously accepts the confidence of those who give him an opportunity of exalting his glory. Christ did not call even the apostles by the tender name of sons. Two persons, who had recourse to him with great confidence in their grievous misfortunes, the paralytic, of whom it is written—"Jesus seeing his faith, said, have confidence, son:" and the woman who suffered from hemorrhage, to whom our Lord said: "Have confidence, daughter, thy faith hath saved thee,"—these two were styled his children. Let us take courage, and placing our whole confidence in God, commence a holy life. "I will arise and go to my father." To animate us still more, let us reflect on this narrative. (*Promp. Ex. V. Miseric.*) A most wicked man who had murdered his father and brother, fled from divine and human justice. One day during Lent, he heard a sermon on the divine mercy, in which he heard explained that passage of *Ezechiel*, xviii. " If the wicked do penance for all his sins which he hath committed, living he shall live, and shall not die." He was so excited to compunction, that he ran to the feet of a confessor, and with most bitter tears told his sins. The zealous confessor absolved him, and obliged him to go to an altar of the most dolorous Virgin, who had Jesus crucified in her arms, and there to continue to weep and implore the mercy of Jesus and Mary. He did so with such lively contrition, that his heart was rent asunder: he fell suddenly dead at the foot of the altar. The following day, as the same priest recommended the soul of the deceased to the prayers of the people, a white dove appeared in the church, holding in his mouth a small paper; after making several turns he let it fall at the feet of the priest, who taking it up, found these words written: "The soul of the deceased had scarcely left the body when it was carried by angels into Heaven. Do you continue to preach the infinite mercy of God." Oh! how good is our God! Certainly, he does great wrong who does not confide in him, much more than the prodigal confided in his father.

THIRD POINT.

The loving welcome of the prodigal son. The prodigal immediately set off for his own country. Having arrived there, as soon as he was in view of the paternal house, he began to tremble from head to foot, and, blushing with shame, thus reflected. What will my father say! What will he do, seeing me in these rags! How can I appear before him, after having acted as I did?" Pensive and sad he paced slowly along, when the father, who was at home, saw him while yet afar off. To see him, to know him, and be excited to a tender compassion towards him, were all the same. As it were, out of himself from joy, he did not walk, but ran with open arms to the prodigal son; who finding that his father, instead of reprehending and punishing him, received him with so much love, threw himself on the ground and embracing his father's feet, shed torrents of tears, and began this beautiful confession: "My father, I have offended you too much, I know it well; however, I am not come to you to consider me as a son, certainly I do not merit it. I will be contented to be treated as one of your hired servants." The father seeing his son humbled and repentant, commenced also to weep, and pressed him to his bosom. The first expression of his love, as St. Jerome reflects, was to press those lips whence issued so beautiful a confession of his faults. "Son," said he, "I forgive you, and that you may be convinced of it, I beg of you to receive this pledge." Thus speaking, he takes a rich ring off his finger, and puts it on that of his son; and orders the servants to procure quickly from the wardrobe, the most beautiful garment to decorate this ragged child; "hasten to prepare for him a sumptuous banquet; kill the best calf, that this poor son may be consoled after so many hardships. The most joyful music shall resound at the table." Thus speaking, he takes him by the hand, and conducts him home, with marks of so much kindness, that he causes envy in the elder brother, who was angry that his father manifested so much more affection for a profligate son, than he had ever shown to him, who had always been obedient; insomuch that the aged father with sweet words was forced to hush his lamentations.

Meditate attentively, that this father of the prodigal was benignant and merciful; but oh! how much more loving and merciful is our good heavenly Father—" our Father who art in Heaven!" The father of the Prodigal Son received him as repentant, but we do not read of any exertion being made to recall him. He did not send a servant, or a messenger to know where he was, he did not adopt any means to bring him to himself; whereas, what does our God do to convert sinners? He calls them, entices them, runs after them in the most tender manner to gain them to his sheepfold.

Own it, beloved, what has God done for you to become a saint? Has he not enlightened your mind? How many inspirations, invitations, how many calls by means of confessors, preachers, good books? How many times have you felt that God required from you a more Christian and holy life? If you have not yielded, it was an effect of your insurmountable obstinacy. Oh! what a good God! what a true Father we possess.

Finally, if our heavenly Father see a sinner converted at his feet, were he even the most wicked in the world, what pleasure does he feel! What a feast! He enjoys it much more than a shepherd regaining the sheep lost in the forest; and he calls all the angels to congratulate with him in Paradise. Whether he be the most wicked creature on Earth—an adulterous David, or a disobedient Jonas, a persecutor Saul, a usurer Zacheus, an assassin Dismas—it is of no consequence, provided he be truly contrite. The deformity, of which the mere mention excites horror in men, does not produce that effect in God, who, to resuscitate Lazarus, who was four days in the grave, did not disdain to view the dead body, cold and decayed, which a sister could not look at. He even holds his arms open to receive all those who return to his love. It was not then without meaning that the Blessed Virgin revealed to St. Bridget, that while enveloping the dead body of Jesus in the holy sepulchre, whatever exertion was made, his extended arms could not be united. He wished thereby to show that his arms were always open to embrace contrite sinners; as his mercy is ever united with the earnest intercession of Mary, who is mother of sinners. When the prodigal returned home, he found the father, not the mother. What would he have felt had he also found a mother, to intercede and weep for him. This advantage of which the prodigal was deprived, we possess, if we be converted to God. Our heavenly Father is most inclined to use mercy towards us; and with his loving designs are united the powerful prayers of our great mother Mary, who is pleased to be called the Mother of Mercy. What confidence then should we conceive of obtaining pardon of our sins from our father? The Prodigal Son not only received from his father a most gracious pardon; he also heard expressions of the most tender description, which were not conferred on his elder brother. Our God not only absolves the penitent sinner; but also places him again in his friendship, invests him with supernatural favors, admits him once more to the eucharistic banquet; and, if he continue to correspond with the assistance of his grace, enriches him with most singular spiritual favors of sanctity. What favors did our Lord grant to Mary Magdalen? He became the panegyrist of her love. "She has loved much." What graces were conferred on Margaret of Cortona? He called her *his* sinner and his net to entice other souls; and so of a thousand other penitents.

It is written of a Roman senator, named Rufus, that having committed a most grievous fault, he finally obtained pardon from Julius Cæsar. Scarcely had he obtained it, than he at once tried to receive from him some special favor in confirmation of the pardon granted to him; for, said he: "Cæsar, no one will believe that you have really pardoned me, if you do not confirm the grace of pardon by the favor of some new benefit."

Our most benign father, God, after having remitted the sins of the penitent sinner, even without having been requested, confirms his love more and more towards him by the expression of the most sincere friendship, and by many new benefits. O infinite charity! O clemency beyond comparison! O inexpressible beneficence! Why should we longer delay hastening, like the Prodigal Son, to the feet of our heavenly Father? He will receive us much better than the evangelical father received his rebellious son. He will console us much more than St. John Chrysostom consoled his persecutors. This great doctor and Bishop of Constantinople, after being unjustly persecuted by the Emperor Arcadius and the Empress Eudoxia, was finally sent into exile, where he died most holily. After his death, Theodosius the younger, son of Arcadius and Eudoxia, wishing to satisfy for the faults of his parents, caused the body of the saint to be brought from exile to the city. Theodosius having arrived at the church of SS. Peter and Paul, laid aside his imperial mantle in the view of an immense concourse of persons, threw himself on the venerable bier, and weeping most bitterly, exclaimed with a loud voice: "Pardon, O holy father and pastor, pardon the sins of my mother." The people cried out in the same manner weeping: "Pardon, O holy father and pastor, pardon the wrongs which we have done you; pardon the insults we have offered you." As it were by divine instinct, having taken the holy body out of the bier, they placed it on the bishop's seat invested with the sacerdotal garments, as if he had been their living prelate. All, on their knees before him, continued to weep and ask pardon. The holy father, appeased by so many signs of true repentance for the evil committed, casting his eyes joyfully around on the people, pronounced these words in a clear tone of voice: " Peace be to you." (*Baron., t. V., an. Chr.* 438). Let us throw ourselves at the feet of our good father and good pastor, Jesus, whom we have so much outraged by many years of a disorderly life; let us weep before him: let us ask pardon a thousand times for our faults. He will certainly be moved to compassion, and will not only forgive us, but will confer on us a thousand other favors, interior peace of soul, and eternal peace in Paradise.

COLLOQUY.

Father, I have sinned against Heaven and before thee. Thou, my Father, "who art in Heaven," too frequently have I hitherto offended thee. I well know it, and as I am enlightened to see it, I wish to weep over my sins incessantly. I have been ungrateful to thy love: I have met thy benefits with outrages. "Father, I have sinned against Heaven and before thee." If as often as I have offended thee, my Creator, I had offended a vile creature, he would persecute me to death. If as often as I turned my back on thee, my Father, a son had acted in the same manner towards his terrestrial father, he would have been disinherited and forever banished from his presence. Yet thou, O my God, instead of condemning me a thousand times, as I have merited, hast awaited my repentance, and now awaitest me with open arms. Most loving heart of Jesus Christ, how benign and beneficent thou art! I wish also, with the prodigal, not to be any longer as a son, for I am unworthy of it, but solely to be as thy servant. " I am no longer worthy to be called thy son; make me as one of thy hired servants." But no: I will not thus wrong thy infinite mercy. Son I shall be, although most unworthy of that name from thee, my heavenly Father; if in the past I have not acted as a son, yet thou hast always been a merciful father to me. Do not then, cast me from thee, when I throw myself contrite at thy feet: but accept these tears and this penance; receive me with thy paternal benignity; absolve me from all past faults, and grant me grace never more to be separated from thee. Grant that in life, I may always be thy adopted child by grace, and that after death I may enter into possession of thy eternal glory. Amen.

MEDITATION XV.

On the Two Standards.

INTRODUCTION.

The present meditation is directed to establish still more the strong resolution already made, to arise with the Prodigal Son to a better life. It is formed by St. Ignatius, according to his military ideas. After having been a captain in an earthly warfare, he became a glorious conqueror in the Society of Jesus. To understand this meditation, it is necessary to suppose that this world, if well considered, is nothing more than a field of battle. " The life of man is a warfare on Earth."—(*Job*, vii. 1): for every man has continually to combat with the attractions of the world, with rebellious passions, and with the Devil's temptings. Every soldier should be enrolled under the standard of a captain. In spiritual warfare, there are two captains, Jesus Christ and Lucifer. It is necessary, that each soul take part, either with the one or the other. There are some who would wish to serve both: to attend a little to piety and devotion, and a little to amusement or profit. Lucifer not being a true or a just captain, but an unjust tyrant, would be contented with this division: as before the throne of Solomon the pretended mother condescended to the division of the child, saying: " Let it neither be mine, nor thine, but let it be divided."—(III. *Kings*, ii. 6.) Jesus Christ, who is our true and legitimate king and captain, is not content with this. On the contrary, he protests clearly in his Gospel that no one can serve two masters: he appears to say to certain persons wavering and inclining sometimes to the side of God and sometimes to that of the demon, what Elias said with great zeal to the Jewish people: "How long do you halt between two sides? If the Lord be God, follow him; but if Baal, then follow him." (III. *Kings*, xviii. 21.)

Choose then according to your pleasure what pleases you most, either to serve God or to serve the Devil and the world.

To make a just and holy election, we shall consider in this meditation: 1. What are the conditions and rewards of those who follow the standard of Christ. 2. What are the conditions and rewards of him who follows the standard of Lucifer. 3. The choice which should be made of the standard of Jesus Christ.

FIRST PRELUDE.

Imagine that you see on a beautiful mountain the captain, Jesus, holding in his hand a white banner, on which are written in characters of gold, these words: "Short the suffering, eternal the reward." With a pleasing and amiable countenance he animates his disciples to go over the world to make a levy of persons for his standard. On the contrary, imagine you see in a horrible cavern, Lucifer seated on a throne of flames and smoke, holding for sceptre a formidable trident, and unfurling a black banner, on which are written in characters of fire, these words: "Short the enjoyment, eternal the suffering." He is surrounded with innumerable demons, and he excites them all to go over the world to enrol followers for his standard.

SECOND PRELUDE.

Say: " My most sweet captain Jesus, I will follow thee whithersoever thou goest." The reason for so doing, will be, because: " Thou only art holy; thou only art Lord; thou only art most high, Jesus Christ!"

FIRST POINT.

What are the conditions and the rewards of those who follow the standard of Jesus Christ.

1. We should consider what Jesus Christ requires from his followers. He, being our captain, our king, and our master, might exact our services by right of justice. But he does not wish for forced soldiers. He wishes to be served " with a great heart and a willing mind." He, who will follow me, let him do so: he who does not desire it, let him act according to his fancy. Our Lord is not as the captains of this world, who will not admit all to the lists, but select the youngest, strongest, and tallest. Our Lord admits all, old or young; sick or healthy; rich or poor. They are to have their motto and arms. Their coat of arms will be a modest and composed deportment, and their armor will be that of incorruptible justice, the shield of faith, the helmet of Christian virtues, and the sword of the divine word.— (*Ephes.*, vi. 14.)

This divine captain wishes that his followers should suffer in this life. What description of sufferings? Does he wish that they should live in deserts or in cloisters—that they should be clothed in sackcloth and ashes—that they should fast on bread and water! No; this is not required. To those who spontaneously wish to make use of these austerities for his love, God gives immeasurable rewards in Heaven: but he does not require so much from them. On the contrary, he allows the wealthy to enjoy their riches lawfully; the nobility, to act according to the decorum of their state; to all, he permits the moderate use of those delights which he created in the world for the benefit of mankind. What then does he require? 1. That a man deny himself. He may still retain human nature, but he must repress those ill bred passions which he has within him of pride, avarice, incontinence, and such like, which cause him to live not as a man, but as a brute.

2. He wills him patiently to carry his cross: but, what cross? That of St. Peter, or of St. Andrew, so bloody and so cruel? No: but the cross of those labors, which the Lord usually sends to every one for his greater good: thus, the good thief was saved, though his cross was not more tormenting than that of the bad thief. Why did he pass from his cross to Heaven, while the bad thief was precipitated from his cross into Hell? The former suffered his pain with resignation, saying: "We indeed suffer justly, but this man, what evil hath he done?" The latter sustained his torture with complaint and cursing.

Finally, our Lord wills, that man should follow the example of his charity, humility, mildness, and other virtues. "Follow me." It is right that the soldier should follow the lead of his captain. A man of wise and holy life, while he is useful to others by his virtues, receives, reciprocally from others, great advantage.

How long does God wish his followers to suffer such pains? For a very short time, for this life; which for all is short, and for the greater part of mankind is very short:—many more die in childhood and in youth, than in old age.

These are the conditions and the laws which the good captain Jesus imposes. Are they not most reasonable and just? Who can deny it? Besides, this most benign Lord does not wait to give all the recompense for such sufferings in the other world, but gives a portion even in this life. He acts more nobly than earthly captains: he gives his soldiers copious assistance whilst they combat, and rich rewards after the victory of salvation. What are these rewards?

1. *Great peace of conscience.* What contentment to be enabled to say: "I am in the grace of God: if I die I shall be saved." Solomon says (*Proverbs*, xv. 16): "A secure mind is like a continual feast." This is an interior good which cannot be taken from us by any one. Riches, dignities, lands can be taken from us by robbers, enemies, or those in power; but who can take peace of soul from us? None. Jesus Christ says: "Your joy no man can take from you."

2. *Spiritual consolations* which God gives to the just: a little Paradise which mitigates all their pains. These internal delights were styled by St. John (*Apoc.*, ii. 17), "the hidden manna which no man knoweth, but he that receiveth it." St. Bernard, though leading a most severe kind of life, asserted, that all he suffered for God appeared to him sweeter than honey. St. Augustine

weeping at the foot of the crucifix for his former faults, declared, that he experienced much greater pleasure in weeping for God, than he had in frequenting the theatre, which formerly had been his delight.

3. *The assistance of divine grace*, which anticipates, accompanies, and strengthens the just man to act uprightly. As a little child, he could not alone form one letter, but when the master holds his hand, he soon writes well. Do not fear, God says to his followers, for I will act in the same manner with you. (*Isaias*, xli. 13.) " I am the Lord thy God, who take thee by the hand. Fear not, I have helped thee."

4. *The example of the captain*, Jesus, who first of all fulfils the laws of charity, patience, and humility, which he prescribes to his soldiers. What comfort, what great courage the hero receives, from his captain always preceding him to the conflict.

The Maccabees coming in sight of their enemies, and beholding a rapid torrent impede their progress, lost courage. Then Simon, their captain, boldly entered the waters and passed them by swimming. Immediately all his troops courageously followed. (I. *Maccab.*, xvi. 6.)

Such then are the rewards, the aids, the graces and the delights that the captain Jesus gives his followers during this life: how much greater are the rewards which he gives them in eternity? After a short suffering he gives them an eternal reward. Then he will say to them : " O my soldiers, who have so well suffered the labors and the fatigues of my warfare, come and triumph with me eternally in Heaven. According to the measure of your pains will be, but immeasurably greater, the measure of your rewards: each of you is always to be more happy, more rich and more powerful than any earthly king, and to possess a much more extensive kingdom, and without comparison more noble than any empire in the world."

The seraphic St. Francis appeared once in a vision to a servant of God. "Know," said he, "that if God created another world far better than this, insomuch, that the mountains were made of diamonds, the country of emerald, the seas of silver, the rivers of balsam, all this fine world could not equal the kingdom which any one of the blessed possesses above." What fine premiums then, and what rich recompenses our Lord grants to his faithful soldiers!

Here meditate, beloved, how great are the advantages of a follower of Christ—what great emoluments! If to acquire a terrestrial kingdom it were necessary to lead during twenty years a good and holy life, oh! how many would become saints through ambition of reigning! God promises in Paradise an eternal kingdom; and we have so little self-love, that we do not care to gain it. In a warfare in which God himself deigns to be captain, shall we be slow in following? What a shame it would be for us, and how mean and cowardly should we appear if we excused ourselves from walking in the royal way of the holy cross, in which God himself did not disdain to walk. What an injury we offer to God, while he erects the standard of the cross, and invites us to his suite, if we turn our backs and leave him alone to suffer?

Plutarch writes of Sulla, that while combating with Archelaus, leader of the army of Mithridates in Bœotia, and assailed in a marshy place, the Roman soldiers not being able to square themselves advantageously, took to a precipitate flight. Sulla sought by prayers and threats to bring them back. All being in vain, he took a standard from one of the ensigns, saying: "Romans—Romans, unworthy of such a name, do you fly? I will remain here firm until my arm loses its strength, and my sword its sharpness, and defend the honor of this ensign. Go and save yourselves; but, should you be asked where you leave your chief, say that you leave him alone to defend the Roman standard against an army. What more do you wish?" The soldiers confused with these words, returned to the field and won a signal victory.

Christians, the captain Jesus appears to say, "Know that I remain firm in sustaining the standard of the cross: if you do not wish to follow me as you should, at least remember you leave a God alone to suffer for you, while you will not suffer anything for yourselves." Reflect if it be right, that while your captain is contented with being humble, poor, and covered with wounds, you, most vile servants, will always be proud and self-interested. How bitter soever these reprehensions of Jesus may be, yet they are most just.

My divine captain, how sweet and loving thou art! Not to be attracted by thy most amiable qualities, we should either be devoid of sense or feeling.

SECOND POINT.

What are the conditions and the rewards of those who follow the standard of Lucifer. Lucifer is not a just captain, but a perfidious tyrant, who has usurped the power of enlisting people against God. He promises his followers what is written on his standard, " Short enjoyment —eternal suffering." He exhibits plays, dances, theatres, banquets, and gives full vent to the most unrestrained passions. " Let us enjoy the good things that are present, and let us speedily use the creatures as in youth."—(*Wisdom*, xx.) This, however, is for the very short time of life, and no longer. The felicity of the impious appears, as St. Augustine says : " a happiness like glass, which breaks, although it shines, and dissolves into powder." It is a mere semblance of good; and the short deceitful appearance of colors soon vanishes. It is a dream of enjoyment; which quickly finishes. This is all the advantage of him who follows Satan and the world. And how this brief and apparent advantage is poisoned by innumerable evils! For the Devil while granting terrestrial pleasures to his soldiers, gives them a dolorous stipend of pains in life, and for reward, eternal torments after death.

1. The brief enjoyment of worldlings is to be embittered by *cruel remorse of conscience*, which continually accuses the sinner, and reminds him, that to die and to be damned, is for him synonymous. As one in a fever, or with a thorn in his foot, at a concert, banquet, or theatre, could not enjoy pleasure ; so he, who feels he is in disgrace with God, whatever pleasure may be afforded

him, can never fully enjoy it. Miserable Cain, having committed the great crime of murdering his brother Abel, wandered through the world, fearing to be murdered by whomsoever he should meet. From whom could he expect death, if no one lived at that time, but Adam his father and Eve his mother? This is the terror which sin brings with it.

2. The brief enjoyment of worldlings is ever accompanied by *labors and heartbreakings*. Plentiful banquets occasion sickness: gambling produces rage and despair: luxurious vanities expend beyond one's income: military honors are succeeded by wounds and toil: the dignities of courts cause envy, rancor, rivalry, irregularity, shortness of life: the acquisition of riches never indemnifies their miserable pursuers. How much solicitude—how much anxiety have worldlings for brief enjoyments? How much do they suffer, even in this world? They have to undergo in a manner, what Jonathan suffered in assailing his enemies, the Philistines, who were encamped among rocks and surrounded by sharp stones: "And Jonathan went up creeping on his hands and feet."—(1. *Kings*, xiv. 13.)

The followers of the world do not obtain riches, honors, or any other terrestrial felicity, without great labor and most bitter remorse: thus Jeremiah said: "They have *labored* to commit iniquity."—(ix. 5.) Those wicked men in Wisdom confessed: "We have walked through hard ways." (v. 7.)

3. Lucifer does not trouble himself to give any *assistance to his followers* to observe the laws of the world. If Jesus Christ command the accom-

plishment of his law, he assists the faithful by his grace. Not so with Lucifer. He commands the nobleman to propose or accept a duel; but he does not give him courage and valor to conquer. He commands pomp and luxury; but should a person have but little fortune, he does not increase it. He commands revenge and guilty passion; but should a person remain impoverished, or be murdered by giving way to degrading vice, it does not in the least concern him. He appears to say, as the Pharisees did to Judas, who, aware of his excess, confessed having committed a perfidious act, saying: "I have sinned in betraying innocent blood." "But," said they, "what is that to us? look thou to it."—(*Matt.* xxvii. 4.)

4. The following of Lucifer and the world, even in this life, often *receives no reward:* not unfrequently, most fatal ruin is the recompense. The servants of God, even whilst alive, have a hundredfold of consolations: not so those of the demon, who often do not obtain any. Soldiers for the most part die in war, without having obtained that rank to which they aspired. Courtiers, after many years of service, do not attain the post they covet. Merchants after much traffic are not enriched. Generally, men at the close of life, ar obliged to confess that the world " is vanity and a great misery."—(*Ecclesiastes*, vi. 2.)

This is the least that happens to the followers of Lucifer. It is far worse, after laboring much for him, to receive no other reward than an unfortunate death. In general, warriors die by the sword; the ambitious die in despair; the avaricious die much lamenting to leave their acquisitions to those to whom they are averse; courtiers die victims of their capricious sovereigns, of which history bears testimony, and continual experience proves it. What Herodotus relates (*book* VIII.) is sufficient.

Xerxes, going by sea from Greece to Asia, was surprised by a violent storm. All the effects in the vessel were cast overboard, and the passengers were on the point of being drowned. Xerxes, dismayed, asked the pilot if there was any chance of safety: the pilot, with a sigh said, there was no other resource but to cast overboard the first noblemen of the court. The king turning towards them, said: "Now is the time for showing your love for your prince. I cannot be saved but by your shipwreck." Xerxes had scarcely finished speaking, than immediately these noble courtiers, one after the other, threw themselves into the sea, never more to rise. The ship being thus disencumbered, Xerxes arrived safely in Asia. On the landing of the king, he wished to recompense the pilot for having saved his life. Extraordinary to relate, he ordered a golden crown to be presented to him; then immediately commanded him to be beheaded for having caused the death of the flower of the Persian nobility.

How much subject for reflection in this instance! What was the recompense which the world gave to those miserable courtiers, after so many years of service? To be drowned in the sea, in homage of their sovereign! What was the reward of that unhappy pilot, after having saved the life of a king? To lose his head under an axe! Oh! how many similar fatal examples have been, and continue amongst men. Lucifer is a tyrant, the world is perfidious: their followers are ill requited during life. What rewards are given them after death? Eternal sufferings: the sole recompense the impious receive in the other life. The rich man, during life, feasted sumptuously every day, attired in purple and fine linen, enjoying human pleasures as much as he could, and was hurled to the lowest abyss of Hell to burn forever. How cruel a captain is Lucifer! How unfortunate are those who follow his standard! How barbarous are the rewards they have in this life—what fatal recompense after death!

THIRD POINT.

The choice of the standard of Jesus Christ. If the conditions of following Christ were not as advantageous as they are, we should still follow his standard through the strictest justice? While he deigns to become our Captain, he is also our Creator, our Redeemer, our Preserver, and our whole good. For us he becomes light to the blind, food to the simple, drink to the thirsty, shepherd to the strayed, master to the ignorant, nurse to his children, defender in conflicts, physician to the infirm, guide in tempests, and briefly, to comprise all, he is the whole good of all. Consequently, were the following of Christ most austere, and that of Lucifer most agreeable, we, through justice, gratitude, and duty, should follow Christ with all our strength. How much more should we follow him, since his yoke and his laws are so sweet and so mild!—the conditions he requires from his soldiers so discreet, the assistance of his grace so copious, and the rewards of his glory so excellent? To the invitations of so worthy and loving a captain, it might be anticipated that all persons in the world would surround him, and, that none should enlist under the standard of Lucifer, who is not less impious than cruel. Yet, O confusion of Christians, O shame of Christianity, it is not so. St. John Chrysostom, reflecting on it, was in great astonishment, and trembled with zeal.

Lucifer calls, and those who follow him are innumerable. Christ calls, and all are deaf to his invitation. The Devil calls to risk life in a duel, and all hasten. Jesus Christ calls to a slight mortification, and no one listens to him. The Devil calls to exchange in a game, goods and conscience, and every one precipitates himself. Jesus Christ calls to a church or an oratory, and no one attends. For a foolish interest there is no labor, how great soever, which does not appear trivial. Every inconvenience is too great to obtain some merit for the soul: even the apostles, when fishing to procure gain, joyfully watched entire nights: " We have labored all the night, and have taken nothing."—(*Luke*, v. 5.) Afterwards, when there was question of accompanying Jesus in the garden, they could not watch one hour: " Could you not watch one hour with me?"—(*Matt.*, xxvi. 40.)

O Jesus, what bad success you have with men! or rather what folly is that of men, who being able to follow Jesus by a plain and agreeable way, and then attain Heaven, prefer following Lucifer by a severe and thorny road, to be thence precipitated into Hell!

Reflect, O beloved, on the years of your past life, during which you were deaf to the divine calls, and followed the standard of Satan. How great was your folly! How much bitterness and anxiety the short pleasures of the world cost? Compare the time in which you lived in the grace of God, and that in which you lived separated from him, and own the truth. When were you more happy and contented—when your conscience enjoyed peace with God, or when, far from God, you gave way to irregular caprice?

St. Augustine having first enjoyed the pleasures of the world, then the delights of the soul, acknowledges his former error.—(*Medit.*, i. 8.)

This is the difference between following Christ and Satan: the following of Christ, according to appearances, is severe and difficult; the following of Satan appears delicious, but in substance is most bitter. Our Lord tells us not to judge of a good life from the first appearance, but to make trial of it: " Taste, and see that the Lord is sweet." Observe all the true servants of God: you will see them all joyful and contented, from the interior delights which God grants them. You will not find it so with the wicked, who continually lament and sigh, saying: " We wearied ourselves in the way of iniquity."—(*Wisdom*, v. 7.) What then, my soul, do you resolve on? Tread under foot the standard of Lucifer, and run to embrace the standard of Jesus Christ. Say to him with all your heart: " My divine captain, you alone I wish to follow, for you alone deserve it: for you I am ready to spend my life, and shed all my blood."

We must admonish whoever has declared himself a soldier of Christ, that he should, 1. *Wear his livery* and colors; these are, a more devout and modest deportment. 2. He should *follow Jesus closely*, by the perfect imitation of his virtues; and not act like St. Peter, on one occasion, who followed him afar off, and perhaps on this account denied him. Finally, he *should follow Christ constantly*, without ever abandoning him; and not resemble the disciples of the Lord, who in time of his greatest want, namely, at his crucifixion, abandoned him. Innumerable heroic souls have followed the captain Jesus, in the course of many centuries, of every sex, state, and condition. Amongst these were five children of the king of Scotland, destined one after the other for the diadem of their father, and who all successively renounced it to become soldiers of Christ, and imitators of his poverty and humility. The first, who was already duke, left the kingdom, and in the habit of a poor pilgrim went to visit the holy places. The second, who ruled a large county, departed privately to live in a hermitage. The third, who was elevated to the dignity of archbishop, renounced the mitre and took the religious habit among the Cistercians. The fourth son was named Alexander, who remained with his sister Matilda. Alexander, at the age of sixteen years, was admitted by his father the king to a share in the government. Matilda, a youthful princess of great sense and piety, called him to a secret conference, and said: " My dear brother, what are we doing? our brothers have renounced a kingdom the better to follow Christ, and shall we remain in the world to follow vanity? For my part, I cannot admit that they should reign more gloriously in Heaven than we. What are we doing?" " I will do what you wish," answered Alexander. Each then by mutual consent resolved on the following morning to disguise themselves as pilgrims, and without taking leave of their parents to quit the palace and the city, and proceed to France. This they effected. Having arrived at a remote country, they stopped at the rustic cottage of a herdsman, where Alexander with heroic humility began to make cheese. Subsequently he requested to be admitted, first as a domestic, then as a lay brother in a Cistercian monastery. Matilda retired to a small hermitage, a short distance from the monastery. Their sole consolation was occasionally to see each other, and converse on celestial topics; but Matilda soon petitioned her brother to make together the last holocaust of their affections to God, and never more to see each other in this world. Alexander almost fainted through grief at this proposition, yet he agreed to it. Matilda having retired to a villa named Lapione, lived and died a great saint.

Saint Alexander also lived to edify. Shortly before his death he was obliged by his abbot (who interrogated him by particular inspiration from God) to acknowledge that he was son to the king of Scotland, brother of three princes, and of the princess Matilda. After this admission, his holy soul, as if to flee human glory, left the body, which was held in veneration. Shortly after a Cistercian monk, having had recourse to him, was cured of an extensive swelling on his chest: Alexander appeared to him more luminous than the Sun, with two most precious crowns, one in his hand, the other on his head, and said: "Know, that the crown I hold is a reward for the regal crown I left for God; the other on my head is the one usually bestowed on all the blessed: as a sign that this vision is not mere fancy, but real, know that already you are cured." Having thus spoken, he disappeared: the monk was completely reëstablished in health.—(*Thomas Cantipratanno, ord Præd., l.* ii. *apum., c.* x. *par.* 34.)

Take courage then, my soul, to follow the captain Jesus, and give a generous refusal to all worldly pleasures which the enemy offers. Be not afraid to attempt what princes effected in the flower of their age amidst the delights of a court.

COLLOQUY.

Most sweet and amiable captain Jesus, here I am at thy feet. I consecrate myself to thee as thy faithful soldier, although most unworthy of such a name. I embrace thy holy standard, and with all my heart, I thank thee for the infinite goodness with which thou deignest to invite me, and to admit me to thy service. How advantageous is it for me to follow thee! I should not spend much time deliberating on this, which, in itself, would be doing thee an injury. Thou art my Creator, my Father, and my King; and is it necessary for thy creature, thy son, and thy vassal, to deliberate upon following thee? I. therefore, trample under foot the impious standard of Lucifer. If, in the past, I have adhered to him, I now detest my error; and if I could, I would efface it with my blood. My Jesus: "Remember not my former iniquity." Know that henceforth I will be entirely thine. I wish, also, to follow thee, carrying the cross, in the way of humility and patience by which thou walkest. I say with St. Bernard (*Ser.* 2, *de Assumpt.*): For thee, to thee; for thou art the way, the truth, and the life: the way in example —the truth in promise—life in reward. I beg, therefore, thy grace, so that having followed thy standard here on Earth, I may afterwards triumph in Heaven. Amen.

MEDITATION XVI.

On the Incarnation and Nativity of Jesus Christ.

INTRODUCTION.

PLINY strongly complains of nature for doing a great injury to man, by causing him to be born disarmed and void of all defence, while all beasts enter into life well supplied. Eagles are armed with claws, lions with tusks, tigers with fangs, horses with feet; man alone enters the world naked, disarmed, and unfurnished with any defence. I do not justify the lamentations of Pliny. Man becomes so versed in the art of war, that he rules every wild beast, how ferocious and cruel soever. I only observe, that if this were true of other men; of Jesus at his nativity it is not only untrue, but that he comes into the world surrounded with a thousand loving darts to wound the hardened hearts of men.—(*Ps.*, xliv.) He appears a lively lance of charity, issuing from the bosom of the eternal Father, and vibrating on this Earth (*Is.*, xl.); so numerous are the most amiable attractions of his goodness, and so great the incomparable benefits with which he enriches the whole human race.

Meditating then on the incarnation and nativity of Jesus Christ, and omitting for the present reflections on the other divine attributes, we shall solely consider the great charity of God, particularly manifested to awaken in our cold breasts some sparks of grateful love towards him who has so much loved us. As the three clearest signs of love are to act, to suffer, and to benefit, let us first consider how much Jesus Christ has *done* in his incarnation and nativity for the love of man: how much he has *suffered* in his incarnation and nativity for the love of man: how much in his incarnation and nativity he has *benefited* man.

FIRST PRELUDE.

Let us imagine that we see the little infant, Jesus, lying in a cave on a heap of straw. Mary and Joseph adore him on their knees as God: with their whole souls they do not cease admiring and considering him. Let us imagine that he extends his little hands towards us, asks for the gift of our hearts, saying: "Son, give me thy heart."

SECOND PRELUDE.

Say with holy David: "I love thee, my God, my strength, my firmament, my refuge, and my deliverer." My dear Jesus, I place myself at thy feet with the holy shepherds. I bring thee the gift of my poor heart, which will certainly be much better in thy hands than in my breast.

FIRST POINT.

How much has Jesus done in his incarnation and birth for the love of man. Love resembles fire, which can never be idle; the beloved is ever occupied in doing as much as possible for the loved object. What has God done for man in his incarnation and birth? By an effort of his omnipotence, he has united his divine, infinite, eternal nature, to weak, miserable human nature, with so strict a tie of hypostatic union, that whatever action one should operate, must be attributed to the other; hence God becomes man, and man becomes God. This is so exalted a work, that Habacuc with a prophetic spirit foreseeing it, spoke as one astounded (i. 5): "Behold ye among the nations and see: wonder and be astonished, for a work is done in your days which no man will believe when it shall be told." This was a work truly of God, which should be called "his work." God has done for man much more than the work of his creation, in which he has given him a noble soul and well organized body. For love of man he created Heaven, the planets, the elements, and a variety of creatures in the world; but in his incarnation and birth what did he give to man? His divine being. This is the greatest effort of God towards man. Is not human gratitude aroused by such obliging traits on the part of God? If, after such benefits, man is not grateful, it cannot be said he is asleep, but dead; for this is the most intimate manner in which divine goodness could communicate itself to creatures. God had already given himself to man, by giving him a being, with all the intrinsic gifts of health, riches, and honors, which accompany it: he had communicated himself by means of grace, enriching him with supernatural gifts: he had communicated himself by means of glory, elevating man to enjoy his divinity unveiled in Heaven. The last way of communicating himself by personal union remained, by which he would give to man, not goods distinct from himself, but his own person, substantially united to human nature. His infinite love effected this by means of the incarnation. No other means remained for immense goodness to diffuse itself to man. What more intimate union can be imagined than that I should give my person to you, so that you may be changed into me, and I into you?—that God may be man and man God. O most astonishing instance of Divine Charity! O inscrutable mysteries of Divine Providence! This great communication, this great wonder God did for man and not for angels. Beings had committed the same fault, of foolishly aspiring to the divinity. Lucifer said: "I will ascend into Heaven, I will be like the Most High."—(*Isa.*, xiv.) Adam sinned in the terrestrial Paradise, being flattered with the promise made to him: "You shall be as God."—(*Genesis*, iii. 5.)

Lucifer was a most noble spirit, and worthy of every consideration. Adam, on the contrary, was a most vile creature, kneaded from the earth. Yet God willed to do for vile man what he never did for a noble angel. He not only did not give divinity to the angel, but he despoiled him of the grace which he had first given him. He not only restored miserable man to lost grace, but gave him personal union with the Word. What partiality of ardent love God shows in his incarnation, doing for us what he never did for the most sublime spirits of Heaven!

Finally, the Lord in his incarnation and birth certainly favored the whole human race; but in the centuries of the New Law he has conferred more privileges than on all those who lived under the Old Law; though there were then many virtuous and heroic souls who ardently sighed to see the future Messiah. How much did the patriarchs and prophets sigh to see the new born Deity? Turning towards the Heavens, they begged he might be sent as a refreshing dew: again they cried to the Earth, that it might open and bud forth a Saviour. Holy David continually said: "Show thy face and we shall be saved."—(*Ps.*, lxxix. 8.) The lawgiver Moses repeated: "Show me thy face, that I may know thee."—(*Exod.*, xxxiii. 13.) From the long expectation in which the world awaited the Messiah, he was " the desired of all nations." Though the Eternal Father knew the vows, prayers, and sighs of so many people very dear to him, yet he did not hearken to them, but deferred the incarnation and birth of the Messiah for four thousand years. Our ages are privileged, for God operated in them what he did not effect for the patriarchs and prophets of the ancient law. The preceding centuries considering us with envy, appear to utter: " Many prophets and kings have desired to see the things that you see, and have not seen them."—(*Luke*, x. 24.) O privileged mortals, to enjoy the happiness of seeing with your own eyes that Messiah whom the most illustrious personages of Judea longed to see, and never beheld ! For you the holy infant is exposed in a cave, without any appearance of majesty. Not only kings and wise men, but the lowest herdsmen, have the liberty of gazing on him when they please, of embracing his feet and caressing him. Consider then how much our Lord has done for our love in his incarnation and birth in a stable. With what obliging partiality he has preferred us even to the angels, and the patriarchs? What are we doing for his love? It is a shame to tell it. To us, ungrateful creatures, everything appears burdensome; whatever is done for God appears too much. If we gave in exchange to God what we are and what we have, certainly we should do nothing; and when there is duty to give him an affection, we do not even thank him. The grateful Tobias seeing what had been done for his love by the angel who appeared to him under the form of a youth, begged of his father to offer him in return the half of what he had brought. (*Tobias*, xii. 4.) What shall we offer to God for all he has done for us? St. Augustine answers (*Ep.* 120, *ad Honar.*): "If you do not know, I will tell you: you can make a return in this manner: he being a pure spirit, became man for the love of you: you, on the contrary, being man, composed of flesh, must make yourself as much as possible a spirit, renouncing terrestrial pleasures. He wishes to converse with you; do you treat continually and willingly with God by means of prayer!"

SECOND POINT.

How much Jesus in his incarnation and nativity suffered for the love of man. Love shows itself by deeds; but much more by suffering for its beloved object. God displayed great charity in creating man, and for man's service creating so many creatures in the world. All this demanded no more from his omnipotence than a fiat. By his incarnation and nativity he had to suffer much; humbling his high majesty, and subjecting it to human miseries. Thus he showed the most evident marks of his immense love.

1. He might have entered the world as a grown up man, without being enclosed in the maternal womb, or exposed to suffer the inconveniences of infancy. But he preferred suffering all that children undergo. Why so? To prove the greatness of his love by the extent of his suffering. He

would be conceived in the womb of Mary, and remain a prisoner there for the space of nine months, to satisfy the debts to divine justice which the world had contracted. All other children remain in the maternal womb without sense, not having the use of reason; not knowing the miserable state they are in, they cannot complain. But God made man, enclosed in the womb of Mary, not only knew his miseries, (being infinite wisdom;) but was also obliged to be closed in an obscure place, as in a portable sepulchre, more as one dead than alive. The prophet explains it for him. " I am become as a man without help, free among the dead."—(*Ps.*, lxxxvii. 5.) How great was this pain! What an insupportable torment! He could have appeared on the Earth, with every species of convenience and delight, yet he did not. Why? To show man by his sufferings, how much he loved him. He would be born in the midst of winter, when the country is cold and desolate; die in spring, when the world rejoices, and displays all its beauty: and all to denote that he did not require anything from the world, except labors and pains to prove his love for man. He so disposed, that at the time of his birth, all the subjects of the Roman empire should be enrolled, by order of Augustus. So great was the concourse of strangers who arrived at Bethlehem, that lodgings could not be procured by Mary and Joseph; notwithstanding their exertions, amongst their relatives and friends, or even in the public hotels. "He came unto his own, and his own received him not." Thus the most blessed Virgin was obliged to give birth to her divine Son in a cold cave, exposed to the winds of the country, and the hard frosts of December. The infant Jesus was of a most delicate constitution. It is said of him: "Behold the stone that I have laid before Jesus; upon one stone there are seven eyes."—(*Zachar.* iii. 9.)

Jesus could not have better accommodation from Mary, than to be enveloped in swathing bands, laid on straw, with a hard pillow for his tender head. An ox and an ass had there taken shelter, and approaching the holy child warmed its delicate members. From the stones in the grotto, as Bede relates, a fountain of limpid water issued. The little child wept, and watched night and day, continually repeating, ah! ah! as if to express, according to the remark of St. Bernard: "Souls, souls, I weep, I suffer, and lament for your love." Mary, on hearing these lamentations, felt her heart burn with compassion, and Joseph was moved to tenderness. What could be done to console Christ in so disagreeable an abode? Mary often took him up in her arms, and pressing him to her heart, refreshed him with milk. Joseph, taking off his mantle, gave it to him as a covering and defence. Who can imagine a more deserving object of compassion and admiration? Who does not feel his heart inflamed to love a God, who suffered so much for love of us? If he whom we see lodged in the stable at Bethlehem, were a strange child not belonging to us, or even a most vile child, the son of a herdsman, humanity would teach us to compassionate and to love him: how much more should we do for our God, Redeemer, the only Son of the Eternal Father, who came purposely into the world to save us?

The daughter of Pharaoh had no sooner seen

the infant Moses, on the waters of the Nile, and heard his tender moaning from the midst of the bulrushes, than, instantly moved by compassion and love, she saved him from the waters and preserved his life, though he was of the Jewish nation, which was greatly hated by her father.

How much more compassion and love should we have for the child Jesus, trembling with cold in a stable, since he is our most amiable and beloved God? We should also correspond to the love of Jesus, by suffering something for him, who suffers so much for us. Our Lord in his nativity teaches us patience, enduring cold, nakedness, and most bitter sufferings. We advance in years and strength, and do not know how to profit by his lessons, nor to practise for his sake some corporal mortification. In our adversities, let us raise our eyes to Jesus in the manger, and say with holy David: "Thou art my patience, O Lord; my hope, O Lord, from my youth."—(*Ps.*, lxx. 5.) I should not complain in my labors, as thy great endurance obliges me to be patient. If we cannot imitate Jesus Christ, in suffering great pains, let us at least endure for him little contradictions, unkind words or actions, and similar things. Let us imagine that our Lord says to us these words of St. Augustine: "Support little things if you are the truly faithful, and elect wheat of Heaven."

St. John of God, travelling from Gibraltar to Granada, met on the road a child of most beautiful aspect, badly clothed, walking barefoot on the frosty path. The charitable saint, moved to tenderness at this sight, not knowing what else to do, said: "Dear child, get on my back; I will willingly carry you." Placing himself on his knees and

THE INCARNATION AND NATIVITY. 317

bowing his head, after tenderly embracing him, he made him ascend and continued his journey. He soon began to feel the weight so great, that he did not seem to sustain a child, but one grown up. Sinking under the weight, and overcome by the heat, the good child, with an amiable countenance, tried to relieve him by wiping off his sweat and tears. John being unable to proceed, begged of the child to descend for a time, in order to be refreshed at a neighboring fountain, and acquire new strength. He consented, and John placed him on a mound near the road, and went to the fountain, when suddenly he heard a voice saying: "John, John:" turning round, he no longer saw a poor, shivering child; but one luminous, as brilliant as the sun, having a most beautiful pomegranate in his hand, at the top of which was a cross: he heard him say: "John of God, in Granada, there is your cross." Having thus spoken, the child disappeared. The saint knew it was Jesus, and he encouraged himself to bear that cross in Granada, which our Lord destined for him, in the care of the hospital (*in Vit.* viii.) What the infant Jesus said to John of God, exhorting him to bear his cross with patience, he says to us, according to St. Ambrose: "Take up thy cross and follow me."—(*b.* viii., *in Luke.*)

THIRD POINT.

How much Jesus in his incarnation and nativity benefited man. It often happens to those who truly love, that though they do and suffer much for the beloved person, they do not succeed in benefiting him in any way, from various human motives which render their designs useless. This could not happen to Jesus, as he is a God of infinite power. Having done much for man in his incarnation and birth; he conferred on him the highest benefits. It is proper to consider some of them.

1. The Divine Word become man has brought all spiritual goods to the soul: he destroyed original sin; and as Origen reflects (*Hom.* xxviii., *in Luc.*), generated from eternity by the Eternal Father, he wished afterwards to be temporally engendered in the bosom of Mary, in order that man, born by the fault of Adam, a child of wrath, should be again born spiritually to grace, becoming the adopted child of God. By his coming into the world, he has opened to mankind the gates of Paradise, which for many centuries had been closed, even to the holiest patriarchs and the most virtuous persons of the ancient Testament. He mitigated the terrors of divine justice, by which God showed himself in chastising the people of the old law. He has changed those terrors into showers of grace and benediction. "He bringeth up clouds from the end of the Earth; he hath made lightning from the rain"—(*Ps.*, cxxxiv. 7.) He made the most clear signs of his divine goodness and mercy appear in the world. Are not these most singular, incomparable, inexpressible benefits? What more? He satisfied divine justice for the sins of the whole world, taking on himself the punishments due to men, who were sinners: he degraded himself even to be born in a stable, to satisfy for human pride: he was pleased to be covered with rags, for our extravagance and indelicacy of dress: he wished to be wrapped in swathing bands for our too great freedom of manners: he willed to be born among beasts for the faults of those who act

like beasts: he took on himself poverty, nakedness, cold, and all the inconveniences of an abandoned cave, for the intemperance of those who attend to nothing else, but the enjoying of all earthly pleasures, even such as are unlawful.—Is not this an infinite love shown by our God?

It is related of Maurice, Duke of Saxony, when at war with the Turks in 1542, that once this animated youth, accompanied by an only page, left the royal pavilion to reconnoitre a body of the enemy. In the conflict his horse was killed; and he falling on the ground, was exposed to the swords of the Turks. The page laid himself down on the body of his sovereign, and took upon himself all the wounds of the barbarians, until other soldiers arrived and saved the life of the duke. The page was conveyed to the tent all deluged in blood, and soon after died. It was certainly great love, which induced the faithful page to take the wounds and death intended for his master. How much greater is the charity of God, our supreme master, who took on himself human miseries to free us, most vile slaves, from miseries and eternal death? Our Lord wished especially to be born in Bethlehem, and appear as an amiable child, thus to animate sinners to come to his feet with more courage, and there with more facility to grant them pardon of their faults. It is usual for children to hush their cries and allay their anger for the small gift of an apple or any similar thing. The infant Jesus remits the wicked all their delinquencies, if coming to his feet they shed a tear of contrition, or offer him the small gift of tender affection.

John Tauler (*Ser.* v., *in Mat.*) says, that God, who conceived so much anger for an apple eaten by Adam, is calmed in Bethlehem, and dispenses immense benefits to whoever offers him the smallest tribute of devotion.

An extraordinary fact is related of John Guarino, a celebrated hermit of Mont Ferrate. He lived about the year 860 in so penitential a manner, and in such great credit for sanctity, that Richilda, daughter of Godfrey, Count of Barcelona, having applied to him to be delivered from evil spirits, was immediately cured. Afterwards, blinded by passion, he took away her honor, and deprived her of life. After other enormous excesses, having been converted, he undertook great penances and commenced living as a brute, walking on his hands and feet in the fields, and solely nourishing himself with the herbs, which he tore up with his teeth. After seven years he was taken by huntsmen for a savage, or rather as a monster, and was conducted into court to the count, who, with his courtiers, looked on him with amazement; when, O prodigy! a child of three months old, son of Godfrey, being in the arms of his nurse, had his tongue loosened, and said in a clear voice: "Arise, John, for God has already pardoned you." The wise Godfrey thus recognized John, and having heard his crimes from himself, answered: "God forbid I should punish a penitent, whom Heaven itself has declared forgiven by so evident a miracle."—(*Villega* ii. *par Flas. SS. et alii.*) This fact appears to be a lively image of what occurred to man at the birth of Christ.

Man was guilty of original sin; therefore he was hated by God as his enemy. He was besides, by perverse manners, become very like to the brutes, not guided by the dictates of reason. When the infant Jesus was born, and come to satisfy the sins of the world, he seemed to say: "Arise, man, for God has already pardoned thee: arise from the abyss of misery, for already God lays aside the arm of his justice, which he held raised against thee: for with him is the fountain of life, and in his light we shall see light."—(*Ps.*, xxxv. 10.) Is not this a great benefit—a great effect of infinite mercy? How much then ought we to love Jesus, who in his incarnation and nativity has done and suffered so much for our love, and who has so much benefited us? We are certainly the most ungrateful creatures of the world, if we do not correspond, by doing for him as much as we can in good works; suffering also our crosses in imitation of him, and in return for so many graces, restoring to him our whole heart and being. Regenerated to grace with so much benignity by Jesus, we should begin a new life, as if we were newly created, confirming the saying of the prophet: "The people that shall be created, shall praise the Lord."—(*Ps.*, ci. 19.) The apostle writes to the Ephesians: "For we are his workmanship, created in Christ Jesus in good works"— (ii. 10.) We should endeavor not to displease him in any way; assuredly he does not deserve it. At his birth he deigned to call himself our eldest brother: let us then love and respect him as such, and not offend him by our sins. Reuben said: "Do not sin against the boy"—(*Genesis*, xlii. 22,) that is, against the youngest of his brethren, Joseph; and I say for our first born Jesus: "Do not sin against the boy, for he is our brother and our flesh."

COLLOQUY.

Most amiable little infant Jesus, I have not the heart to look on thee among thy many hardships in the stable of Bethlehem. My dear Saviour, how couldst thou have suffered in thy tender members so much cold and poverty? It was thy infinite charity which made thee suffer so much for us, miserable creatures! Be thou blessed, my Jesus, a thousand times: blessed be thy providence, thy wisdom, thy benignity. How could man imagine that thou, O great God, who art seated in Heaven, above the seraphim, shouldst deign to humble thyself, and suffer so much for him? "What is man, that thou art mindful of him; or the son of man, that thou visitest him?" Thou hast honored and benefited our miserable humanity too much! nor can our gratitude sufficiently correspond to thy immense benefits! Accept, however, our most humble thanks, and the devout tribute which we offer thee of our hearts! My most sweet Jesus, turn, I beseech thee, thy loving eyes on our souls, and grant us the grace to attain the end of thy incarnation and death. Offer to the eternal Father one of thy precious tears to efface our sins; and raising from the manger thy tender little hand, bless us all in body and soul, for time and for eternity. Amen.

MEDITATION XVII.

On the Institution of the most Holy Sacrament of the Eucharist.

INTRODUCTION.

Though the sun is always admirable in the Heavens, for its great light and beneficent influence, yet it is never more considered and admired by the world, than when it becomes obscure and eclipsed. When brilliant in the zenith, scarcely any one will turn his eyes to Heaven to consider its light; but when it becomes darkened, and is eclipsed, then every one turns to observe its occultations; it is viewed in mirrors and waters. This observation is from Seneca. God, the Son, shows himself admirable in every attribute. In the choicest benefits which he confers on the world, he never is more worthy of our admiration, than when he instituted the most holy Eucharist. In it, in a certain manner, he is eclipsed and hidden under the sacred accidents. How great is this wonder, in which God displays the greatest charity towards man: " He loved them to the end." It is true that he conceals himself under the sacred accidents; but then, precisely, he more perfectly unveils all his divine perfections. Pliny writes of Timante, a celebrated painter, who never better displayed his art than when, by his admirable touches, he appeared to conceal the members of those personages whom he painted. The Lord in the sacrament unveils his omnipotence in such a manner, that the angelic doctor, (*Opusc.*, v. 7,) seeking why the mystery of the Eucharist was not inserted in the symbol of the faith—the creed, answers, that it appears to him it is well comprehended in the creed, under these words: "Almighty God," by the many miracles contained in the Eucharist. He shows his wisdom by the admirable manner in which he communicates himself to man; he discloses his providence, whereby he assists us in our necessities; thus also he unveils his other attributes,

In the present meditation we shall more particularly reflect on three excesses, which our Lord shows in this sacrament. 1. An excess of condescension. 2. An excess of beneficence. 3. An excess of charity.

FIRST PRELUDE.

Let us imagine that we see the holy child, Jesus, in the consecrated host, in that attire in which a remarkably virtuous man, of the Society of Jesus, named Father Balthazzar Alvarez, saw him. Being in prayer before celebrating, he saw the holy infant in the sacrament, with hands and arms laden with most precious jewels. As if he could no longer bear so great a weight, the sacred Infant begged him to enrich himself with those treasures by the communion, which he was about to receive.

SECOND PRELUDE.

Let us say to God, with holy Job: "What is man that thou shouldst magnify him? or, why dost thou set thy heart upon him?"—(vii. 17.)

FIRST POINT.

In the Eucharist our Lord shows excessive con-

descension. In the incarnation the condescension of God was certainly great. He there humbled himself so much, that although an infinite and omnipotent God, he became a lowly man. He appeared to annihilate his great majesty under the vile semblance of a servant. "If I be made a victim upon the sacrifice and service of your faith, I rejoice and congratulate with you all." (*Phil.*, ii. 17.) In the Eucharist his condescension is much greater; for here he makes himself the food of man. In the incarnation he assumes the form of a reasonable creature; in the Eucharist he takes the appearance of insensible creatures; namely, bread and wine. In the incarnation he hid his divinity; in the Eucharist he also hides his humanity. In the incarnation he deigned to unite himself to one individual nature, which was holy and replenished with every grace; in the Eucharist he condescends to unite himself to each particular person, even though he may have been a sinner and rebellious to his love. Certainly this is infinite condescension. If God had been pleased to remain in the society of man, in the most magnificent kingdom of the world, this would be an excess of condescension: how much greater then, not only to live with man, but to live within him, making his chest a living pyx, an animated cyborium of his entire body and blood.

After Solomon erected, with many years of labor and the expenditure of vast treasures, his celebrated temple, which was a miracle of art, and the wonder of the universe, he could not persuade himself that God would condescend to dwell within it. What then would he now say, seeing the same God not only dwell with men, but even within their breasts! To whom does he dispense this incomparable favor? To the sovereign pontiff, to kings, or only to saints? He grants it to all, even to the poorest, the lowest class, to the most miserable in the world. Our Lord in the most holy sacrament, does not disdain to go and seek them in hospitals, in prisons, in the galleys, in the most vile and loathsome places. That every one may easily and at pleasure enjoy this great benefit at all times, he instituted this sacrament under the ordinary and common matter of bread. He gave all priests the power of consecrating on any altar: although the King of kings, he does not disdain to obey the voice and enter the hands of any priest, how unworthy soever, who pronounces the words of consecration. What more? He is contented always to remain enclosed as a prisoner in the tabernacles, to give audience to whoever wishes to have recourse to him at any hour of the day or night. O condescension! O charity! O infinite benignity! What earthly king did ever half so much for his earthly vassals? What king ever was obliged to give audience to his subjects during the night and day? O infinite benignity of Jesus in the holy sacrament!

The greatest act of condescension which our Lord deigns to give in the Eucharist is, to communicate himself to souls that are tepid and indisposed; even to sinners, to the sacrilegious, if they approach to receive him. Oh! this is an accumulation of humiliation worthy of astonishment; if God is pleased to enter the bosom of sinners who are poor and low, at least poverty and lowliness are not hated by God; but tepidity in the just, and the wickedness of sinners, are abominable to God.

The condescension of Christ in the sacrament extends to granting the Eucharistic manna even to those who, unwilling and indisposed, make no account of this celestial gift, saying with the Hebrews in the desert: " Our soul now loatheth this very light food."—(*Numbers*, xxi. 5.) Can we say more? He has arrived so far, as to feed with his divine flesh and to refresh with his blood even the most ungrateful sinners. " He shall entertain and feed and give drink to the unthankful, and moreover he shall hear bitter words."—(*Eccles.*, xxix. 31.) If Jesus, in the holy sacrament, were capable of grief, what bitterness would he feel in approaching the lips of him who communicates without affection, and without any disposition? What immense regret must his be on entering the bosom of a filthy and irregular sinner? He would be crucified again; he would feel sinful thoughts more sharp than thorns; unmeasured words more bitter than gall: the evil ways of life harder than his cross. This our Lord indicated in the celebrated vision that recalled Videchindo, Duke of Saxony, from infidelity to the true faith. He was vanquished in battle by the emperor Charlemagne: having made a treaty with him, he went in disguise to the imperial army to observe the sacred rights performed during Holy Week and at Easter: being much surprised, he said to the emperor: " Know, that whilst the priest distributed the Eucharistic bread for the paschal communion, I saw in each particle a most beautiful child, who entered into your mouth and that of many of your soldiers full of joy and delight; but to others he appeared melancholy and retiring, turning himself about as if he refused to be placed on their lips." Charles persuaded him to embrace the holy faith, and Videchindo was converted; and by St. Erimbert, a holy bishop, was baptized in a most solemn manner. The emperor was his godfather: and in a short time the whole of Saxony came over to the true faith.—(*Albertus Cranzius, l.* ii. *Saxon, c.* 23.)

In this vision, our Lord showed how much it displeases him to enter the breast of sinners; yet by infinite condescension, and worthy of all admiration, he is received by them.

From this great consideration I can draw two very important consequences.

1. What great disgust I give Jesus in the holy sacrament, when I approach to receive him not only with coldness and without preparation, but with the soul all stained with defects. Our most beloved Lord, in approaching my lips, cannot but be disgusted with my imperfections. If he were not restrained by his infinite goodness, he would expel me from his presence. How sad it would be, if, finding himself in my breast, I should even then remain cold, distracted, and without affection! If, after communion, I did not know how to thank him, and should quickly depart from him, how much would he feel this ingratitude! Could not Jesus Christ renew his ancient lamentations—" For if my enemy had reviled me, I would verily have borne with it. But thou, a man of one mind, my guide and my familiar, who didst take sweet meats together with me; in the house of God we walked with consent."—(*Ps.,* liv. 13.) That a man should offend me whilst far from me, is cer-

tainly wrong; but that he should offend me, whilst I, with infinite condescension, admit him to my table and feed him with my flesh, oh! this cannot be borne!

How do the seraphim in Heaven wonder, seeing a God treated so ill by so vile a worm of the Earth!—a God whom they adore with the most profound awe. Even the devils in Hell are greatly astonished.

The excess at which human ingratitude arrives towards Jesus in the holy sacrament is such, that even demons have left Hell to reprehend and reprove it.—(*Specul. Exemp., dist.* 10, *ex.* 28.)

2. The second consequence is, that if God in the Eucharist shows an excess of condescension, inclining his great majesty to dwell in the breasts of miserable men, how much more should we, in receiving this sacrament, humble ourselves, and protest that we not only do not merit such a favor, but that we deserve to be deprived of it. Filled with amazement, we should exclaim with the seraphic St. Francis of Assisium: "Lord, who am I! and who art thou? I, a worm of the earth, a miserable sinner, am to receive a God! Thou, God of infinite majesty, art to be received by a worm—a sinner, such as I am!"

We should also repeat the words with which Miphoboseth, the son of Jonathan, answered David, when, with too obliging courtesy, he invited him to be seated at the same table with him: "Thou shalt eat bread at my table always. He bowed down to him, and said: Who am I, thy servant, that thou shouldst look upon such a dead dog as I am?"—(II. *Kings*, ix. 7.) With such sentiments of most just humility should we correspond to the great condescension of Jesus Christ in the holy sacrament.

SECOND POINT.

In the Eucharist our Saviour shows the excess of his great beneficence. What Joseph did to recall his ungrateful brothers from their wanderings, was not without mystery. He hid a great sum of money in their sacks of wheat, and a rich silver cup.—(*Gen.*, xliv. 2.) Having caused his brethren to be conducted before him as if guilty of theft, he enriched them all with gifts and singular benefits. This was a symbol of the immense treasures which Providence has hidden in the Eucharistic manna: thus we can say with Jeremias, (xliv. 17): " We were filled with bread."

In the sacrament God gives us his entire being. What more can be said? What more can man desire?* He gives us all he has divine: he gives us all he has as man: he gives us all his merits and his satisfaction.

The lot of Magdalen was certainly very enviable, for with her tears she bathed the feet of her Redeemer. The lot of the apostle Thomas was not less happy, who with his finger touched his open side. A greater privilege was that of St. John, who leaned his head on the breast of Jesus. How do these compare with the happiness we enjoy in this sacrament, in which we receive Jesus in our breast? We can say with truth: " Already God has become all to me; already God is entirely in me!"

A refinement of love never before heard of, is related of what our Redeemer effected for St. Catherine of Sienna. He placed her hand within his breast, and taking out his heart, turning towards her, he said: "Here, Catherine, take my divine heart." Oh! what an astonishing excess of infinite charity, of love beyond comparison!

Holy faith! enlighten our minds to know what is most true! Whenever a faithful soul receives the holy Eucharist, he receives within himself the inestimable gift not only of the heart of Jesus, but of Jesus himself. Is not this an excess of infinite beneficence? What more? The sacrament of the Eucharist, as St. Paschasius well observes (*lib. de sacr.*, xix.), is a wonderful extension of the redemption to human nature. The whole man, composed of soul and body, was saved by the redemption: so by the Eucharist he is nourished and benefited in the soul as well as in the body. The stream of divine beneficence never diffuses itself with more plenitude on souls than in the Eucharist. "Thou hast visited the Earth, and hast plentifully watered it; thou hast many ways enriched it."—(*Ps.*, lxiv. 10.) Here our Lord communicates his sanctifying grace more copiously than in all the other sacraments; for in the others grace is infused in order to perfect in us some particular virtue, or to preserve us from some particular evil: thus baptism to cleanse us from the stain of original sin: confirmation to fortify us against persecution; so of the others: whilst the Eucharist perfects all virtues in us, and frees us from all evils. With it not only grace is given, but even the fountain of grace, who is God. He does not send us his supernatural gifts by an angel, nor shower them from Heaven as manna or celestial dew, but he comes in person to bring them to us. Oh! what great benignity! It was certainly great benignity towards the holy fathers who were in Limbo (in making them participators of the fruit of redemption), not to call them from their prison, as the Redeemer called Lazarus from the tomb: not to send an angel, as to St. Peter in chains; but with infinite condescension to go in person to Limbo, to afford them more ample enjoyment of the consolation of his presence by the beatific vision. Greater, however, is the kindness of our God in the Eucharist, for as the abbot Rupert observes, (*lib.* xii. *de vict. verb Die, cap.* xii.) when Jesus descended into Limbo, his soul alone went down to the fathers. To sanctify us both in soul and body, according to our capacity, the Eucharist communicates to the soul all supernatural gifts requisite for salvation and sanctification.

The angelic doctor proposes this question (*Opusc.* xlviii. *de sacram.*)—Why our Lord instituted this sacrament under the species of bread and wine? He resolves the doubt, saying: "These are the most vigorous nourishment of human life." Thus the Eucharist preserves the spiritual life of the soul, fortifies it against all the temptations of the Devil, and all the perilous occasions of the world.

1. It so preserves the life of grace, that the primitive Christians, according to St. Augustine, (*l.* i. *de pec. meritis, c.* 24,) did not call the Eucharist by any other name but the sacrament of life. Being a living food, namely, Jesus, with his soul and divinity, he prepares us for immortal life.

2. It fortifies the soul against all enemies, renders it strong against the demons, who dare not molest too much, by temptation, him who has God

with him in the sacrament; so that he can say with David: "I fear no evil because thou art with me." It renders him also strong against rebellious passions, mitigating the ardor of concupiscence. John Mosco relates *(in Prado Spirit., c.* xxix.), that an impious heretic having with great fury thrown a consecrated host into a cauldron of water which boiled on a great fire, the host not only remained untouched, but suddenly the water became cold, notwithstanding the burning coals on which it remained. How much better does the Eucharist extinguish in man the fire of sensual appetite! There is no better preservative against impure molestations, than frequently to receive the most holy Eucharist.

Finally, besides many other goods which this sacrament brings with it, it communicates to the soul an interior sweetness, as the bread truly descending from Heaven: so great is this spiritual delight, that after having tasted it, several saints languished more and more from their great desire of partaking of it; thus they could not live without the holy communion.

St. Thomas moves this question (3 *p.* iv. 82): Did the Saviour at the last supper communicate to himself? Should we not answer in the negative. 1. The Gospel does not mention it. 2. He who receives should be distinct from the thing received. 3. Jesus was incapable of receiving an increase of grace, being the fountain of the same grace. Notwithstanding, he answers in the affirmative, and approves St. Jerome *(ad Lactanc.)*, who affirms it. Cajetan assigns the reasons. Of the two principal effects of this sacrament, one is the augmentation of grace; of this the Lord was not capable. The other, the interior sweetness of this most holy food, which could well be enjoyed by the soul of Christ. Such is the great and inexpressible sweetness contained in the Eucharist, that the Redeemer appeared as if he wished to taste and enjoy it himself.

If the Eucharist diffuse so many benefits on the soul, it does not omit conferring them on the body. In the ancient Testament when the people wished to soothe the anger of an irritated God, and to avert the strokes of his justice, they had no sacrifices to offer but beasts; and such sacrifices were so little acceptable to God, that he once said with anger: "Shall I eat the flesh of bullocks? or shall I drink the blood of goats?"—(*Ps.*, xlix. 13.) In the new law of grace the world has the most worthy and the most acceptable sacrifice to offer to God that can be imagined, namely, the adorable sacrifice of the Eucharist, by which the only Son of God offers himself to the Eternal Father. What cannot be obtained, and what evils avoided by such an offering? Woe to the world, woe to cities, to the people, if there were not the holy Eucharist! How much more frequent would there be plagues, wars, desolations! Hence holy Church in public afflictions, causes the most holy sacrament to be exposed on the altars for adoration. She acts as the prudent Abigail who allayed the anger of David, coming to destroy the cattle and vines of Nabol, her husband. She brought a present of bread, with which the king laid aside every sentiment of revenge. Holy Church offers to the Eternal Father the Eucharistic bread, and with it the adorable sacrifice of Jesus in the holy sacrament, which restores the faithful to grace, and obtains for them every benediction.

From what we have said, we should first deduce, how deeply indebted we are to God for having given us this great sacrament. "There is no end of their treasures."—(*Isaias*, ii. 7.)

From the holy altars he invites us to come to him, for he wishes to enrich us. "With me are riches and glory, that I may enrich them that love me, and may fill their treasures."—(*Prov.*, viii. 18.) O infinite benignity! O inexpressible beneficence! What can a God give us more, than himself, and with himself all good!

What father, mother, or friend, has ever done so much for any one? My God! if all our members were so many tongues, they would not suffice to thank thee so much as we should.

How much should I condemn myself, seeing how little I profit by so great a benefit! Whence does it happen that, partaking of a divine nourishment, I do not become divine?

St. Mary Magdalen de Pazzi used to say, that "one communion well made, sufficed to make a person a saint." I make many, and am more irregular than ever. What does this indicate? This proceeds from my negligence and perfidy, by which I approach the holy altar so indisposed, that I even restrain the infinite beneficence of God, so that he does not enrich me, even when he has every desire to do so. What folly, what perversity is mine!

Joseph, after having entertained his brethren at a costly banquet, commanded his steward to fill their sacks with corn. (*Gen.*, xliv. 1.) Those received more, who had the greater number of sacks. The same happens to those who approach Jesus in the holy sacrament: those whose hearts are most void of the affections of the world, and most capable of containing the gifts of God, enrich themselves most. If I do not enrich myself with graces in communion, it is not God, but my indisposition, prevents my being benefited to the fullest extent.

THIRD POINT.

Our Lord in the Eucharist shows an excess of charity. Amongst all the divine attributes, charity is principally displayed in the Eucharist; insomuch that the angelic St. Thomas entitled it the sacrament of charity. 1. Because in this sacrament, our Lord wished to be always with us: " Behold I am with you all days, even to the consummation of the world."—(*Mat.*, xxviii. 20.) The most congenial and dear friends wish to converse together—to eat together. They cannot experience greater displeasure than to be divided from each other. Eliseus, several times commanded by Elias to go from him, could not obey the order to abandon his most beloved; and he said (IV. *Kings*, ii. 27): " As the Lord liveth, I will not leave thee." How clearly, by this, is the love of Jesus seen towards us? After having conversed for thirty-three years with men, receiving from them continual outrages, at the end of his life, though he was to receive the most cruel death of the cross, yet he shows more displeasure at his departure from the world and from mankind, than for his death; so that he found an admirable manner of remaining with them, even after his death, by means of the institution of the Eucharist. " In this we know that he abideth in us, by the spirit which he hath given us."—(I. *John*, iii. 24.) Is not this an excess of infinite charity?

The institution of the Eucharist was a work long desired by Jesus Christ: "With desire I have desired to eat this pasch with you."

Before the incarnation, our Lord willed to be desired for many centuries by mankind. In the Eucharist, he desired to be with us: "With desire I have desired." What more can be imagined, to know the immense love of Jesus Christ towards us? Yet there is much more; for he not only wished to be with us in the sacrament, but he also wished to be within us. What great excess of benevolence this is! The divine Word become man, showed great love towards Mary; conferred most singular honor on her, when he deigned to inhabit her womb for nine months. She was the most pure and holy mortal in the world; and yet holy Church is ever saying: "Thou didst not abhor the Virgin's womb." What then can be said of the love and honor which our Lord shows to us, by coming into our breasts, taking up his abode within us, who are laden with so many sins? The friends of Job, through the great love they bore him, said, emphatically, that they would wish to eat him alive, to place him in their hearts. "Who will give us of his flesh, that we may be filled?"—(*Job*, xxxi. 31.) What they said through exaggeration, we can say with all truth. Whilst in the Eucharist we eat the flesh of Jesus Christ, and drink his blood, our Lord coming within us, wishes to place himself in our breasts as *a seal of love*. O inexpressible goodness of Jesus in this holy sacrament!

MEDITATION XVII.

The centurion was amazed and confounded when the Redeemer offered to enter his house. He exclaimed: "Lord, I am not worthy that thou shouldst enter under my roof." How much more astonished should we be, seeing the same Redeemer even entering within our breasts? He comes willingly and with pleasure. He has often gone so far as to work miracles, in order to come more quickly; which may be observed in what happened to the Emperor Otho IV., who, in his last agony, desired most earnestly to receive the holy Eucharist: but could not, from the state of his illness, which caused him to reject every kind of food. He requested the assisting priest to bring the divine sacrament to him, that if he could not receive it, he might at least behold it. The priest immediately took from the pyx a sacred host and presented it to his view. The dying person then arose to adore the most holy sacrament, and extending his arms towards it, he appeared to wish to embrace and receive it. O prodigy! the adorable particle detaches itself from the hands of the priest, and with rapid flight goes to the breast of Otho, and with a mild wound penetrates even to his heart; and he, as it were, disgusted with life, happily expired. There remained after death a beautiful sign of the wound in his breast. A similar circumstance is related of the seraphic St. Bonaventure. At the end of life, suffering from continual rejection of food, he durst not receive the holy viaticum, for fear of irreverence towards the blessed sacrament. He requested and obtained that the Eucharistic pyx uncovered, should be reverently placed on his chest, when immediately a sweet wound opened on his heart, like a vermillion rose, by which a divine particle entered: (*Theoph. Raynaud de Euch. par.* 182.) Our Lord enters willingly into us, having often performed miracles to come quickly. Can a greater excess of charity be imagined?

Finally, the greatest excess of divine love is, that Jesus in the Eucharist not only wishes to be with us, but to become, as it were, the same substance with us. "He who eats my flesh and drinks my blood, abideth in me and I in him." Ordinary food is converted into the substance of him who eats it. The Eucharistic food changes into itself those who receive it. Thus, in a certain manner, all becomes divine, according to St. Leo. What great love Christ shows in wishing to unite himself intimately with man!

In the incarnation the Divine Word was only united with the humanity which it assumed; but in the Eucharist, Jesus unites himself with each individual who receives him, and is spiritually engrafted in him, according to St. Denis. (*de Eccl. Hier.*, ciii.) A fair branch engrafted on a rough trunk, beautifies the wild tree, and causes it to produce better leaves and more noble fruit. Jesus in the holy sacrament, uniting himself to man, sanctifies and enriches him with graces, and causes him to produce fruits of merit and virtues.

It is related of the venerable Maria Vela, a Cistercian nun, that one morning, after receiving the holy Eucharist, she was wrapt in ecstacy in which she had this vision. It appeared to her that our Saviour with his divine hand took her heart, and placed it in the wound of his sacred side, and pressing it with his most holy heart, of two he made but one, that each of them should be uniform in seeking the divine glory.—(*In vita Marchese Pan, quotid.* 23 *Sept.*) This singular privilege of this servant of God, may in some manner be obtained by just souls, in holy communion: the soul being intimately united to Christ, seems to make but one with him. My soul admire, and bless, and know, the infinite charity of Christ in this holy sacrament. He, infinite sanctity and majesty, unites himself with man, a most vile worm and guilty of a thousand misdeeds! O depth of divine love! We can say of the faithful, what Moses said in favor of the people of Israel: Neither is there any other nation so great, that hath gods so nigh them, as our God is present to all our petitions." (*Deut.* iv. 7.)

No. Never was known in all the ancient centuries, so great a prodigy of charity as God shows us in this sacrament of the law of grace. How is it possible to know and meditate divine goodness, and not dissolve in love towards him, and conceive sentiments of loving gratitude? Yet it is true, and it cannot be recalled without weeping, that many in the world receive the holy Eucharist, and are favored by God with infinite benignity; and still remain cold, distracted, without charity. The great fire of the love of God does not cause them to feel a spark of warm affection. Should not these deserve to be forever excluded from the holy altar as too unworthy of the Eucharistic benefit? David inflicted this punishment on Miphiboseth. David at first, with singular condescension, allowed him daily to partake at his table: " Miphiboseth shall always eat bread at my table"—(II. *Kings,* viii. 10): but in a short time he dismissed him: " Miphiboseth, the son of Saul, came down to meet the king, and he had neither washed his feet, nor trimmed his beard, nor washed his garments."—(II. *Kings*, xiv. 24.)

How much more should they merit to be rejected from the Eucharistic banquet, who approach not only ill-disposed as to the exterior, which is of little consequence, but cold and indisposed in the interior of the soul? How much should I be confounded. Let me reflect on this!

COLLOQUY.

My Jesus in the most holy sacrament, behold me at thy feet, prostrate on the earth; and whilst the seraphim adore thee unveiled in Heaven on the throne of thy glory, I adore thee with a lively faith, veiled in the holy species, here on Earth. I bless a thousand times thy beneficent hand, which dispenses this bread of angels, not to angels, but to us mortals, to make us pure, holy, and like to the angels. I thank thy providence, which has enclosed in this food all celestial treasures; and, above all, I admire thy infinite charity, which has urged thee to remain with us and within us, and to become almost one with us.

I cannot refrain from exclaiming: " Bless the Lord, all ye works of the Lord; praise and exalt him forever." How can I show a just return of gratitude for so great a benefit? " What shall I give," I say with Peter Cellenses, (*lib. de Panib., cap.* xiii.), " that I may come to thee, and receive thee." I have neither the gold of charity for God, nor silver of charity towards my neighbor, nor riches of virtues and merits, to compensate for thy gifts, and to correspond with thy love. What shall I do? I will act as mendicants do to those who benefit them; simply, to accept of gifts, be pleased with them, and not only thank my benefactor, but take courage to return and implore his help and assistance. In the same manner, O my Jesus, in the holy sacrament, I continually return to show thee the desire I have to be restored by this divine food, and to be enriched with thy celestial treasures. O my Jesus! be moved to compassion at my miseries, and grant me, in this sacrament, the plenitude of thy graces, which will be to me a pledge and foretaste of the eternal enjoyments of Paradise. Amen.

MEDITATION XVIII.

On the Passion.

INTRODUCTION.

The celebrated Michael Angelo once painted our Lord expiring on the cross. The representation was so expressive, that the beholder felt himself moved to weeping at the bloody eyes, the pale and emaciated countenance, the livid lips, the swollen chest, and the torn members. What caused much reflection in the audience was the motto at the foot—" No one thinks of it."

How profound are those brief words! A God has such excess of love for man, that, in order to save him, he allowed himself to be mangled, tortured, and crucified. He was content to die in a cruel and disgraceful manner, between two thieves, and on a cross. Man, saved by his death, should correspond, by giving life a thousand times for him: yet his ingratitude goes so far, that he does not even remember or think of him. " No one thinks of it."—(*Ps.*, cv. 21.) " They forget God who saved them, who had done great things." David wept over human ingratitude. If the Redeemer had shed one drop of his blood for us, or had he died without any torture—had he even died of pure joy, as it has sometimes happened, yet not to think of it would be great ingratitude. What then, not to think of it, after his dying in such excruciating torture? This ingratitude, or rather injustice, our Lord is compelled to suffer from unthinking men. On Calvary's cross, the perfidious Jews considered not his pains. They even abused him. Sinners very rarely remember the passion of our Lord; and not only do not compassionate him, but a thousand times crucify him by their sins. Can anything more cruel be imagined! Let us not act thus; but let us earnestly consider the sufferings of Christ, and compassionate them with the most lively affection.

How shall we meditate on the entire passion of Christ, which is an ocean of suffering? "I am come into the depth of the sea, and a tempest hath overwhelmed me."—(*Ps.*, lxviii. 3.) To meditate on one stage of the passion, many months would not suffice; for we can say of each of these mysteries what Seneca said of the seven mouths of the Nile: "Each one is itself a sea."

We will meditate the commencement, continuation, and termination of the passion. In each point we will consider a particular pain of our Redeemer. 1. In the garden, his total abandonment. 2. In the prætorium, his complete ignominy. 3. On Calvary, his dying grief.

FIRST PRELUDE.

Reflecting on Jesus, humble, patient, and meek, let us know ourselves, as proud, irritable, and unmortified.

SECOND PRELUDE.

Let us beg of our Lord to give us grace to practise the virtues he has taught us by his passion, and thus correspond to his love.

FIRST POINT.

At the commencement of the passion in the garden, our Lord particularly suffered total abandon-

ment. Men feel nothing more intensely than to be deserted by their dearest friends and relations in their greatest calamities. Holy Job, in his grievous misfortunes, instead of complaining of his sufferings, complained of the friends who had abandoned him. Even from afar, he requested their pity and assistance. "Have mercy on me, have mercy on me, at least you my friends."

St. Teresa suffered aridity of soul in prayer for several years, and felt as if abandoned by God: she said that this was the greatest pain imaginable.

Jesus Christ, at the beginning of his passion particularly, wished to suffer the pain of entire abandonment. He could well allay all his cares by infusing into the inferior part a little of the enjoyment which he experienced in the superior portion of his soul by means of the beatifical vision: which, purposely, he did not do. This caused much wonder in the angelic St. Thomas, and made him assert, that the grief of Christ in the garden was pure grief, and without any comfort. There is no person on Earth, however miserable, or afflicted, or abandoned, but tries with agreeable thoughts and pleasing promises to mitigate his grief and console himself. Our Lord not only did not console himself, but gave license to his passions, which had heretofore been hushed and obedient to reason, to assail him furiously, as so many untamed animals; so that "he began to fear and to be heavy."—(*St. Mark*, xiv. 33.) He placed before his imagination all the torments and the sad scene of his passion: "his soul grew sorrowful unto death." He reflected, that after the effusion of so much blood, a great number of men would be lost, without drawing fruit from his sufferings. Finally, seeing that his passion should be unfruitful to many, and overcome with great sadness, in suffering so much for a perverse and ungrateful people, his sorrow became even as an agony. His generosity of mind wished the redemption of the world at any cost; weakness of the flesh was unwilling to procure it, at least in so cruel a manner. Amidst these combats, the soul of Christ sustained such grievous sufferings and pains, that he was reduced almost to death; therefore he said: "My soul is sorrowful, even unto death."

The abandonment he sustained from his eternal Father was not less grievous. Whoever heard that a father on Earth abandoned his son, and while easily able to assist him in his grievous pains, would not do so? If the love of an earthly father for a son, though ungrateful, should effect so much, how much more can be said of the love of the Heavenly Father towards his only Son, who is innocence and sanctity itself? The same eternal Parent has ever been the consoler of all the afflicted. He delivered Isaac from the fatal stroke; he allayed the heat of the burning furnace for the three Babylonian children; he delivered innocent Daniel from the lions; how much more should he console, in the garden, his consubstantial Son? He could easily do it. Other means would not be wanting to redeem the world, says St. Austin. Jesus implores his assistance in the most humble and tender manner that can be imagined; he begged it of him on his knees, with his face prostrate on the ground: "He fell flat on the ground"—(*St. Mark*, xiv. 35,) and begged it of him three times. If the sacred text did not mention it, who could believe that the eternal Father, not in the least moved by so many prayers and humiliations from such a Son, did not console him? He sent an angel from Heaven, who quickly took flight to Gethsemane, first adored Christ as his God, then showed him a chalice of bitter gall, announced to him the irrevocable decree of Heaven, that he should die, and by the most cruel and ignominious of deaths on the cross. O God! who can relate the interior sorrow of Jesus, thus abandoned by his eternal Father? He is abandoned by his dearest disciples. Has he not brought to his assistance three of his most beloved apostles? What do they do? Do they run to raise him from the ground, wipe away the sweat and blood, and restore his strength? Nothing of all this; on the contrary, all three are placidly asleep, without thinking of their Master. This loving Lord could not refrain from complaining sweetly: " Couldst thou not watch one hour?"—(*St. Mark*, xiv. 37.) Oh! how ungrateful in the disciples!

From the lively apprehension which Jesus conceived of the most cruel death which awaited him —he began to sweat blood, and so copiously, that his garments were bathed in it, and it began to flow by drops on the ground—even to run like a small rivulet. The stones even had compassion, as the venerable Bede relates: " Our Lord, finding himself on his knees on a marble stone, it liquefied like wax, insomuch that the print of the knees remained profoundly impressed upon it. Poor Nazarean, how great must have been your grief, since it caused you to sweat blood ! It could not be otherwise; for if men feel so much at being abandoned by their friends, what bitterness must have been that of Jesus? How unjust, how undeserved his desolation! Yet this was nothing in comparison to what another apostle did towards him. While Jesus was agonizing, and sweating blood for the benefit of the world, Judas went to the scribes and pharisees, and sold to them the life of his divine Master, for no more than thirty pieces of money. Placing himself at the head of a squadron of men, he went with spears, torches, halberds, and chains, to surprise Jesus in the garden. Jesus remembering his ancient love, goes to salute him, saying: " Friend, whereto art thou come ?"—(*Matt.*, xxvi. 50.) The divine countenance inclines to the hardened Judas, and receives the perfidious kiss of the traitor, who remains obstinate. Jesus sweetly upbraids him: " Judas, dost thou betray the Son of Man with a kiss?" Judas, inexorable in his perfidious attempt, does not cease until Jesus is loaded with chains, and conducted by the soldiers to Jerusalem. Our divine Lord was abandoned in the garden by all those who were most dear to him; and by one betrayed unto death. He seemed typified by that tree described by Daniel, which as long as it remained standing and bearing leaves, was visited by the birds of the air; but scarcely was the voice heard, " Cut down the tree"—(*Dan.*, iv. 11,) than the birds fled from its branches. The prophecy of David relating to him, was confirmed: " They surrounded me like bees"—(*Ps.*, cxvii. 12): as bees surround flowers while they can find any sweet to extract; but having gathered the honey, depart. As long as the Redeemer was praised by the multitude, and worked prodigies in Jerusalem, all his disciples surrounded him, and every one followed him; but in the garden, when he is reduced to the agonies of death, "being in an agony"—(*St. Luke*, xxii. 43), there is not even one to help him; one even is found plotting his death.

From this point, we are to draw various profitable fruits: 1. Lively compassion for the abandonment of our Redeemer. It was a great matter for Job, in his pains, to have friends to console him. The poor beggar who travelled from Jerusalem towards Jericho, had a courteous Samaritan, who comforted him in many ways. Jesus alone has no one in the garden to console him: "I stick fast in the mire of the deep, and there is no sure standing"—(*Ps.*, lviii. 2): yet he had always done good to every person. There never appeared before him an infirm, blind, or deceased person, that he did not console, cure, or resuscitate. The infirm man at the pond called Probatica, abandoned by all, who said: "I have no man"—(*John*, v. 7), was immediately assisted by our loving Lord. After giving consolation to all, now, in his greatest necessity, no one affords him any. My Jesus, how grievous must thy torment have been, and much more so, as thy eternal Father had turned from thee! Cesarius relates, that in a monastery of ancient fathers, Christ crucified appeared to a tepid monk, but with his back turned towards him, and thus reproved him: "Because thou art tepid, thou art not worthy to behold my countenance." At this intelligence, the miserable man was near dying with fright. How much greater must have been the bitterness of Jesus Christ, since without any demerit on his part, it appeared as if his eternal Father were averse to him!

The second fruit is a firm resolution never to abandon Jesus Christ in the occasions that present themselves. How often is good omitted through human respect; in order not to displease a creature, displeasure is given to God! My soul, reflect well on it. Perhaps you are among those of whom our Lord complained: "My people have done two evils: they have forsaken me, the fountain of living water, and have digged to themselves cisterns, broken cisterns that can hold no water."—(*Jer.*, ii. 13.)

Finally, the third fruit is the patience we should have when creatures abandon us, and the uniformity with the divine will when the Creator appears to abandon us.

1. When our friends forget us, when our parents do not assist us, and when those who are most indebted to us are ungrateful, we should not despair, saying: "I have no one for me." How can that be, since the providence of God assists all? If he permits ingratitude, it is for our good, to detach us from creatures and make us know that the only true friend, who never abandons us, is God.

2. We should not be dismayed when we are not heard or consoled in our prayers; nor should we break out into these inconsiderate expressions: "God appears as if he had forgotten me; even the saints do not listen to me." What boldness in us to wish to be always heard in our prayers, when the Son of God in the garden was not heard, after having thrice prayed for the same thing: "He prayed the third time, saying the self-same word." (*Matt.*, xxvi. 44.)

It is not true that God ever abandons us,

though sometimes he appears to do so to make a trial of our virtue.

St. Catherine of Sienna was once very melancholy on account of the aridities she experienced in prayer; it seeming to her that her celestial spouse had abandoned her, when suddenly our Lord appeared to her and she said: "My Jesus, where wert thou?" "Where was I?" replied our Lord. "I was hidden within your heart, and I assisted you, that you might not fall into distrust."

SECOND POINT.

In the Prætorium, our Lord particularly suffered utter ignominy. In the continuation of the passion, the ignominies were not less than the pains: not being able to meditate on both together, let us solely meditate on the ignominies.

It is most certain that all men, especially the wise and noble, feel in a much more lively manner, prejudices against reputation, than corporal suffering; honor being frequently more esteemed than life itself. King Saul, defeated in battle, said to his armor bearer: "Draw thy sword and kill me, lest these uncircumcised come and slay me, and mock at me."—(I. *Kings*, xxxi. 4.)

The valiant Razias, being surrounded by five hundred soldiers of King Antiochus, chose "to die nobly rather than fall into the hands of the wicked, and thus suffer abuses unbecoming his noble birth."—(II. *Mach.*, xiv. 42.)

The divine Nazarean as God, was the supreme monarch of all kings: as man he descended from the royal race of David: as preacher of the New Law, he was the person who had most credit in all Jerusalem, insomuch that the people flocked in thousands to hear his heavenly doctrine, and to see the wonderful prodigies which he worked; yet he condescended to satisfy for the faults of human pride, by suffering so many and such great ignominies, as to surpass all expectation. "I have been humbled exceedingly."—(*Ps.*, cxv. 1.)

1. How great was the confusion of Jesus Christ, when captured in the garden, he entered Jerusalem, bound with ropes and chains like an assassin, in the midst of a perfidious mob, who purposely led him through the most populous streets, where he had received applause and veneration? O God! what an affront was this to Jesus Christ! All certainly should have crowded to recognize him and laud him, saying: "There is Jesus the Nazarean; who can suppose him to be an infamous person? But Jesus holds his peace." (*Mat.* xvi. 63.) With downcast head and shame in his countenance, he pursued his way. When Aman was obliged by King Assuerus to go through the street of the city as groom, holding the bridle of the horse of Mardochai, whom he so much hated, the sacred text says, Aman felt so much confused that he "made haste to go to his house, mourning and having his head covered."—(*Esther*, vi. 12.) How much greater must have been the confusion of Jesus Christ appearing in the most public streets, not as a servant, but as a robber and malefactor!

2. What confusion for Jesus Christ to be conducted to so many tribunals, namely, to Annas, Caiphas, Pilate, Herod, and to be there accused, calumniated as a drunkard, as one possessed, a seducer of the people? Not only not to find his innocence justified by so many judges, but to have

them all against him, insomuch that one of them seeing an insolent soldier, who, in his presence, and without any cause, gave him a blow on the countenance, did not resent it: another despising him as a man void of sense, sent him through the city, arrayed in a white robe as a fool: another, after having recognized his innocence and declared it, condemned him first to be scourged, then to be crucified. What outrages were these against Christ!

3. How great the injury thus offered to Christ by condemning him to be scourged? If those impious wretches, contrary to all laws of justice, wished to punish him, at least they might have done so with one of the chastisements usually given to persons of noble birth. They punished him with stripes, a pain which was inflicted on wicked slaves (*Eccl.*, xlii. 5) and on robbers, who thence were called latrones, from the punishment they sustained in their sides by lashes. They chastise him after having tied him to the pillar.

Abner, captain of Saul, accepted death; but his hands were not bound, nor his feet laden with fetters.—(II. *Kings*, iii. 34.)

Jesus, besides, was scourged naked, which was a source of immense confusion to him. Finally, they strike him, not alone with thirty-nine strokes, according to the statute of the Jews, nor with forty, against the sentence in *Deuteronomy*, but with an immense number of stripes, which would have been endless, if a Roman soldier of the court of Pilate, enraged at so much wickedness, had not unsheathed his sword and cut the ropes which bound him. How injurious to Jesus was this scourging? Even if it had not been most cruel, the shame alone which the Redeemer sustained in it, would have been for him a great torment.

4. The crowning with thorns was in a singular manner outrageous to Jesus. The perfidious Jews, intending at the same time to torment him as guilty, and deride him as a mock king, pressed on his head a crown of most cruel thorns: they put an old purple garment around him, and a reed in his hand as a sceptre. Who can relate the scoffs they added? "They have added to the grief of my wounds."—(*Ps.*, lxvii. 27.) The prophet David testified, that he could not express what they added, to show us that their insults cannot be uttered. Others bending the knee before him, pretended to adore him: then, they beat the thorns into his head: others with affected irony, salute him as King of the Jews: some tear his hair, others pluck his beard, others give him kicks; some give him such blows, that even from afar off the noise was heard, as was revealed to St. Bridget.—(I. *Book, Rev.* vi.) All derided him in a thousand ways: that the gravity of his majesty should not deter them, they bandaged his eyes and countenance. O God! what more can be said? Pilate, the judge, exposes Jesus in this opprobrious condition in a balcony in sight of all the people, saying: "Behold the man." The ungrateful Jews cry out with a loud voice: "Let him be crucified; release unto us Barabbas." A robber, a seditious man in preference to Jesus! The timid judge consenting to their iniquitous wishes, condemned him to the infamous death of the cross: for greater scorn he causes him and not Barabbas to go to Calvary, bearing his cross upon his shoulders. Such is the mockery which was made in the Præ-

torium of the honor, esteem, and reputation of Jesus Christ.

From this point we may draw two most important fruits. 1. A most lively and tender compassion for Jesus Christ. Where on Earth was there ever seen a contempt like to his? Truly was fulfilled the prophecy (*Thren.*, iii. 30), that he should not only be filled, but saturated with opprobriums. With great reason he was likened to a flower of the field: " I am the flower of the field."—(*Cant.*, ii. 1.) Why from the field and not from the garden? Because little flowers in the field are trodden on without any consideration. He is called a worm of the earth, for little worms are crushed by the passers by. My Jesus, how much from my heart do I compassionate thee! I do not know how thou couldst survive so much ignominy; nor why I do not die through compassion for the many insults which thou didst receive!

The second fruit is, to reflect on the cause of Jesus suffering so much scorn and confusion. Our Lord willed it, to confound our pride and to teach us evangelical humility. How many are there in the world, who, though otherwise good, know not how to yield or humble themselves in anything; they think it lawful for them to say: "My esteem and reputation are here concerned." True esteem for a Christian is, to be humble, after the example of his divine master: he will acquire more honor before God, when he seems to lose it with the world. A God could suffer so much contempt and ignominy for the love of man! What more can be said, than a God? Man, a worm of the Earth, cannot suffer, for the love of the same God, some slight prejudice to his esteem! St.

Ignatius the martyr did not feel thus. Conducted to Rome to be martyred, and receiving on the road a thousand scorns and blows, full of joy, he exclaimed: "Now, I begin to be a disciple of Christ." My soul, resolve then to cure your excessive pride, by the humility of Jesus.

THIRD POINT.

On Calvary, our Lord particularly suffered excessive grief. The whole course of the passion of our Lord was truly interspersed with most bitter sorrow and pain. The severest of all the torments suffered by Jesus, was at his crucifixion on Calvary: 1. To die on the cross, as the angelic doctor says, (III. *p.*, 33 *q.*, *art.* 6,) is the most cruel of all deaths. Whoever dies on the cross, expires of pure torture, and has to suffer the most intense and lengthened pain. Provident nature has so disposed of other pains, either that they be tedious and tolerable, or violent and short. Thus, the pain of death being the greatest of all pains, is also the shortest; but he who is crucified, suffers both intense pain from the severe wounds which he receives from the nails in the most nervous and sensitive parts, the hands and feet; he also suffers very tedious pain, for he does not die at one stroke, like one pierced with a sword, or strangled; but he loses life by slow degrees, the blood flowing from the wounds drop by drop.

2. The punishment of crucifixion was much more tormenting to Jesus than to others; for the thieves were strong and robust, therefore better able to resist the violence of pain. Jesus Christ, on the contrary, was most delicate and sensitive to every pain; besides, from the scourging, his veins were

exhausted, his strength diminished, and all his members scarified and wounded.

3. The crucifixion of Jesus was executed with extraordinary fierceness. If the Jews had no pity when crucifying robbers, at least they had humanity by not tearing them more than was necessary, as they had no ill-will or rage against them. They did not thus act in crucifying the Redeemer, for they had implacable hatred against him, and desired nothing more earnestly than to see him dead. When on Calvary they had attained their object, of being able to crucify him with their own hands, O God! who can relate with what ferocity and inhumanity they executed the sentence of Pilate! Paying but little regard to the two robbers, they turned towards Jesus; one quickly polished the nails, another excavated the hole for the cross, another extended the same cross on the ground, then furiously tearing off the garments of Jesus, they did not lay him, but threw him on the murderous wood; the fiercest of the executioners, clasping the divine right hand, and, O God! with what agonizing torture, piercing it with a large pointed nail, with repeated blows of the hammer fixed it on the right side of the cross; then—who can relate it without horror?—placing his impious foot on the side of Christ, and dragging the left hand, nailed it to the other side; finally, placing one foot over the other, with a larger and more penetrating nail, he pierces them with intense torture. Those barbarians, raising the cross on high, bearing our crucified Lord, whose blood flowed in rivulets from his wounds, caused it to fall suddenly into the destined hole, thereby jarring all

the members of Jesus, opening still more his wounds, and causing him most intense agony.

My afflicted Jesus, how couldst thou suffer such cruel torture! If only to think of it makes us shudder, what must thou have felt in suffering it?

St. Francis of Assisium used to say, that rather than suffer the pain of his wounds, he would tolerate the most cruel death; yet he was not suspended by nails: his nails were not of iron, but of flesh. What martyrdom was thine, O Lord, in being suspended thus from the gibbet by cruel nails! I cannot understand why thou didst not die by the excess of intense pain, and how thou couldst survive for several hours after thy crucifixion. It did not suffice for thee solely to die for the love of man; but in one death thou didst unite a thousand deaths.

Our Lord agonized in torture for several hours on the cross, without any relief. If he rested his head, he found the thorns piercing still deeper; if he threw himself forward, the wounds opened still wider; wherever he turned his eyes, he met something tormenting: here, his mother in desolation; there, a robber who outraged him; all around, the Jews, who insulted him; an eclipse in the Heavens, darkness in the air, earthquakes on the Earth. Amidst so many sorrows, he had no one to give him assistance; he asked for some relief to assuage his thirst, and he was saturated with gall and vinegar. He could not receive aid from his disciples, for they had all fled; nor from his mother, as it would not be permitted by the Jews; besides, she was so feeble and exhausted, she required some one to console herself. Even the eternal Father appears to have so abandoned him, that the afflicted Redeemer did not refrain from sweetly complaining: "My God, my God, why hast thou forsaken me?" Thus martyred by interior grief, bloody and wounded in all his members, his death agony begins. His countenance grows pale, his lips become livid, his chest swells, his eyes close, he bows his head and breathes his last sigh. O God! O God! What a cruel death! what a tormenting martyrdom was that of Jesus? Who can ever think of it without being moved to compassion! Let us then weep bitterly for the death of our Lord, more than children weep at the death of their parents. If the angels of peace wept so bitterly at the death of Jesus, for whom he did not die, how much more should we weep, for whom Jesus died!

Let us reflect on the infinite love which our Lord showed us by his death. "By this hath the charity of God appeared towards us."—(I. *John*, iv. 9.) Who on Earth, even father or friend, caused himself to be put to death as Jesus did for us? Consider the manner in which he dies. He expires with his arms open to embrace sinners, with his head inclined, to give them the kiss of peace, and with his side opened, to show to the world his loving heart. O infinite charity! O love without comparison, and without measure! "It is true, by this hath the charity of God appeared to us." Let us be confounded at our ingratitude; we, who do not know how to correspond to a God crucified for us, not even by patiently bearing with the smallest crosses. It was too little for the love of Jesus, to die for us by his bloody torture; and the slightest mortification we suffer for God appears too much.

St. Peter, Martyr, was imprisoned for several months. Tired of suffering, he thus complained before the crucifix: "Lord, what evil have I done to thee, that I should always remain in this prison?" He was then answered in a wonderful manner from the crucifix: "Peter, what evil have I done, that I should remain on this cross?" The saint, humbled and weeping, begged pardon of Jesus for complaining. To how many who complain in their crosses, could our Lord make a similar answer?

Seeing Jesus crucified for our sins, we should compassionate, thank, and bless him; above all, we should firmly resolve not to crucify him anew by our sins. This proposition should seem useless: for it would be ingratitude not to give one's life for him who died for us. Who could imagine that any one should wish to cause him again to die? Human perversity is, however, so great, that in order not again to crucify Jesus, we are constrained to make resolutions; and these resolutions are not often observed. O God! what cruelty! Longinus showed great ferocity by wounding the side of Christ after his death. What would it be again to crucify him with a thousand wounds?

An extraordinary case is written of one who was enclosed in a garden of sanctity, amidst flowers of virtue, though a venomous serpent lay hid. Once, during night, she wished to speak to a friend, who led a bad life. At the top of a corridor, she cast her eyes on the image of a crucifix, which coming before her with open arms stopped her passage; she, blinded by passion, did not retire, but turned her steps towards another corridor; at the end of it the crucifix again with extended arms impeded her steps, and did not permit her to advance; she, still obstinate, turned another way. How far ungoverned passion will go! The same thing again occurring to her, she became so contrite, that throwing herself before an image of Mary, she craved her assistance. She fell into a swoon, and was thus found by the nuns the following morning. The miserable creature recovered from the faint, changed her manners, and lived virtuously. He, who really wishes not to commit sin, is to act thus: should he wish to go to plays and expose himself to the occasions of sin, let him imagine that Jesus crucified, with open arms appears before him, and impedes his passage, exclaiming: Stop, or you will again crucify me. Have you courage to act thus! If you are so rash, you are not a man, but a beast, a monster of ingratitude.

COLLOQUY.

My crucified Jesus, here I am at thy feet humbled and weeping. I adore thee most humbly as my God, and my Redeemer. I admire thy infinite charity and mercy, which have excited thee to die for us, miserable men. I thank thee without end for so singular a benefit which thou hast conferred on us, by redeeming and saving us. I compassionate thee, in the most lively manner, for the many torments and affronts which thou hast suffered in satisfaction for our sins. This punishment and this death was not due to thee, who art innocence itself; it was due to me, who am the most wretched. I am the one guilty of thy chastisements, and more than the Jews I have crucified thee by my sin. I have as often crucified thee as I have sinned. Death is due to me, and not to thee; I will die at thy feet from contrition and repentance for having offended thee.

Accursed sins, which have occasioned the death of a God; I detest and abominate you; and sooner than commit you again, I would wish to die a thousand times.

Forgive, O Jesus, forgive. On the cross, thou didst pray to the Eternal Father for thy crucifiers: " Father, forgive them; for they know not what they do." Pray, then, to the Eternal Father for me, who am ignorant; who have committed faults without well knowing their malice. And thou, Eternal Father, " look on the face of thy Christ." I should not dare to appear before thee, being the murderer of thy Son; yet that Son, crucified by me, asks thee to pardon my sins. " For pardon," these wounds cry to thee: " Pardon," this wounded heart cries; " Pardon," these bloody and scarified members cry out; " Pardon," then, O Eternal Father.

In the meantime, I resolve, with thy assistance, to compensate Jesus with love for my past ingratitude; and now that he has died for me, I wish to bury him in my heart. I wish to please him by renewing and cleansing this heart of mine. Henceforth, I wish to conceive new affections, new manners, new thoughts, and new life.

MEDITATION XIX.

On the sorrows of Mary at the foot of the Cross.

INTRODUCTION.

MARY at the foot of the cross was certainly a martyr, and queen of martyrs. For her most singular purity, she is called Virgin of Virgins. For her most dolorous martyrdom, she is styled Martyr of Martyrs. It is well to reflect on her martyrdom—noble, and worthy of a Mother of God! It is well known, that human justice, even in inflicting death, the greatest of all torments, wishes those persons to be honored who are especially respected: thus, nobles and soldiers are generally despatched by the sword, and not hanged; others of highest rank have been strangled with a golden rope. Abner, captain of Saul, being condemned to die, said: "I will die; but I will never consent to die as a coward, with hands and feet fettered:" and David said: "Not as cowards are wont to die, hath Abner died." (II. *Kings*, iii. 33.) When Cassendro sent a squadron of soldiers to murder Olimpia, mother of Alexander the Great, she went out to meet them, decked in royal attire, to die as a queen, and showed such courage, that even in death she could be recognized as the mother of the great Alexander. God wishing Mary to be martyred in the world, by a high counsel of his providence, disposed that she should receive a most noble martyrdom; such as was suitable to the Mother of God; he did not will that she should be tormented by the hatred of wicked men, but by the love of God himself.

According to the teaching of the angelic doctor, love is much stronger than hatred; thus the martyrdom of Mary was more noble, also more severe than that of the other martyrs; for her love was strong as death.

This is our present meditation, in which we shall consider that Mary was martyred by the strong love of three persons. 1. By the love of the Eternal Father, which obliged him to will the death of his Son. 2. By the love of the Son, who obliged her to assist at his death. 3. By the love of man, which obliged her to love and benefit him, even while he was crucifying her Son.

FIRST PRELUDE.

Imagine Mary on Calvary, at the foot of the cross: pale, and with her hands crossed on her breast, and all covered with blood falling on her from the wounds of her Son.

SECOND PRELUDE.

Let us say from our heart to Mary: Sorrowful Mother, you suffer for my love; do not permit that I shall be ungrateful to you: share your pains with me, that I also may weep through compassion for your suffering.

FIRST POINT.

Mary was martyred with love for the Eternal Father, that obliged her to will the death of her Son. It is common to friends and to all those who love each other reciprocally, to have the same will in all things. Who then is not aware that Mary always loved God most ardently, and more than all creatures in the world? Who does not know that Mary had ever one sole will and sentiment with Jesus? Each appeared to have but one heart, as it was revealed by Mary herself to St. Bridget. Mary knowing it to be the will of the Eternal Father that Christ should die—knowing, besides, that it was the will of Christ to accomplish the decrees of his Father, she was also constrained, through love, to will the death of him whom she loved more than herself, and to will it with such ardor, that St. Anselm attests, if executioners had been wanting, she would have placed him with her own hands on the cross.

Although Abraham most tenderly loved his son Isaac, yet as soon as he heard that it was the will of God that he should sacrifice his child on the mountain, he obeyed. Thus Mary, gifted with much greater virtue than Abraham, knowing that the Eternal Father willed the death of his Son, also willed it. Although Mary, through the force of love, willed a thing so sad to her heart, still she had to sustain the most cruel of all martyrdoms.

The unfortunate daughter of Jeptha, knowing she was destined for sacrifice by the vow of her father, accepted death; but she felt such lively grief, that she entreated and obtained two months to weep over her misfortune. During the interval she did nothing but wander about, making the hills and forests resound with her sobs and groans. How much more must Mary have felt to the heart's core the severe necessity of consenting to the death of her most beloved Jesus? She had to say, I must will the death and torments of him whom I love far more than myself. O most cruel martyrdom! There is, however, great difference between Mary and the daughter of Jeptha; for if the latter felt great grief in accepting her own death, she had some means of alleviating it by weeping for two months. Mary had not this solace in accepting the death of her Son. To show her love for the Eternal Father, notwithstanding her immense grief, she executed the divine will with intrepidity and courage; not shedding a tear, not breathing a sigh, not falling down in a faint. "There *stood* by the cross of Jesus his mother."

The angels mourned the death of Christ; the sun was darkened; the moon refused her light; the earth trembled; all creatures were in commotion; and Mary was unmoved. In suffering grief without alleviation, she sustained a martyrdom beyond comparison, or example; such as would be that of any feeling mother, seeing her only son dead before her, and at the same time constrained not to weep or complain. What is, however, most worthy of astonishment, Mary not only conformed to the divine will concerning the death of her Son, and suffered it with intrepidity; but she also concurred in it, as an intrepid priestess, offering to the Eternal Father the holocaust of her expiring Son. Mary did not remain at the foot of the cross like the ancient Resfa before two of her sons, crucified by the Gabaonites, to defend them from wild beasts, but she remained to concur in the great sacrifice which was offered for the redemption of mankind.

It was revealed to St. Bridget, that as Adam and Eve had ruined the world together; so Jesus and Mary had restored it on Calvary; with this difference, adds Salmeron, that the ruin of the world commenced by Eve, who gave the forbidden apple to Adam: whereas, the reparation of the world commenced by Christ, who having tasted the bitter wood of the cross, gave it to his mother. Whoever wishes to comprehend the most bitter agony felt in the heart of Mary, let him imagine a mother constrained to immolate a son. O God! how great the struggle! What tears, what fainting! How the hand would tremble! How often would the arm be raised; then, losing courage, would stop when but half lifted? It would surely be less for a parent to be murdered, than to murder a son. Afflicted Mary! She is on Calvary, as one that sacrificed the Son in the presence of the Father.—(*Eccles.*, xxxiv. 24.) She is more than mother and priestess; concurring by her sufferings to the sacrifice for human nature, and offering him to the Eternal Father. O torment! O martyrdom! Easier to be imagined than expressed! Hence we should conceive tender compassion for Mary. How was her heart torn by the vehemence of grief! How much a father suffers when obliged to correct his son! How much does he desire some one to intercede for him! How immeasurably more had Mary to suffer, concurring on Calvary, to the holocaust of her Son!

Nicephorus relates (*l.* xii., *c.* 4), that in the horrid butchery made in Thessalonica, by order of the Emperor Theodosius, amongst the rest, two children of a most afflicted father were conducted to death. He wept so bitterly, and offered so much money to the soldiers, that, finally, they consented to liberate one. The miserable father, shedding a torrent of tears, said: "No; I cannot make this cruel choice between those whom I equally and passionately love:" so the soldiers dragged both to death. It was less painful to the unfortunate parent to see both of them dead, than to seem to decide the death of one. What a cruel martyrdom was it for Mary, when, through love for the Eternal Father, she accepted, and even concurred in the death of her Son, whom she loved more than any earthly parent ever loved a child!

We should learn from Mary conformity to the divine will, even in the things most displeasing to us. How different we are from her! If we are touched by God by any adversity, by the death of some intimate relative, what despair we feel; how many lamentations we utter, as if God were too severe with us! Mary could conform to the divine will in the death of the Son of God; and yet we cannot be resigned, and restrain our grief in the death of a relative or a friend. Mary conformed to the divine dispensations, for she knew them to be most just and holy, and directed for the salvation of the world. Why should not we also be resigned, well knowing that whatever God does is for our good? When he afflicts the body with chastisement, then he more than ever instructs and sanctifies the soul. Let us reflect on this, and make a firm resolution of amendment.

SECOND POINT.

Mary was martyred by the love of her Son, which obliged her to assist at his death. Mary certainly could have shut herself within her own dwelling, and not be present at the crucifixion of her Son: and not to suffer the great pain she foresaw from such a spectacle. The ancient Agar, when travelling through the wilderness of Bersabee, and seeing her little child in agony, placed him on a stone; then retiring, she began to sob, saying: " No, I cannot bear to see my son die."

Mary's virginal modesty shrunk from those wicked Jews, who, in crucifying her Son, cursed and scorned her also, as mother of a man most odious to them.

It is usual to keep away parents, wives, and children, from the apartments of the dying, that pain be not increased on either side. Mary might thus have exempted herself from assisting at the agony on Calvary, and at the death of her Son. Why did she not? Because the exceeding great love she bore her Son, obliged her to assist at his death, and thus suffer a most cruel martyrdom.

The apostles fled from Calvary, and all the other Hebrews who had received benefits from Christ, because their love, was not fervent; fear had greater power over them. Mary, who loved Jesus without measure, did not fear the Jews, minded not the repugnance of her virginal modesty, or the intense grief she was to suffer. She could not detach herself from him whom she loved more than herself: intrepid, constant, and faithful, she kept him company to the bitter end. This most prudent virgin well knew, that if at the sight of her crucified Son, she did not weep, she would appear cruel: if she grieved too much, she should much increase the sufferings of Jesus. Mary, torn by contrary affections, by a sovereign grief, and by a sovereign fear of increasing the sufferings of her Son, remains immovable, as if astounded by the horror she felt at an expiring God. "Now there *stood* by the cross of Jesus his mother." Who could express the pangs of her heart? If the celebrated mother of the Machabees was called by St. Augustine (*ser.* 300) seven times a martyr, because she compassionately considered the martyrdom of seven of her children; Mary, constrained by her love to see the martyrdom of her Son, who was above all value, certainly may be styled a thousand times a martyr. To speak properly, she, viewing the agonies of Jesus, suffered more than the object of her compassion: for according to the angelic doctor (2. 2. *qu.* 30. *a.* 1) compassion concerns the pains of others, not one's own: hence, one who compassionates the sufferings of a son or a father, who is, as it were, another self, to speak correctly, suffers, rather than sympathizes.

How great a martyrdom was it for Mary to be under the cross near her agonizing Son? When Jesus, bowing down his thorny head from the cross to consider his mother, and Mary raising her eyes to look at her Son, their eyes reciprocally met. How sad that mutual gaze! Jesus, with a bloody and expiring countenance, begged assistance from Mary, who would have died to procure it for him; however, she was totally unable to afford him any help. O Lord! what pain did she feel when Jesus groaned—when he agonized—when he sighed from thirst. What sorrowful echoes were in the heart of Mary! The afflicted mother, unable to stand upright, embraced the cross and placed her head upon it; she felt the blood flowing from the divine wounds: her mantle was sprinkled with the same blood, and she sobbed and groaned, and could not refrain from embracing the purpled cloth, and pressing it lovingly to her bosom. She desired a thousand hearts to compassionate her Son, and the more, as she saw him bereft of compassion: the bad thief she heard blaspheme him, and the perfidious Jews mock and insult him. She said within herself: "My poor Son, what a bad return you receive from mankind, whom you have so much benefited!" The height of Mary's sorrows was when the Redeemer, after having been tortured for several hours on the cross, was reduced to the last agony. It was a stupendous miracle that she did not die, when she saw the breast of Jesus swelled, and his lips pale. Bowing his head towards her, and collecting on his bloody lips the last sigh, "he sent forth his spirit." O God! what inexplicable martyrdom! How willingly would she have died a thousand times rather than see her Jesus dead! How miserable did it appear to her to survive him, who was her life and her soul!

Most afflicted mother, who can be found so hard-hearted as not to compassionate your pain? Who would not mingle his tears with your lamentations? This, however, does not suffice. We should also learn from Mary, who remained so faithful at the foot of the cross, a tender devotion to the holy crucifix, by remaining often at its feet, meditating its pains, and begging pardon for our sins, which were the cause of the death of Jesus. Let us often in spirit, seek to dwell in the prints of his wounds. God ordered Noah to construct numerous little rooms in the ark for every different species of animal, that one might not be injured by another. (*Gen.*, vi.) So Jesus crucified is now a mystical ark for us; and our place of refuge is in his wounds. Let us close ourselves within them;

and be there sheltered from the Devil and the world. If we had continually before us the holy crucifix, how much more patient, humble, and mortified should we be! We ought to learn from Mary, constancy in good. How many are there in the world who commence following Jesus by a more Christian life, and immediately abandon him to follow the world? Mary did not thus act: faithful and intrepid, she never abandoned him, though all others did; but she accompanied him to his last breath. Thus also did Jesus for us; he was importuned by the Jews to descend from the cross, and they would then believe him to be God. The Redeemer, ever firm in his resolution, would not descend until he had breathed his last sigh.

THIRD POINT.

Mary was martyred by the love of man, which induced her to benefit him, even when her Son was being crucified. To understand this point, suppose, as Rachel had two children, Joseph and Benjamin, who was called "the son of her grief:" so Mary had two children, namely, the Man-God and guilty man: she brought forth Jesus in the world: she produced the second spiritually to grace: the first she brought forth in Bethlehem, without any pain: the second she produced on Calvary, suffering the most acute pains, says Damascene. Mary on Calvary, seeing her divine Son crucified for the faults of sinful man, who likewise was her son, she felt her heart as it were rent in two; she could not hate him who crucified her Jesus, for she loved man and considered him as her son.

Such was the grief Eve felt when she saw her

son Abel murdered by her son Cain; though the death of the innocent was extremely painful, she could not hate the perfidious murderer, who was likewise her son. The heart of Mary obliged her to love those who crucified her most beloved Son. Mary on Calvary, not only loved man, while he tore and murdered her child, but blessed him by concurring in the great sacrifice which was offered for the redemption of the world. It is true, our Redeemer did not require the assistance of others to save man, his divine blood being sufficient to save a thousand worlds; yet Mary wished to show her love for man, and the excessive desire she had for his salvation, by coöperating, as much as she could, in his redemption. She offered to the Eternal Father, for the good of the world, the sacrifice of the body of her Son, and the sacrifice of her suffering soul.

Adam and Eve together caused the ruin of the world. Jesus and Mary offer together their holocaust; one of the blood of his veins, the other the tears of her heart. Mary, on Calvary, pleaded for man to the Eternal Father; while our Redeemer, on the cross, prayed for those who crucified him. "Father, forgive them, for they know not what they do." Mary, also, prayed for them and for all sinners, as in all things, she was conformable to the sentiments of her Son. Although she abhorred the deicide of the Jews, yet she also prayed for them. She was as the woman of Thecua, who shrouded in a black mantle and shedding torrents of tears, spoke to king David in favor of Absalom; she related to him the parable of two children, one murdered by the other, "And behold the whole kindred rising, saith: Deliver up him that hath slain his brother."—(II. *Kings*, xiv. 7.) In the same manner, Mary spoke on Calvary in favor of man. "Eternal Father, I am the mother of thy only Son, and I am also the mother of sinful man, who, impiously murders my divine Son. Man merits eternal death; but shouldst thou punish him as he deserves, as an afflicted mother I must weep bitterly for the death of both. Deign to be moved with compassion at my grief; now that I sigh and suffer for the death of my Jesus, do not permit me to grieve and lament for the eternal death of sinful man, who is also my son." Who can explain the interior martyrdom of the heart of Mary! St. Bernardine of Sienna, says: "She suffered as many grievous pains as there were innumerable men, whom she thus brought forth to grace." Hence, we may draw many different affections towards our Lady of sorrows. First, of *gratitude*, giving her thanks for all she has done and suffered for us. On Calvary she conducted herself as a tender and compassionate mother: in bringing us forth again to grace, she suffered much more than mothers do in bringing their children to light. How much then are we obliged to her? Certainly, after Jesus, we owe most to Mary. We should then imagine that Jesus himself admonishes us with those words, which the ancient Tobias said to his youthful son (*Tobias*, iv. 3): "Thou shalt honor thy mother all the days of her life." Why? Because you should ever remember how much labor and pain she suffered for love of you.

Second, *sorrow for our sins*, which have afflicted and crucified Mary, by crucifying her only Son.

Herodias writes, that Anthony Caracalla and

Geta, brothers, who were equals in the empire, being unable to agree, at first thought of dividing the government. The impious Caracalla unsheathed his sword, and ran towards Geta, who took refuge in the arms of his mother. Even there, the wretch barbarously murdered him. The miserable parent remained but half alive, being transfixed with intense agony.

Wretches that we are! we have acted in like manner by our sins, and even with greater cruelty, towards Mary, murdering and crucifying in her arms the Son of God. What is worse, we continually commit sin, and thus renew his torments and her suffering.

It is written of a youth devoted to our Lady, that, having committed a grievous sin, he went as usual to recite his devotions before an image of Mary of sorrow. He perceived her transfixed, not with seven, but with eight swords. Being astounded, he scarcely credited what he saw, until he heard a voice saying, that his sins had added the eighth sword to the heart of Mary. (*Revelation Fascett. di rose, par.* iv.) Miserable sinners that we are! who by the continual commission of sin, pierce every day with a hundred and a thousand swords the most sweet heart of Mary! What confusion should we feel, and how many penitential tears should we shed!

The last affection, which is the principal fruit of this meditation, is, to try *to console Mary in her misfortune.* We shall do so,. if, throwing ourselves at her feet, we ask pardon again and again for the bitterness we have occasioned her; above all, promising her never to relapse, by offending and crucifying her Son. Thus a youth in India acted, of whom mention is made in the annual letters of the Society of Jesus. He had in his room a little statue of Mary of Dolours, with a sword piercing her heart. One day assailed by a youthful passion, he resolved to violate his conscience, which reminded him that he would thereby grievously offend God. Blinded by passion, he went to the door of his room to execute his wicked purpose, when suddenly he heard a voice, saying: "Stop; whither are you going?" He returned back, and saw the image of Mary of Dolours detach her arm from her side, and snatch the sword from her heart. Turning towards him, she said: "Here take this sword, and wound me rather than my Son, by your sin." At these words, the youth fell to the ground, and with a torrent of tears begged of God and our Lady of Dolours pardon for his fault, promising her in future to lead an innocent and holy life. Sinful soul, if such you be who read these lines, imagine that Mary of Sorrows also repeats to you: "Stop; what are you doing? For a long time, by your evil habits, you have been crucifying my Son, and wounding me: now have done. If you are so cruel as not to cease your evil ways, strike at me rather than the only Son of my heart." Who can be so hardened as not to be moved by these words? Let us throw ourselves at the feet of our Lady of Sorrows, and with hearts filled with liveliest contrition, let us thus address her: Most holy Virgin, if I had at my disposal the hearts of all mankind, I could not sufficiently compassionate your grief, which is sorrow without measure and beyond example.

COLLOQUY.

Ah! most afflicted Mother, how worthy are you of the liveliest compassion! and how much reason have we to be grateful to you? To have suffered so much for the love of the Eternal Father, and your divine Son, was not wonderful, as it is most just to conform to the divine will; but to wish to suffer so much for the love of mankind—we, who are so wicked, disobedient, and ungrateful, this, indeed, is a prodigy of excessive goodness. Mary, I ought not to appear before you, after having crucified your divine Son by my sins; for a slave would not dare to appear before a queen after having murdered her only son, the heir to her kingdom. Yet, you are the mother of all mankind and mother of mercy; we take the liberty of throwing ourselves at your feet, we embrace them a thousand times, and with tears ask pardon for all the offences we have been guilty of towards you and your divine Son. Forgive, O Mary, forgive! Have mercy upon us, miserable sinners! If you wish to punish us, do so, and pierce us with your sword of sorrow; and the pain shall be dear to us, for it will render us more compassionate towards your sufferings. Do not permit that we should be ungrateful to your love. Whilst you weep at the foot of the cross, grant that we may also weep through compassion for your sufferings, and through grief for our sins. Finally, now while you gaze on the agonies of your divine Son, grant us the grace, although most unworthy children, to be assisted by you in our agony and death. Amen.

MEDITATION XX.

On Heaven.

INTRODUCTION.

The commencement and termination of the holy exercises admirably correspond. How are the exercises begun? By meditating on the end for which we were created—to see, love, and enjoy God in Paradise. How are the exercises ended? By meditating on the same Paradise, in which we are to see, love, and enjoy God. What a great thought is this! How efficacious, to strengthen, and as it were, seal all the resolutions made in the former meditations. No more powerful motive could be urged to induce man to undergo great labor, than the hope of an extensive reward. The Israelites sustained a disastrous and tedious journey through the deserts of Arabia during forty years—and why? From their hopes of the promised land. Those mysterious animals mentioned in *Ezechiel* (i. 22), that were drawing the chariot of the glory of God, moved through the air like lightning; for they had on their heads an image of the firmament. How much more will the thought of Paradise animate us to suffer in this life, and to run forward in the road of Christian perfection!

St. Ignatius, the Patriarch, during the summer nights remained entire hours with his eyes fixed on the firmament. After long contemplating the beautiful azure, and the stars all bright and vivid, and then turning to look on the earth, which is so dense, thorny, and deformed, he uttered this lamentation: "How mean the earth appears to me, when I contemplate Heaven!" In Rome this sign was given to recognize St. Ignatius: "He is always looking up to Heaven, and speaks continually of God."

Let us also raise our eyes from this miserable earth, and consider the beauty of Heaven.

We shall divide this meditation into three points. We shall consider in the blessed—1. The Heaven of sense. 2. The Heaven of soul. 3. The Heaven of eternity.

FIRST PRELUDE.

Imagine that you see the New Jerusalem; a most luminous city, enlightened by a thousand suns: with streets of sapphire; entire habitations of diamonds; the air perfumed with a thousand odors, and rich in harmonious music. This description is not of Heaven: it is but a shadow of Paradise.

SECOND PRELUDE.

Say to God from your heart with holy David: "One thing have I asked of the Lord, that I may dwell in his house all the days of my life."—(*Psalm*, xxii. 6.) My God! this is the most important grace I beg of thee; that thou conduct me to Heaven. If thou wilt not grant me other graces, I am content. I wish for Heaven. Thou didst merit it for me by thy blood.

FIRST POINT.

The Heaven of sense. What is said of Heaven should not appear exaggerated, but be considered as much less in description than what it truly is,

Let us discourse on the clearest reasons, which show Heaven to be beyond all human understanding. The first reason is from St. Bernard. "Raise your eyes," says the saint, "and consider Heaven. What brilliant stars! What luminous planets! What beautiful azure! What do we see? It is the pavement of Heaven. If such be the pavement, what then is the place itself where the blessed are, and where God dwells!"

The second reason is from St. Augustine, who says: "Turn your eyes around the universe: what a fine world this is! What delights therein! How many seas, rivers, mountains, mines, plants, flowers, cattle, birds, and fish? It is such, that men seldom wish to die, or quit it." Yet, what is all this world compared to Paradise? It is a prison, an exile, a valley of tears. For whom did God make this world? He made it, not only for the habitation of men, but also for beasts, serpents, and dragons. He made it not only as a shelter for his friends, the just; but also for his enemies, schismatics, heretics, Turks. Heaven is not a prison, but a place of freedom; not an exile, but a home; not a valley of tears, but a place of pleasure. It is purposely and solely made for the friends of God. What then must it be! How beautiful, how rich, how delightful! If you were conducted to see the palace of a great king, and entering the palace gates, were introduced into the stable, and there beheld statues of porphyry, engravings on ivory, Flemish tapestry, exquisite paintings, what would you feel? If the stable of this king is so admirable, what must be the drawing-rooms, the galleries, the chambers, of the king? This world, inhabited by beasts, in regard to Paradise, is but a stable; and yet is noble and delightful. The kingdom of the saints, of Mary, and of God himself, who is the Monarch of monarchs, what must it be!

The third reason may be drawn from two similitudes: 1. Imagine a king with immense treasures, expert in architecture, and occupied in constructing a palace for himself, surpassing all ever before seen in the world. What a palace would it be? God is King of kings, of infinite power, who can do as he pleases: of infinite wisdom, who can devise what he wishes; and of infinite goodness, in rewarding his servants in Paradise. What then must Heaven be? 2. A jeweller most skilled in his art, had one hundred thousand crowns. A precious stone is presented to him by a peasant, who says: "This jewel is beyond all price." The artist answers: "I wish to buy it of you with my one hundred thousand crowns." How valuable would this jewel be? Heaven was sold by Adam to the demon for an apple. Jesus Christ, who has the greatest knowledge of Paradise, thought well to purchase it by shedding all his blood, which is of infinite value. What great things then should be thought of Heaven!

Fourth. In Hell, God chastises his enemies much less than they merit; yet inflicts on them indescribable torments. In Paradise, he rewards the just with much greater joy than they merit. What enjoyment then must there be in Heaven!

Finally, Cæsar Arelatensis (*Hom* viii. *de Pasch.*) says: "Observe how much the Devil does and labors to rob men of Heaven." The Devil, having first been in this most happy place, and envying man his fortune in being able to go there, even while Satan uses so many efforts to prevent him, clearly gives us to understand, that it is a habitation of sovereign delight.

Let us now meditate the point proposed; and before any other, let us consider, *the first entrance of a soul into Heaven.* O God! what joy is hers? Scarcely has she seen herself raised above the stars, than turning her eyes around to the world she has left, she exclaims: " Blessed be God that I am no longer subject to human miseries, sickness, pains, torments, infirmities, plagues, or even death: these are no longer for me. Blessed be God, I am secure of my eternal salvation, I have no fear now of being lost."

What pleasure for the saved, to be free from all those anxious solicitudes that mankind have concerning salvation?

The blessed come to meet the soul to receive her and to congratulate with her; and her parents and friends who are saved, and those souls who were freed from Purgatory by her suffrages; and above all, with what joy does her angel-guardian come before her? Welcoming her tenderly, he says: " Come with me, beatified soul, who so well profited by my direction and guidance: blessed be whatever I have done for you." Thus the soul is introduced into the blissful country of the living. How overpowered the soul must be at first seeing her greatness. St. Bernardine of Sienna said (*Ser. de dign. art.* i. *cap.* 1): " That if God created as many worlds as there are grains of sand in the sea, they could scarcely be equal to the immensity of the highest Heaven." The farther the soul advances into that blessed mansion, she becomes more astounded, as at every step she treads on sapphire; at every look, she sees a new prospect; at every pulsation, she breathes the balsamic breeze of a thousand odors.

Finally, arrived at the throne of God, the saved soul will experience much more than what happened to the queen of Saba, who, approaching king Solomon, seeing him seated on a throne of gold, as it were a sun surrounded by a thousand planets of most noble courtiers, she in amazement cried out: "She had no longer any spirit in her." (III. *Kings*, x. 5.) So the soul, beholding the most august Trinity, amidst the glories of a thousand suns, and surrounded by innumerable choirs of angels, will remain overpowered with astonishment. What enjoyment will it be for the blessed, when they are invested with the rays of the divine Sun, and transformed into his likeness? "Who will reform the body of our lowness, made like to the body of his glory."—(*Phil.* iii. 21.) This is a great mystery, says the apostle St. Paul. "We shall all indeed rise again."—(I. *Cor.*, xv. 51.) All the blessed at their resurrection will be changed in Paradise from what they were. All their senses will become glorious and beautiful, according to the sufferings they sustained in life for God. Those eyes that were so modest, and shed so many penitential tears, will appear like stars, and will brighten with the sight of the saints and angels, of Mary, and of the glorious humanity of Christ, whose sacred wounds the blessed can embrace, and approach his glorious feet even as does Magdalen. "Mary, sitting at the Lord's feet, heard his word." (*Luke*, x. 39.) The abbot Silvan having once had a glimpse of Paradise, said: "May my eyes be forever closed, to behold nothing created." What then will it be to a blessed soul who can view Paradise unceasingly!

The hearing, which was heretofore mortified by refusing to listen to murmuring and indelicate words, will be delighted with most sweet and angelic melodies. St. Francis of Assisium having once heard, for a very short time, the sound of an angelic instrument, was suddenly caught up in rapturous ecstacy. What will it be to hear forever the harmonious concerts of innumerable angels?

The scent will be continually consoled with a thousand odors. Every blessed soul will appear a rich perfume.

The palate, formerly afflicted with fasts and abstinence, will taste the most exquisite flavors. Suarez says: "God will produce in the palate of each of the blessed a quality, which, much better than manna, contains all kinds of sweetness."

Finally, the feeling will be glorified with the four gifts of beatitude—namely, with *agility;* by which it can in an instant descend from the height of Heaven to Earth: by *charity* each blessed soul is as much more luminous than the sun, as the monarch of day is brighter than any celestial body, which St. Augustine attests (*Tr.* 46): by *subtility* a blessed soul can penetrate a mountain as a ray passes through crystal: by *impassibility* the blessed soul is an immortal lover, and can never more suffer, complain, or die.

In Heaven there will be, besides the enjoyments

common to all, special rewards for particular pains sustained for God during life. If the Lord willed, even in this world, that the hair of Magdalene, which wiped the feet of Christ, should remain unchanged—the tongue of St. Anthony of Padua, which propagated the glory of God, should be ever fresh—and the charitable hand of St. Edward incorrupt; how much more will he glorify those same members in Heaven!

St. Augustine adds: "If God has rendered glorious and miraculous on earth the instruments of punishment of the saints, such as the chains of St. Peter, and the scourges of many confessors, what will he do for the saints in Heaven?"

All bliss the blessed enjoy together, and at the same time. It is not so with earthly pleasures. He who reposes does not enjoy theatres; he who dances does not enjoy banquets, and so of the rest. "In Heaven," says Boetius, "there is every good at the same time." The blessed enjoy all flavors, odors, and harmony; all happiness, the quintescence of all good at the same time. As the prophet Joel says: "The mountains shall drop down sweetness."—(iii. 18) Each drop of these celestial delights is such, that if it fell into Hell, it would immediately mitigate that great sea of bitter pains. The rich glutton begged of Abraham one sole drop of celestial refreshment.—(*Luke*, xvi. 21.) He knew that one such drop of celestial sweetness could give him more relief in his cruel burning, than all the waters of the sea could effect.

Reflect then, beloved! Is it not of faith that in Heaven all delights and joys are contained, even for the body? How is it that you who are so solicitous for pleasures, do not wish for them? The vile and brief enjoyments of the world ravish you; and the eternal and inexpressible bliss of Paradise does not gain your affections and desires? What does this mean? If you wish for enjoyments, seek them; but let them be celestial and immortal. You are contented to suffer inconveniences and expense that you may enjoy the pastimes of earth. To attain eternal happiness, it is not much to suffer something for God. You wish to enjoy two Heavens; one on earth, the other in Paradise; but this is impossible. Be contented then to suffer a little here, that you may rejoice eternally in Heaven.

Similar sentiments animated the youngest brother of St. Bernard, named Nivardo. His brothers having become religious at Clairvaux, said to him: "Dear little Nivardo, you will be the sole inheritor of all our worldly substance; remain in the world for the relief of our father." The wise child shaking his head, answered; "O no! amongst brothers, portions should be equally divided; why then do you wish to gain Heaven for yourselves, and leave earth to me? The division is not just: if you wish for Heaven, I desire it also." He accompanied them to Clairvaux. How wisely did this child speak? While many, though advanced in years, speak like children. How many Christians do not mind Heaven, provided they enjoy the pleasures of the earth? Rather than bear the slight yoke of Jesus Christ, they renounce Paradise.

SECOND POINT.

The Heaven of soul. The very Heaven of Heavens, as St. Augustine remarks, is God himself, seen and enjoyed face to face. St. Anselm observes, that as a fish in the sea is surrounded on all sides by water, so the blessed soul, immersed in the happiness of God, finds in all his powers inexpressible enjoyment. Great will be the enjoyment of the memory, by recalling the benefits conferred by God, especially the regulated chain of graces which secured the soul's salvation.

The martyrs recollecting their torments, the confessors their penances, the virgins the strictness of their cloisters, will exclaim, " Blessed be God, who gave us strength and light to suffer those pains, which gained for us so blissful a Paradise! Blessed prayers, blessed fasts, blessed alms! Blessed be that day on which we turned from the world, to follow more closely the example of our Redeemer." The intellect will be in enjoyment, because the most ignorant will know in Heaven in one moment all sciences better than all the wise of this world : and, much more, as it will see God, the infinite beauty, unveiled. This is such great happiness, that theologians agree, that beatitude consists in the sight of God: this vision is an infinite good, its object being infinite in perfection. If the eye is pleased in seeing a palace splendidly adorned, or a king arrayed in majesty and glory, what will it be to see God himself in his infinite majesty, who has immutability for his throne—omnipotence for his sceptre—eternity for his crown, and glory for his mantle. What will it be to see all good in God! What will it be to see the most august Trinity ; and in the Trinity an essence, which, though participated by several, is still undivided! Add to this, that to see God, is not like considering any created good; for those who see a king, do not, consequently, become kings: he who sees a banquet, does not become satiated; but he who sees unveiled the greatness of God, becomes great; he who sees his riches, becomes rich; he who sees his felicity, becomes happy; he who sees his divinity, becomes divine: "We shall be like to him, because we shall see him as he is."—(I. *John*, iii. 2.)

As the sun pouring its rays on a dewy cloud, transfers its own beauty and splendor, so God, unveiled and enjoyed by the blessed soul, communicates to it the divine perfections, and causes it to appear in Heaven almost as God. O what happiness! What bliss! What glory!

Finally, great shall be the pleasure enjoyed by the will; for in loving God, the last end will be possessed, which includes all goods, so that every desire will be fully satisfied. In this world no one possesses so much that he does not wish to enjoy still more. What could be desired more by David, than to pass from the condition of shepherd to that of King of Palestine? Yet, not contented, he said: "I shall be satisfied when thy glory shall appear."—(*Ps.* xvi. 15.) The will of the blessed, having all it desires, will abound in God, who is a sea of infinite perfections.

Herodotus relates of Crœsus, king of Lydia, (*l.* vi., *Sabel*, *l.* 3), that wishing to show gratitude to Alcmeone, who had graciously received his ambassador, he introduced him into an extensive gallery in which his immense treasures were placed, and gave him permission to take as much as he could carry. Alcmeone, being in great delight and solicitude, took with both hands whatever he found was most precious, filled his pockets and loaded himself with gold and jewels. How much happier is the lot of the blessed, who continually and always can possess God, the inexhaustible source of all good. To possess him, no fatigues or sufferings are to be endured: it suffices only to will it.

If a man had a ring gifted with this virtue, that by touching it, he could have what he desired: for example, if he wished for wealth, he touches the ring, and immediately he sees before him a mountain of gold: he desires dainties, he touches the ring, and instantly a banquet appears before him; how much would he be envied by all! My soul, if you are saved, how much happier will you be in Heaven! To have there what you wish, you will not have to endure the slightest inconvenience. You will scarcely desire music, honors, perfumes, or riches, before at once you will enjoy them superabundantly. Is not this bliss, inexpressible happiness! What wonder then, if St. Giles, of the seraphic order, was raised in an ecstacy, contemplating eternal beatitude. Even the name of Paradise placed him in ecstacy.

Dearly beloved, does not the thought of these celestial delights animate your fancy? The hope of one day attaining by the divine grace such felicity, is it not consoling! What then will it be, says St. Augustine, to possess it? Know, that God has created this beautiful Paradise purposely for you; and has also promised it to you. Do you wish for Paradise or not? Wish for it! I do certainly. "Who is the man that desireth life: who loveth to see good days: who wishes for Heaven?"—(*Psalm*, xxxiii. 13.) Every one answers: "I wish for it." If it be so, then Heaven is yours. If you are poor, no matter: to go to Paradise, riches are not wanting. If you are ignobly descended, it is of no consequence: nobility is not required. If you are ignorant, it is no obstacle: science is not necessary. What is required is the will, which is in the power of every one. "All you that thirst, come to the waters; and you that have no money, make haste, buy and eat."—(*Isaias*, lv. 1.) Here note the strange speaking of the prophet: "Come and buy without money." If money be not required, it is not a purchase, but a gift.

Nazianzen says (*Or.*, xxv.): "Even without money, heaven is purchased; for God esteems the will, and the sole desire of man." The will of man is true and efficacious, when he uses the means to attain the end. The means for obtaining heaven is the observance of the divine precepts: "If thou wilt enter into life, keep the commandments." Many, at the mere mention of the observance of the divine precepts, immediately show repugnance, and their works contradict their expressed desire of salvation. "What a shame," exclaims St. Augustine, "Do men expect to be carried by the hair of the head to Heaven, as Habacuc was borne through the air!" This is folly. If we really wish for Paradise, while God assists us to it by his grace, we should also assist ourselves by holy coöperation.

THIRD POINT.

The Heaven of eternity. Paradise is such, says St. Augustine (*l.* iii., *de lib arbitr.*, 25), and enriched with so many delights, that to enjoy it for one day and no more, it would be well to pass innumerable years in this life in suffering and in the privation of all temporal pleasure.

The prophet asserts this: " Better is one day in thy courts above thousands."—(*Psalm*, lxxxiii. 11.) It is not for one day, or for one year, or one century, but for innumerable centuries, for all eternity. Paradise and its goods are true. According to the maxim of St. Augustine, there is no true good if it be not eternal: the goods of this world cannot be true, because they all end. If one were king of the most flourishing dominions, the certainty of his rule coming to an end, prevents him from being completely happy so long as he reigns. This was alluded to in the keen reply given by an ambassador of Pyrrhus, monarch of Epirus. Having gone to Rome while it was at the zenith of its greatness, he admired the splendid architecture and the prodigious works of art in that illustrious metropolis. One day some of the noblemen who paid him court, enjoying the praises given to their country by a stranger, asked him : " Have you found any defect in our city ?" " Yes," answered the ambassador, " I observe a very great one." " What is it?" " In Rome, also, people die." This statesman wished to signify, that how great soever was Roman felicity, still it should terminate. This cannot be said of the celestial Jerusalem; thence were expelled forever death and sickness.—(*Apoc.* xxi. 4.) The inhabitants of Heaven will be like stars, fixed in eternity. " They shall shine as stars for all eternity."—(*Daniel*, xii. 3.) The duration of their reign will not be for the space of a century alone, but for all centuries. " I will praise thy name forever, yea for ever and ever."—(*Ps.*, clxiv. 2.)

The permanence of those blessed spirits will always be firm; as the prophet says: "Our feet were standing in thy courts, O Jerusalem."—(*Ps.*, cxi. 2.) What great joy will every blessed soul experience, at every instant, from the certainty of a most happy eternity! He will say: "These excessive delights will never have an end! Never. This glory I can never lose: no one can diminish it, or take it from me? Never. This great God, who made Heaven for me, I am always to see, to love, to enjoy. Always. Oh! what happiness!"

The soul will always be the same, without ever losing any of its first bliss; because God will always be enjoyed, infinite in beauty and perfection; and because, the blessed who enjoy him, will always be in the grace of God.

Here below, the most harmonious music, the most exquisite food, or the most agreeable employment, if prolonged, gives more pain than enjoyment. The pleasures of Heaven last eternally, yet they do not annoy, but are ever new, as if they were only beginning: hence it is said, that the angels in Heaven always chant new canticles.

Here below, greatness and honors are subjects of envy, rivalship, and persecution. If a person could live for one year in a city, peopled only by the just, what great happiness it would be? It would be the home of charity and peace; the inequality of citizens would not occasion discord, reciprocal love would cause each to recognize as his own the good of others. The blessed, not for a year alone, but forever, inhabit a city solely peopled by the just, without fear that in that holy company there should arise division or discord. What incomparable happiness! What inexpressible joy! It is such, says the learned Scotus, that the blessed soul, who occupies the last place in Paradise, would not leave it, even to be the greatest monarch in the world.—(*Scot. in* IV., liii. *q.* 3.)

The better to understand this, imagine a holy man, a worker of *miracles*, seeing the corpse of a peasant, whose soul is already in Heaven. He places his hand on the bier, and with an imperious voice, says: " In the name of God, let the soul be restored to the body; let him revive; not to be, as he was, a beggar, but to be monarch of the entire world." That soul would make the most bitter lamentations, and could not be induced to leave the last post in Heaven for the greatest throne on earth. If it be so, O souls whose affections are buried in the filth of this miserable earth, raise your eyes and consider Paradise. Remember that God formed man with the head upward, that he might easily look to Heaven. To view Heaven kindles our hope, and strengthens our weakness. " Lo! this was our hope."—(*Isa.*, xx. 6.)

St. Ambrose says: " The hope of reward removes the pain of toil."

If Paradise were nothing more than what we have meditated, would it not merit that every labor should be endured for its acquisition! How much more does it deserve, since it is incomparably greater than what has been said?

Suppose this proposition were made: " If for one year you do not offend mortally, you shall become a King." What fool could be induced to sin, and thus lose a kingdom? Here is offered, to those who do not commit sin, an eternal kingdom; and yet, not only sin is committed, but on every slight occasion. O good Lord! what folly!

How rash soever a gambler may be; still, before he ventures a large sum of money in play, he stops to think of the risk he runs. Many for every little caprice, seem by their deeds to say: "Away with Heaven!" Consider what you say and what you do. To insure Paradise to us, Jesus Christ shed his blood on a cross. And we, to acquire Paradise, will not overcome our passions. Let us remove those affections which keep us tied to the earth, and prevent us from flying towards Heaven.

Herodotus relates of Egisistratus Eleo, that being bound by the Lacedæmonians, he cut off his foot with his own hand to set himself free. Let us do as much, but in a better way: "If thy hand or thy foot scandalize thee, cut it off and cast it from thee." If the hand be inclined to sin, or the foot to walk in evil ways, let it be cut off for the love of God. To acquire Paradise, whatever is done or suffered is little indeed.

COLLOQUY.

Be thou forever blessed, my good God, for having created Heaven. Blessed be thy wisdom, which hast devised it in so noble a manner. Blessed be thy omnipotence, which has constructed it so deliciously. Blessed be thy charity, which has formed it purposely for us. "Possess the kingdom which was prepared for you from the beginning of the world." We lost it by the sin of Adam, and thou didst purchase it for us by the shedding of all thy blood. Be thou forever blessed, my good God. I call all angels and creatures to bless and praise thee. "Bless the Lord, all ye works of the Lord; praise and exalt him forever." Yet know, above all the other delights of Paradise, I desire most ardently to see, to love, and to enjoy thee. The sole thought of this makes me languish with desire. Thou alone, infinite goodness, can satisfy my heart. My heart, which is an abyss of capacity in power, sighs after thee, who art an abyss of capacity in essence.

I am, O my God, an unfortunate exile in this world; "for we have not here a lasting city, but seek one that is to come." Let me enter into the beautiful country of the living; conduct me to eternal life. I am a pilgrim, and have lost my way to Heaven, strayed in sin and passion. Oh! place me in the right way. "Show me thy ways, O Lord." I am as a vessel in the tempestuous sea of this world, which is steering towards eternity. O! grant that I may arrive at the port of happiness.

It is true—oh! how it pains me to think of it!—it is true that I have little merited this Heaven. But it is likewise true that thou hast purchased it for me with thy blood. As Chrysologus says, "Before Christ came, even Abraham was in hell; after Christ, even a thief enters Paradise." Thou hast said, that in Heaven there are distinct places for every condition of persons. "In my Father's house there are many mansions."—(*John*, xiv. 2.) If I cannot find a place among the innocent, or the martyrs, or the virgins, admit me among the penitent sinners. I implore it, my God, through the bowels of thy infinite mercy. If thou dost not wish to grant me other graces, act as thou pleasest but for Paradise I pray. I wish it not through my merits, for I have them not; but through the merits of thy divine blood. "One thing I have asked of the Lord, and this I will seek: to inhabit the house of the Lord all the days of my life." Amen.

MEDITATION XXI.

On the Love of God.

INTRODUCTION.

THE words which God said to the prophet Isaias are very mysterious. "I will lead the blind into the way which they know not; I will make darkness light before them."—(*Isa.*, xlii. 16.) Thus, at the same time can one be blind and seeing! The word of God, who is infallible truth, can never fail.

There lived in those times, as well as in our days, a description of persons who are at once blind to the Creator and clear-sighted for creatures: blind to the knowledge of the true good, and clear-sighted to every earthly beauty. Such persons do not merit to be with true Christians. To such, the demon appears to have acted as the Ammonites, when they threatened to remove the right eyes from the besiegers of Galaad. (I. *Kings*, xi. 2.)

Worldlings want the right eye, to consider God; but have the left, to gaze on creatures. As they have not eyes to contemplate the divine goodness, they have not a heart to love him. Of this kind of people it can be said, that they are "become as a dove that is decoyed, not having a heart."—(*Osee*, vii. 11.) More stolid than stone, and colder than ice, they have not one affection for God. But, for the things of this world they are observed to be possessed, not alone of one heart, but of as many different hearts as there are objects to idolize. The greatest account is made of fallacious earthly goods; and of God, the uncreated good, there appears to be no esteem. This is exemplified in Judas, the traitor. When he saw the ointment prepared for God by Magdalen, he considered it a mere waste of three hundred pieces of money; but when selling our Redeemer, he thought it well to betray him for the price of thirty pieces! What inconsistency! Let us for the future labor to employ our affections with better economy, esteeming and loving God alone, and uniting ourselves to him, who is our last end.

Let us earnestly contemplate the attributes of God, which render him infinitely amiable; for, as St. Thomas says, (12, *qu.* 27, *ar.* 2,) "as the sight of a beautiful object enkindles cupidity of sense, so the contemplation of divine goodness inflames our spirits with holy love."

We shall divide this meditation into three points, in which we shall consider three most powerful motives to love God. 1. Because God is infinitely amiable. 2. Because he is infinitely beneficent. 3. Because he is infinitely desirous of being loved.

FIRST PRELUDE.

The Blessed Virgin visibly appeared to St. Frances of Rome, with the Divine Infant in her arms, and said: "Daughter, love him who has so much loved you." Let us suppose that Mary says also to each of us: "Ungrateful and insensible man, learn to love a God who has so much loved you."

SECOND PRELUDE.

Let us beg of the Holy Spirit to inflame our hearts with his charity.

FIRST POINT.

We should love God, because he is infinitely amiable. It is certain that the object of love is goodness; and where goodness fails, love also is wanting: as fire becomes extinct without combustible matter. God, then, is a good, uniting in himself all goods. " I will show thee all good."— (*Exod.*, xxxiii. 19.) He unites them in himself, as the angelic doctor mentions (*D. Th. l.* 1. *contra Gen.* i. 29), with universality, fulness, and unity.

1. With *universality*. Creatures possess their own perfections, but not those of others: so that man has the being only of man, not that of an element, or a planet; but God, who is all good, contains in himself all the good of men, of angels, planets, heavens, plants, flowers, precious stones; and he contains good purified from every imperfection.

2. With *plenitude*. Other creatures possess goods with measure and limit: but God contains good with excess of infinite advantage, even every fullest perfection: thus we say an angel is good, but he is not goodness; he is rich, but not riches; great, but not greatness; whereas God is goodness itself, riches, and greatness. Because God is infinite in power, he can create a thousand worlds; because he is infinite in goodness, the beatific vision is bliss to innumerable spirits in Heaven; because infinite in mercy, he even assumed human nature for fallen man.

3. With *unity;* as all the divine attributes are indivisible in God! In man the soul is not the body; wisdom is not sanctity; and so of the rest. In God, all perfections are the same essence,

with innumerable beautiful semblances to cause love. "Stop here, miserable lover of the world," says St. Augustine: "you go in search of beauty, riches, honors; seek them if you will, but not in the world, where everything is foul; seek them in God, where beauty, riches, and honors are real." God has dispensed beauty, strength, riches, to creatures. How much more beautiful, strong, and rich is he than they! If you see in a friend—I will say more, if you see in an enemy—any singular prerogative of wisdom, valor, comeliness, your affections are immediately entwined around him, and you cannot detach yourself from him. How does it occur, that every prerogative being in God, you not only do not attach yourself to him, but you rather disgust and offend him? Is it because in God all perfections being united and infinite, they cease to be amiable? What is there in the world, for which you should cease to love God? If every good here below is vain, short, fallacious, treacherous, "what will you love if not God?" asks St. Augustine. You may say, it is true all perfections are united in God, and all are infinite; but not being well known to man, they cannot be loved. God became man, and descended on earth purposely to be known to men? So long as God remained retired within himself, and did not speak but amidst the flames of Sinai, man could in a certain manner excuse himself from the knowledge of God; but since his birth in a stable, his dwelling in the world for the period of thirty-three years, loading all with benefits, who can excuse himself and say he does not know him? "If I had not come and spoken to them, they would not have sin: but now they have no excuse."—(*Jo.*, xv. 26.) By his incarnation he became like unto us; so that the very likeness should persuade us to love him. He wished to treat familiarly with us, to draw us to love him. He assumed the most tender appearance, to gain our affections. "He was the most beautiful of the children of men." His words were most gracious: insomuch that the disciple said: "Thou hast the words of eternal life."—(*John*, vi. 69.) St. Bridget writes, that the Jews in their greatest labors recurred to him for comfort, saying: "Let us go to the Son of Mary to receive consolation." He was beneficent towards all: "He went about doing good, and healing all that were diseased." How many infirm, blind, and lame presented themselves? He cured and consoled them, and never rejected any, not even publicans and sinners. He assumed for us various most loving titles, alternately calling himself Lamb, Pastor, Father, Mother, Spouse, Nurse, or King. With this knowledge, how can any object but God ever be loved?

What appears incredible is daily seen in the world: relatives are loved, even though they be unkind; friends also, though faithless; companions, too, although traitors: but God is not loved. Creatures are loved, who have some slight participation of the divine perfections; but God, the fountain of all good, is not loved.

St. Ambrose had great reason to wonder at the folly of Holofernes. When Judith came before him with a most pleasing countenance, and with celestial beauty, he, not minding her beautiful countenance, fixed his eyes on the sandals of her feet, and with these alone was enchanted.—(*Judith*, xvi. 11.)

How much greater is the folly of men, who never raise their eyes to Heaven to contemplate the infinite beauty and goodness of God, but always keep them turned towards miserable creatures. They thus show themselves to be very unwise, loving mere creatures, and not the divinity who formed them.

My soul, enter into yourself, and consider how ill you have employed your affections; and weeping, say to God with St. Augustine: "There was a time in which I did not love thee." Reflect that in loving the paltry goods of this world, you have also rendered yourself base and hateful. "They became abominable, as those things were which they loved."—(*Osee*, ix. 10.)

Remember the chastisement inflicted by God on the children of Aaron, Nadab and Abiu: "The Lord destroyed them, and they died before the Lord."—(*Levit.* x. 2.) Why? Because they offered before God strange fire. You are wretched, if in your heart, in which should always burn the flames of divine love, there should be placed the coals of profane love.

SECOND POINT.

We should love God because he is infinitely beneficent. Holy David wondered that the God of infinite majesty should condescend so far as to remember man.—(*Ps.*, lxxxv.) "What is man that thou art mindful of him!" If it be so great a favor to have a place in the memory of God, and to be the object of his thoughts, what will it be, to be honored with his affection, to be the object of his love?

It is certain that *Ecclesiasticus* (xlvi. 16) could not utter a greater eulogium on Samuel than to say: "He was the beloved of the Lord his God." How great a wonder is this, that God should deign to love man? The angelic doctor teaches (1, 2, q. 27, a. 1), three causes are apt to conciliate love; namely, beauty, goodness, and resemblance: which of these things can be found in man? Not one. Where is beauty, if he is made hideous by sin? Where is goodness, if he is full of malice and ingratitude? Certainly, no resemblance is to be seen in him, for God is a pure spirit, and man is material. God is light, man darkness. God is all, man nothing. Thus in man, there is nothing whatever that can win the love of God; yet God loves him through the goodness of the divine heart. O ineffable charity! In loving us, God does not consider our demerits, but is moved by his own goodness. What a fund for thought! how powerful to make us languish and dissolve in love!

Nyssen relates, that as he was walking he saw a man absorbed in deep thought, who did nothing but weep most bitterly. He asked him why he wept. Sighing profoundly, the man answered: "I weep because, being but a miserable man and an impious creature, yet God loves me: this thought transfixes my heart, and gives me every motive for weeping unceasingly." Most just and sweet tears! why do I not melt, reflecting on this truth—*God loves me.* How much our Lord deigns to honor me! Who loves me? God: infinite majesty. Whom does he love? He loves me!

Me, made of clay, an ungrateful creature, who outrage and rebel against him. Why does he love me? He loves me solely on account of his incomprehensible goodness. My dear Jesus, tell me why do you love me so much? Why dying on the cross do you sigh and agonize for me? Why do you shed from your wounds your precious blood? Why do you die in so ignominious a manner; and yet so lovingly, with your arms extended and with your side open? St. Thomas of Villanova answers for Jesus. (*Conc. de S. Martha.*) " Jesus loves me for no interest of his own, but for my good." He loves me to make me blessed with his love. Should I not love him in return? Can I refrain from loving him, to love a beauty that betrays me, an animal that flatters me? Can I refuse to correspond to so loving a God, my sole good and my last end?

Our God loves us, as every father loves his son, every artist his work, every gardener his plant; for we are his children and the work of his hands. According to the angelic doctor, there is a difference between human and divine love. Human love cannot infuse good into others, by wishing well to the beings selected as the objects of love. It is not so with God: as he occasions in others the good which he loves, he is excited to love without any extrinsic motive: he loves us with his whole being, because his love is himself.

St. Bernard says (*ser.* xv.): that the Father, Son, and Holy Ghost love us. Omnipotence loves us, preserving what he created in us: immensity, being always present to us: wisdom, governing us: and so of all his divine attributes. He loves us more than all: he has not done for angels what he has accomplished for man: he assumed human nature, and died on a cross for us: "For nowhere doth he take hold of the angels; but of the seed of Abraham he taketh hold." (*Hebr.*, ii. 6.) He loves us with more affection than our own father: with more tenderness than our mother: he loves us more than we love ourselves: for God has done and suffered for us, what we neither do nor suffer for ourselves. St. Bonaventure says, "That God seems to hate himself that He may give us life." He loves us always: his love towards us, is not only sovereign in intensity, but also in extent. He has loved us (*Ps.*, cii. 17) from eternity and unto eternity: he loved us before we existed: "With perpetual charity, I love thee." He continues to love us, even whilst we offend him, for he awaits our return to penance, and defers the chastisement of our sins. Finally, his love does not end in words and in affections, but he shows it by the acts of excessive beneficence.

Reflect, O man! that what you are and what you have, all came from God. Consider the heavens, earth, elements: all are benefits from God, which make us know that God has loved us, says St. Augustine, in order to enrich us with delights. God has shown us infinite goodness. Who could ever have imagined that a God would become man for the love of us! Yet God has done this. Who could ever suppose that a God offended by man, would wish to die for him on a cross? Yet God has done this for us. Who could ever have thought of the extraordinary invention by which, even after death, our Lord remains in the world, and in the august sacrifice of the Eucharist, continually renews the sacrifice of the cross? He has done all this for us. How infinite is Divine goodness!

Consider the special benefits which God has conferred on you more than on others. How many are there in the world, poor, ignorant, infirm, persecuted; and you, on the contrary, are wealthy, or educated, or healthful, or in pleasure? What merit have you more than they? Rather, what demerit have you for your sins, which they have not? God has acted towards you with much more mercy than with them. How much more love then has God shown to you? How much more obliged are you to love him in return?

Blessed Camilla Varani, afterwards Sister Baptist, nun of St. Clare, for her illustrious virtues obtained this singular reward, that Jesus Christ once visibly appeared to her, and opening his breast, showed her written in golden characters, in the midst of his Divine heart, these sweet words: "I love thee, Camilla."—(*Papebroch*, 18 *May*.) What a grace, what a subject of envy even to the seraphim! Each of us can see in the heart of God, that he loves us with infinite, eternal love, and far more than he loves innumerable other creatures. "What do you do, my soul?" exclaims St. Augustine. How stone-like is your heart, if after so many benefits it does not show some affection! When will you resolve to make some return to your Divine lover and great benefactor? I am resolved, most amiable and beloved Lord! I know, as St. Bernard says, that there is not in the world a love like to yours. Exclaim with St. Thomas of Villanova: "O ecstatic love! O most fervent excess: without number, measure, weight, thou hast loved me."—(*Ser. de Transfix.*)

THIRD POINT.

We should love God, because he is infinitely desirous of being loved. He is a God of such great majesty, and man is so vile in himself, that it would be great condescension on the part of God, if he only permitted himself to be loved by man. God not only accepts the love of man, but he desires it most ardently. St. Augustine, meditating on this, says: "O Lord, why shouldst thou be mindful of me? What advantage accrues to thee from my love? Whence arises this anxiety for my perfidious and obstinate heart?"

He created all creatures for man; and created man solely for himself. He wished that man should have a natural tendency to love God, his last end. He disdains not to beg man's heart: "My son, give me thy heart."—(*Prov.*, xxii. 26.) He declares he will have it all, without any division with others. To those who love him, he promises Paradise for a reward: "What things God hath prepared for those that love him."—(I. *Cor.*, ii. 9.) He threatens eternal death, as a chastisement to him who does not love him: "He that loveth not, abideth in death."—(I. *John,* xxx. 14.) He declares that the basis and the fulness of his law is to fear him and to love him: "Love, therefore, is the fulfilling of the law."—(*Rom.*, xiii. 10.) He orders all sacrifices offered to him to be seasoned with salt: by salt is meant love: "Whatsoever sacrifice thou offerest, thou shalt season it with salt."—(*Levit.* ii. 13.) If sometimes a cold heart fly from his tenderness, he sweetly complains of it: "Their heart is far from me."—(*Isa.*, xix. 13.) Not contented with all this, he commands his love by a most binding precept: "Thou shalt love the Lord thy God with thy whole heart."

How much is here for our meditation! Why is there a necessity to command the love of what is infinitely good and beautiful? Oh! blindness and perfidiousness of human nature!

If God had commanded us to fear him, and had prohibited us to love him, this would have been a very severe law to the heart of man inclined to love, and yet unable to love the sovereign good. One of the greatest pains of the damned is, to know that God is most worthy of love, and still to be obliged to only fear him. We owe much to God, who has imposed on us what is so dear to our soul, that is, to love him.

This is an incomprehensible honor; for God commanding us to love him, shows how much he appreciates our affection.

St. Augustine cannot understand (*l.* 1, *Conf.* 10) why God commands his love under grievous penalties, while the soul cannot endure greater pain or greater misery, than not to love God. Can we imagine more to persuade us, that God desires to be sovereignly loved by man?

In Ecclesiastical Chronicles it is written, that sometimes our Lord appeared to some holy virgins; he seemed to remove their hearts, and carry them off. The infant Jesus, with a sweet violence, took away the heart of Catherine de Raconigi, and restored it to her with this motto engraved upon it: "Jesus is my hope." He also seemed to take the heart of the virgin Passitea, foundress of the religious Capucines in Sienna. The Author of Life supplied the vital functions in her, and by a great prodigy, she survived twenty-three years without a heart. When Passitea died, the Lord Archbishop Petrucci, of Sienna, caused her chest to be opened in presence of doctors and surgeons. She was without a heart. Who can doubt of our Lord's ardent desire for the heart of his creatures, when he thus takes hearts to himself?

How is it possible for man not to yield to these ardent desires of God? Earthly monarchs need not command what they wish from their subjects; it suffices that they show their inclination, and all try to second it. O confusion of the world! God alone appears not to be obeyed by men when he commands. Moses struck a rock with his rod, and immediately it poured forth water. God with powerful benefits strikes the human heart, and it does not respond with one affection! Man alone denies to his God what he asks of him, his love and his heart. Is this precept of loving God too hard and too severe? Certainly not; there is nothing more natural to every creature than to love him by whom he is loved and benefited. The lamb, among the bleatings of a hundred sheep, knows the voice of its dam, and runs after her. Even wolves and tigers love and caress their offspring. Is it a precept which cannot be practised by all? No. An invalid may well be excused from fasting; the poor, from almsgiving; but who can excuse himself from loving God? Why should we not obey this sweet commandment! Man, ungrateful man, have you a heart to refuse your God, who is so loving, and to follow creatures that are nothingness! You have a very small heart, of which you wish to make a hundred shares; and bestow one on relatives, another on friends, another on dress, and only reserve a small portion for God. But God is not contented with this most unjust division; for he expressly declares: "I am alone, and there is no other God beside me"—(*Deut.*, xxxii. 39): he wishes to have our hearts entirely for himself; "with thy whole heart:" he will not suffer the slightest affection therein which is not referred to him. It is told of St. Rose of Lima, that she had detached herself from the world, and lived solely for God in continual prayer. Occasionally, wishing to unbend her mind from her lengthened contemplations, she watered and cultivated a plant of sweet basil, which having grown flourishing and beautiful, the saint enjoyed the innocent pleasure of seeing it before her; when, one day returning to look at her basil, she suddenly saw her vase overturned, the earth scattered about, and the leaves all pulled off the plant. "Oh!" said the saint, "who has thus ruined my sweet basil?" Having thus spoken, casting her eyes around, she saw our Saviour, who thus addressed her: "I spoiled your sweet basil, because I do not wish that any of your affections should be employed on any other object but myself." The saint became confused at these words, and throwing herself on the ground, begged of her celestial Spouse to pardon her fault.

My soul, here meditate: Can an affection be more innocently bestowed than this? Yet it displeased Jesus, who wishes to be alone in the human heart. How much more offensive are your affections, which are vain, base and sinful! Weep bitterly at the feet of Jesus for your grievous excesses.

COLLOQUY.

My good, most amiable, and beloved God; I do not wish to retain this frozen heart; I desire to have the hearts of all the saints, that I may return in some degree the infinite love with which thou hast always loved me, and now lovest me, without any merit on my part. I unite my poor affections with the love of all the saints and angels, and with them I exclaim: "Be blessed a thousand times, and thanked for so much goodness towards a miserable creature such as I am!" I owe this heart to thee, for to thee alone it belongs, by every title of justice and gratitude. Thou alone art sovereign and infinite good: for "Thou alone art holy, thou alone art Lord, thou alone art most high." I know well that in giving thee my heart, I bestow but a small gift; therefore I exclaim with the fervent St. Philip Neri: "Lord, having to love a God of infinite goodness, why should I have but one heart, and that so small?" What can I do to correspond with the love and benefits of God? Holy Spirit! thou who didst fill the soul of Mary with charity, and the minds of the apostles, inflame our hearts; consume in them with thy Heavenly fire all profane love, that the fire of charity may always burn within us. Divine Spirit, be moved to compassion towards me: "Pour forth thy grace into our hearts, and strengthen us with the spirit of love;" that by thus loving God during life, we may afterwards love him for all eternity in Heaven. Amen.

MEDITATION XXII.

Of the spiritual fruit we should draw from the Exercises.

INTRODUCTION.

St. Jerome, writing to the holy virgin Eustochium, who, by his directions, had arrived at great perfection, said to her: "Daughter, I admonish you not to allow the Devil to despoil you of those treasures of virtues and merits, which with much labor you have acquired. Remember that a traveller goes more cautiously, and is more guarded against robbers, when he is charged with gold and silver." The same advice I repeat to whoever has terminated the Exercises with fervor. He has in this holy time well learned eternal truths: he has conceived strong desires to amend his life, and he has collected much merit from the practice of many sacred duties. What remains to be done, to preserve well what is already acquired, and to strongly guard against the devils, who, like so many pirates, always have in view the ships most rich in merchandise? They attack especially the most fervent souls, who are full of strong resolutions: they wish them to lose in one day what they had gained in eight or ten.

Seneca thought entire centuries were necessary to bring a city to full magnificence as to buildings, population, and commerce; and to destroy it, one day—one hour sufficed; a shock of an earthquake, a sacking by an enemy's army, a raging plague, in a very short time reduces it to nothing.

To place the mystic citadel of the soul in a state

of Christian security, how much is wanting? how many sermons? how many meditations? how much retirement? how many resolutions? To destroy it—(oh! how sorrowful!)—a few moments suffice, a perilous occasion, or human respect, or fear of what may be said. Let us now seriously think on the manner of preserving the good which is done, according to what the apostle advises: "Hold what thou hast." Let us draw from the holy exercises practical and permanent fruit for our lives.

We shall divide this meditation into three points. 1. We must draw practical fruit from the exercises. 2. Permanent fruit. 3. The means to draw this practical and permanent fruit.

FIRST PRELUDE.

Let us imagine that we see our Redeemer after curing the invalid at the pond of Probatica; he reasons with him, and admonishes him thus: "Behold thou art made whole: sin no more, lest some worse thing happen to thee."—(*John*, v. 14.) Let us suppose he says the same to each of us. In these exercises, with penitential tears and exact confessions, you have been cured of the wounds of your sins. I admonish you not to return again, lest something worse happen, if you relapse into your former faults.

SECOND PRELUDE.

Say to the Holy Ghost: Divine Spirit, thou hast given me light to know the eternal maxims; thou hast given me a desire to correspond with thy lights; give me also efficacious graces to perform thy inspirations.

35*

FIRST POINT.

We must draw practical fruit from the exercises. Man considers his countenance in a mirror to cleanse what is soiled, and to reinstate what is out of order; he is deficient in reason, if after having seen in the glass many deformities in his person, he does not think of removing them.

The spiritual exercises are like a clear looking-glass, in which, by the light of faith, all the irregularities of the soul are seen. What folly would it be, if, having well observed and known them for eight or ten days, a person should neglect reforming them?

The apostle St. James preached with great zeal on this subject to his faithful: "Be ye doers of the word, and not hearers only, deceiving your own selves. For if a man be a hearer of the word and not a doer, he shall be compared to a man beholding his own countenance in a glass; for he beheld himself and went his way, and presently forgot what manner of man he was."— (*James*, i. 22.) As a bucket while in water cannot be declared sound or the contrary; but removed from the well it shows whether it leaks: thus when many make the exercises together, we cannot distinguish who profited, because all appear modest and full of compunction. After the exercises it will be known if the lights received are put in practice, if the holy resolutions are followed, if a person live with more devotion and modesty, without ever returning to former disorders. We should endeavor to procure this practical fruit after the exercises, by every possible means, and from numerous powerful motives.

1. Because we shall have to render a most strict account to God for all the lights he has brought to our minds, for all the impulses he has given our hearts, for all the graces he has conferred on us at this period. After having shed on our souls so many showers of knowledge and fervent inspirations, if he saw that instead of producing flowers and fruits of virtue, we showed forth thorns and briers of vices, how indignant must he be! He would certainly act as the husbandman, who, having for a long time watered and cultivated a plant, if he find that it becomes dry, immediately roots it up. "For the earth that drinketh in the rain which cometh often upon it—which bringeth forth thorns and briers, is reprobate and very near unto a curse, whose end is to be burnt."—(*Hebrews*, vi. 7.) Besides, we shall have to render an account to God for the repeated promises we have made to sin no more, and commence a new life. If after the exercises any one return to his former wickedness, what would this outraged Lord say to him? Perfidious and unfaithful creature, deceiver, is God thus treated? If once you fail in word to a fellow-man, he considers himself offended? You fail in your promise to a God of infinite majesty, and do you expect that he should not be offended? Remember the tears and sobs with which you asked pardon for your sins. Remember the words you so often uttered: "Never more sin." Now, you are precisely like the wicked one of whom Jeremias said (iii. 3): "Her treacherous sister Juda hath not returned to me with her whole heart, but with falsehood." How treacherous were your tears and how unfaithful your hearts. "With their

tongue they lied unto him: but their heart was not right with him."—(*Ps.*, lxxvii. 36.) Your worst evil is, that your false penance has added to former faults a still greater one.

2. He who prevaricates after the exercises, renders himself more inexcusable than ever in his faults: a worldling who never considered in earnest the meaning of death or Hell, or the terror of eternity, could have some appearance of excuse before God, saying, that, blinded by passion, he had never minded great truths. But after one has long meditated upon them, and clearly known them in the exercises, can he allege a similar excuse? Certainly not. God, who is most just, would reprove him! Having seen the great abyss of sin and the horrible torments of Hell, yet for a momentary pleasure, you voluntarily returned to your ruin! After having known that God alone is your last end, and that all things else are vanity, yet of your own free will you have turned your back on God, to serve the world and the Devil? How many, from one such thought, have become saints; and you, with so clear knowledge of eternal things, become worse than you were.

How many, if they had this spiritual assistance of the holy exercises, would change their living and become devoted to God? While you, harder than stone, do not yield to the strokes of divine inspiration. "Woe to thee, Corozain: woe to thee, Bethsaida: for if in Tyre and Sidon had been wrought the miracles that have been wrought in you, they had long ago done penance in sackcloth and ashes."—(*Mat.*, xi. 21.)

3. Because these exercises may be the last of your life. How great an evil would it be to

resume former evil habits, without hope of being able to amend by future spiritual exercises! These may be the last concerning efficacious grace; and God may not again bestow it, if what is now given is not corresponded to. " A long sickness is troublesome to the physician."—(*Eccl.*, x. 11.)

Who can deny that the spiritual exercises are amongst the most powerful and efficacious remedies to cure and convert souls? If God see that they are not available with obstinate hearts, what does he do? In anger he often punishes them, as he did infamous Babylon—he abandons them, and never gives them the efficacious assistance of his grace, even though they should again return to the exercises. " We would have cured Babylon, but she is not healed: let us forsake her."—(*Jer.* li. 9.) The miserable creatures may return to implore the divine mercy, but an angry God will not again be moved to compassionate them. " They shall cry out, and I will not hear, saith the Lord." Reflect seriously. Tremble from head to foot, and do not refuse to listen to his words, or show him such ingratitude, as not to fulfil what he has inspired you with for your good, and what you have promised him with so many tears.

SECOND POINT.

We must draw from the exercises permanent fruit. They are not few, who, having terminated the exercises, show by their deeds that they have gathered much fruit: hence, they are more modest in deportment; more cautious in conversation; more devout and frequent in approaching the holy sacraments. But all this fine fruit lasts only a short time. As a vessel of water when on the fire boils and bubbles, and when removed, cools until it returns to its former state: thus they, who in the first fervor of the exercises, burned with the holy desire of becoming saints, having left retirement, by degrees grow tepid in their spiritual exercises, and then recommence a disorderly life. The reproof could justly be made to them which the apostle gave to the Galatians, calling them senseless: " Are you so foolish that whereas you began in the spirit, you would now be made perfect by the flesh?"—(*Gal.*, iii. 3.) He adds, that not having followed the good commenced, they labored in vain and without fruit! The better to understand this, let us imagine that a merchant, after traversing the ocean for forty years, having successfully encountered innumerable perils, at last, enriched with silver, gold, and most precious jewels, arrives in port. Scarcely has he landed, than he commences gambling, and ventures at one sole game of dice all he had acquired by the labors of so many years. What would be said of him? Foolish man! What good accrued to him in having amassed his great riches during many years, if he be content to impoverish himself in one minute? Such is the case of those who, having labored much in the exercises, and even, for some time after, endeavor to perfect their lives; yet, in one instant venture their salvation for a vile satisfaction. How miserable and blind are they, not only to render useless all the good works before performed, but by relapsing into former errors, to make themselves more odious to God. " For it had been better for them not to have known the way of justice, than after they had known it, to turn back from that holy commandment which was delivered to them."—(II. *Peter*, ii. 21.) A similitude will clearly show this. If a soldier from the enemy be conducted prisoner before a captain who always waged war against him, he easily grants him pardon. If, on the contrary, a soldier should be conducted before him who received pay for many years, and fought under his banner, but who rebelled against him, and finally deserted to the enemy's army: such traitor would be punished by death for his felony. Such is our case. If one who was wicked returns to penance, he obtains with ease pardon from God: but if, after having for some time walked in the way of God and devotion, he again rebel and give himself up to vice, he will be most severely chastised by God with eternal death. The Psalmist says so: " The enemies of the Lord have lied to him; and their time shall be forever." Most terrible chastisement! Grant then that the fruit of the exercises may be fruit worthy of true penance. " Bring forth therefore fruits worthy of penance."—(*Luke*, iii. 8.) Such was the penance of St. Peter, who repenting of his fault in denying his divine Master, began to weep; and so long as he lived he never ceased weeping. Such was the penance of Magdalen, who as the first light of divine grace darted on her mind, " did not cease to kiss his feet" during life. She never ceased to be faithful to Christ: at the death of our Saviour, all the disciples having fled, she remained firm beside his cross.

The fruit of the exercises should be *durable:* whoever quits them to commence a more Christian life, should continue it, until God rewards him in

Heaven. We must have patience, until it please God to give us the reward of our labors. St. Augustine adds, if God waited long for us to do penance, it is right that we, performing long penance, should also wait for that period, in which God considers it suitable to remunerate us.

How many of the damned weep in Hell, after having for a long time led a good life; but they had not patience to continue. How unfortunate was Judas, who, having commenced well, finished with deicide!

Think well on it, O beloved! reflect seriously: as St. Laurence Justinian says: "Perseverance alone is the gate of Paradise."

THIRD POINT.

The means to draw practical and permanent fruit from the exercises. There are many means which preserve the fruits of the exercises. It is well to consider the chief: 1. To break at once the chain of our sins. "Thou shalt cry, and he shall say: Here I am. If thou wilt take away the chain out of the midst of thee."—(*Isaias,* lviii. 9.) Thus God spoke to the Israelites, who were fasting and performing great penance, yet continued to commit some grievous faults. God made them understand that they never could have peace with him, if they did not remove the last link of the long chain of their sins. How many flatter themselves that they can reform their manners by degrees; thus they may divest themselves of minor vices, but never can overcome their former bad habits, or their predominant passion.

Herod, by the fervent exhortation of St. John, Baptist, must have abstained from many vices and practised, many good works: "For he heard him willingly, and did many things for him:" but he never rid himself of his incestuous habits; so all the rest was of no avail.

Understand well, beloved, that it will be useless, after the exercises, to be very devout and exempt from other faults, if you preserve some sinful affection or hatred, if you do not immediately restore what you should to your neighbor. St. James says: "Whosoever shall keep the whole law, but offend in one point, is become guilty of all"—(ii. 10).

2. Most important means is to fly the occasions of sin. Holy David earnestly begged of God to remove him from the way that conducts to evil: "Remove from me the way of iniquity."—(*Ps.*, cxviii. 29.) Now, this way is the occasion of sinning. Remove occasions and sin ceases. If the occasion be not avoided, your resolutions, prayers, and penances will not secure you. The epithet Chrysologus gives to those occasions (*ser.* cxvi.) is very expressive; he calls them "smoky." Have you observed a lamp not well extinguished? What smoke comes from it! If a small light approach even at a distance, it immediately rekindles. By means of the exercises and of sacramental confession, the fire of impure passion should be extinguished; yet, if evil inclinations remain alive, the memory of past pleasure, and the suggestions of the Devil, then the smallest spark of an indelicate word, or a curious look, or a salute, or gesture approaching this smoke, immediately the first fire is rekindled. It is not enough to say: "I will resist temptation, and to resist it is

in my power:" for as St. Cyprian says (*lib. de sing. Cler.*): "Who can promise himself not to feel heat, when he places himself in the midst of flames?" He who walks through the air on ropes hopes to support himself, notwithstanding at every instant he is in danger of falling. "Short sighted souls," cries out Tertullian (*lib. de pud. c.* 10), "who, by placing yourselves in the occasion of sinning, put yourselves in danger of falling every moment." St. Jerome adds: "What imprudence to go to those places, into those houses, to those conversations, in which of necessity, we are either to overcome, or be vanquished!" We should well understand the great saying of St. Philip Neri; "That in wars with the senses, the most cowardly vanquish; those who fly, conquer!"

A third means is, to overcome human respect. How many are there in the world who would wish to lead a holy life, but will not venture to do so, from their great fear, that some worldling of little sense might say: "Oh! he wishes to act like a saint. What does he intend by so much affectation? for my part, I do not credit him." For such speeches, they withdraw themselves from good. What weakness! What misery! for all the good and wise approve repentance. If even the whole world were to speak against you, only mind what Jesus Christ, who is infallible truth, says by St. Paul: "If I yet please men, I shall not be the servant of God." Miserable man! if you were damned, all these worldlings could not free you from Hell! You would eternally cry out with the foolish wise of the world: "We fools esteemed their lives madness." What then are we to do? We must follow the example of holy David, who, although a great king, was not ashamed to dance publicly and play before the Ark, in sight of all the people: he answered his proud consort Michol, who reproved him: "No, it is not meanness, but sovereign glory, to serve that God whom the seraphim adore."—(II. *Kings*, vi. 22.) " I shall appear more glorious." If it should cause any prejudice to my majesty, how gladly would I lower myself, for the love of that God, who from a poor shepherd raised me to the throne of Israel. " I will make myself meaner than I have done, and I will be little in my own eyes."—(II. *Kings*, vi. 22.) In the same manner, we should answer whoever censures a more Christian manner of life: " Such a mode of living merits every praise; even if it be disapproved by men, it is sufficient that it pleases God, and is very useful to my soul."

Finally, the fourth means is, to be diffident of self, and to confide entirely in God. We should not confide in ourselves. Although a man may be good and holy, he is always earthly: all then should live in the holy fear of God, and continually pray to our Lord to bestow his assisting grace. " With fear and trembling work out your salvation."—(*Phil.*, ii. 12.) How holy was St. Philip Neri; yet very often, extended on the ground, he exclaimed: " Lord, keep thy hand over Philip, otherwise Philip will betray thee!" How much more, should he distrust himself, who is not virtuous and holy, more frail than a reed, and inclined to fall at every breath of temptation? It is necessary that every man, in the great affair of salvation, should tremble, and daily fortify himself by prayer; and frequent Holy Communion, thence to receive powerful assistance to live well.

Inasmuch as we learn to distrust ourselves, we must place all our confidence in God, hoping that in his infinite mercy, he will assist and help us in executing his inspirations and the resolutions made in the holy exercises. In practising a Christian and holy life, you will not be alone! God will be with you, and will assist you with his grace, without which you can do nothing.

Who can tell how well God treats those who serve him? He strengthens their weakness, defends them in temptations, encourages them in the most arduous undertakings, saying to them, as to his timid apostles: "It is I, fear not." Even more: he lightens the practice of virtue, renders it sweet, infuses celestial delights in prayer, gives a great interior peace of conscience, which surpasses all human enjoyment. "How good is God to them that are of a right heart."—(*Ps.*, lxxii. 1.) Ask those who, from a wicked course of life, have returned to be regular. Let them acknowledge how much more happy they are now, how they experience the truth of David's saying: "He will speak peace unto his people, and unto them that are converted in the heart."—(*Ps.*, lxxxiv. 9.) Take courage, and confide in God; if you are in earnest, you can easily with his assistance do all the good which you have proposed.

In conclusion of the whole, dearly beloved, on leaving the exercises, I wish you to represent to your imagination, that God sends an angel to you, or rather, that the same God of whom we treat in these meditations, says to you: "Come, be convinced, that for so many years of life which you have misspent, you deserve to be banished from the world as useless for your end, and condemned to Hell for your many sins: but, because you have done penance in these exercises, I pardon the past evil, and I grant you a short time longer to live. Profit well by this new mercy, and hereafter in multiplying good works, try to make amends for former failings."

I repeat, represent this in a lively manner to your imagination, and begin to spend well the short remainder of your life. Thus did a person living in the city of Rodriguez, as is related in the chronicles of St. Francis. This man led a very vicious life: he was, however, singularly devoted to St. Francis of Assisium, who, moved with compassion towards him, by means of frightful visions thrice admonished him to confess: at length he confessed, and had no sooner finished than a sudden faint terminated his life. During the funeral ceremony, to the surprise of every one present, the body arose, and sitting on the bier, threw the bystanders into such consternation, that they all took to flight: when he with a rough voice, said: "Do not fly from me; you have no cause to fear, because, though it be true I was dead, yet now, by the grace of God, I am alive. Know, that no sooner had my soul left the body, than it was presented before the Divine tribunal, where it was to receive sentence of eternal condemnation, not having had in the last confession true and sincere sorrow, but merely servile grief for fear of imminent death: then, through the intercession of my great Father, St. Francis, the Sovereign Judge granted me to return again to life for a short time, in order to do penance, after which I shall die." Having thus spoken, he left the coffin. He distributed all he possessed to the poor and to hospitals. For the twenty days he afterwards lived, he did nothing but pray, and perform penance. Nourished with the Holy Sacraments, he again died, and his body was buried with great solemnity in the cathedral of the city of Rodriguez (*P. Marcus ab Ulyssipone in chr. Min. P.ir. II. l. viii. c. 50.*)

From this relation may we draw the useful conclusion which I before mentioned, that God, who, on account of our numerous sins, could have taken away our lives and condemned us to Hell, being now moved to pity us, through his infinite mercy grants us a short time longer to live, that we may be disposed for eternity. With this thought imprinted on the mind, let us seriously reform our manners, and practise as many good works as possible. What matter for reflection! How much will it avail us to profit by it! Let us know well how to avail ourselves of the time God gives us. "If to-day you hear his voice, harden not your hearts."

COLLOQUY.

Most benignant Lord, how grateful I am to thee for so much mercy! How much hast thou done, and still do to convert me, and recall me as a wandering sheep to the fold! May thou, O Lord, be blessed a thousand times! If all my members were as many tongues, yet they would not suffice to exalt thy infinite clemency. I cannot refrain from admiring thy great patience for so many years, with an inconstant sinner such as I am. I hate myself, knowing my infidelities and coldness, after so many benefits received. Thou hast called me in so many ways, and I have turned to thee a deaf ear. Thou hast threatened me with chastisement, and I have remained obstinate. Thou hast promised me rewards, and I have not considered them. Thou hast drawn me with thy benefits, and I have remained ungrateful.

When shall there be an end of all my wickedness? When shall I arouse myself from the lethargy of so many bad habits? What have I gained by committing sin? What evil has it not done me? How short soever the pleasure I experienced, yet I had to expiate it with so much bitterness and remorse. On the contrary, when I have been united to thee by grace, even pain has been sweet to me—even tears have consoled me.

O most benign Jesus! as in all these holy exercises thou hast given me light to know these truths, give me now the graces necessary to put them into practice. Thou knowest well my misery and my frailty: deign to strengthen me, I beg of thee, with the powerful assistance of thy grace. Do not permit that I should ever return to my past irregularities; and give me strength to execute well the holy resolutions which I have already made, to serve thee during life, and afterwards to see, love, and enjoy thee, my last end, eternally in Heaven. Amen.

THE PRAYER "ANIMA CHRISTI."

Soul of Christ, sanctify me.
Body of Christ, save me.
Blood of Christ, inebriate me.
Water out of the side of Christ, cleanse me.
Passion of Christ, strengthen me.
O good Jesus! hear me.
Hide me in thy sacred wounds.
Do not permit me to be separated from thee.
From the malignant enemy defend me.
Call me at the hour of death;
And tell me to come to thee;
That with thy saints and angels I may praise thee forever and ever. Amen.

A. M. D. G.

Laus Deo et B. V. Mariae.

SPIRITUAL READING FROM THE NEW TESTAMENT AND FROM THE "IMITATION OF CHRIST."

End of Man.	*N. T.* Matt. xvi. 14-28; Luke vi. 20-39. *Imit* Bk. iii. ch. 9. 22, 26.
Mortal sin.	*N. T.* Matt. xxv. 1-31. *Imit.* Bk. i. chap. 21, 22; ii. ch. 5; iv. ch. 7.
Death.	*N. T.* Luke xii. 33-43; Apoc. iii. *Imit.* Bk. i. ch. 23.
Judgment.	*N. T.* Matt. xxv. 31. 46. *Imit.* Bk. iii. ch. 14.
Hell.	*N. T.* Luke xvi. 19-31. *Imit.* Bk. i. ch. 25.
Reign of Christ.	*N. T.* John xv.; Col. iii. *Imit.* Bk. i. ch. 1; iii. ch. 13-32.
The Incarnation.	*N. T.* Luke i. 26-56. *Imit.* Bk. ii. ch. 1, 7, 8.
The Nativity.	*N. T.* Luke ii. 1-21. *Imit.* Bk. iii. ch. 1, 2, 18.
The hidden life of Jesus Christ.	*N. T.* Luke ii. 40-52. *Imit.* Bk. i. ch. 20; iii. ch. 44, 53.
Public life of Jesus Christ.	*N. T.* Matt. x. *Imit.* Bk. i. ch. 15, 16; iii. ch. 4.
The two standards, three classes, and three degrees of humility.	*N. T.* Matt. xix. *Imit.* Bk. iii. ch. 23, 27, 31, 56.
Change of a state.	*Imit.* Bk. iii. ch. 54.
The Eucharist.	*N. T.* Matt. xxvi. 17-30. *Imit.* Bk. iv. ch. 1, 2.
The Passion.	*N. T.* Matt. xxvi. 36-75; xxvii. *Imit.* Bk. ii. ch. 11, 12; iv. ch. 8.
The Resurrection and Ascension.	*N. T.* Matt. xxviii.; Mark xvi.; Luke xxiv.; Acts i. *Imit.* Bk. iii. ch. 47, 48.
Love of God.	*N. T.* John xvii.; 1 John iv. *Imit.* Bk. iii. ch. 5, 6, 34.
Holy Communion.	*N. T.* Luke xxii. 14-21; John vi; 1 Cor. ii. 23-31. *Imit.* Bk. iv. ch. 17.

CATHOLIC BOOKS

PUBLISHED BY

PETER F. CUNNINGHAM & SON,

817 Arch St., Philadelphia.

Catholic Doctrine as Defined by the Council of Trent:

Expounded in a series of Conferences delivered in Geneva. By Rev. A. Nampon, S. J., the most complete work on Catholic Doctrine yet published in the English Language; approved by the Bishop of Philadelphia, the Archbishops of Baltimore, New York and Cincinnati. 1 vol. octavo, of 7 0 pages, splendidly bound in cloth $3 50

The Celebrated Sanctuaries of the Madonna.

By Rev. J. Spencer Northcote. D D. Published with the approbation of the *Right Rev. James Frederick Wood, Bishop of Philadelphia.* 1 vol., 12mo.

Price—Cloth, extra beveled..$1 50

The Year of Mary; or, The True Servant of the Blessed Virgin.

Translated from the French of Rev. M D Arville, Apostolic Prothonotary, and published with the approbation of the *Right Rev. Bishop of Philadelphia*, the *Most Rev. Archbishop of Baltimore*, and the *Most Rev. Archbishop of New York*. 1 neat 12mo volume.

Price—In cloth..$1.50

This is a delightful book; brimful of sweet flowers; a lovely garland in honor of Mary our Mother and powerful intercessor before the throne of her Son.

Well has the *Magnificat* said, "all generations shall call me blessed;" all times, and in all lands, wherever the symbol, upon which her Divine Son ransomed a wicked and undeserving world with his excruciating sufferings and death has a votary, her name, spotless and beautiful, shall be pronounced with reverence, and her protection implored.

The tome before us is a collection of the honors paid to Mary by the great and good of all lands; by those who, with the diadem of earthly grandeur adorning their brows, and vexed political commonwealths to guard and pacify, found time to honor the daughter of St. Anna, the beloved Mother of our Lord and Saviour.

Buy the book. Read one or two pages We promise a feast, a desire to read the whole, a determination to do so.—*Catholic Telegraph.*

This work is divided into seventy-two Exercises, corresponding with the number of years which the Blessed Virgin passed on earth, with a consecration

(3)

to Mary of the twelve months of the year, in reference to her virtues; also a method of using certain of the Exercises by a way of devotion for the "Month of Mary," a Novena in honor of the Immaculate Conception, and other matters both interesting and advantageous to the true servant of Mary, and those who would become so.

"BALTIMORE, *April* 6, 1865.

"We willingly unite with the Ordinary of Philadelphia and the Metropolitan of New York in approving 'The Year of Mary,' republished by Peter F. Cunningham, of Philadelphia.
"M. J. SPALDING,
"*Archbishop of Baltimore.*"

A work presented to the Catholics with such recommendations does not need any word of encouragement from us.—*Pilot.*

This work meets a want long ungratified. The devotional exercises which make up the book are ingeniously arranged in reference, 1st, to each year of the Blessed Virgin's long residence on earth; 2d, to every Sunday and festival throughout the year. The Exercises are therefore seventy-two in number, corresponding to the generally received belief of the duration of her terrestrial life.

The First Exercise is thus appropriated to the Immaculate Conception, and may be used both for the 8th of December and for the first day of the year. The seventy-second celebrates the Assumption, and may be profitably read on the 15th of August and on the last day of the year.

Each Instruction is prefaced by a text from holy writ, and followed by an example, a historical fact, a practice and a prayer.

The Approbations are:
1st. By the Roman Theological Censor.
2d. By a favorable letter from his Holiness, Gregory XVI.
3d. By the recommendatory signatures of the Archbishops of Baltimore and New York, and the Bishop of Philadelphia.

This Devotional is a deeply interesting and practical manual, and Mrs. Sadlier, who has very skilfully reduced the originally free translation into graceful conformity to the original, has rendered the Christian public a most essential service. We wish it the widest circulation.—*N. Y. Table*.

"The Year of Mary" is one of the most beautiful tributes to the Mother of God that a Catholic family could desire to have. We are free, however, to confess our partiality in noticing any book that treats of the pre-eminent glory of her whom God exalted above all created beings.

But, independently of this consideration, the present volume can be recommended on its own special merits. Besides being replete with spiritual instruction, it presents a detailed account of the life of the Blessed Virgin from the Conception to the Assumption, and views her under every possible aspect, both as regards herself and her relations with man. It lays down the rules by which we are to be guided in our practical devotions towards her; displays its genuine characteristics, and indicates the sublime sentiments by which we ought to be actuated when we pay her our homage or invoke her assistance.

"The Year of Mary" contains seventy-two Exercises, in accordance with the received opinion of the Church that the Blessed Virgin lived that number of years on earth. In these Instructions, the reader shall learn her life, her prerogatives, her glory in Heaven, and her boundless goodness to mankind. We would like to see this book in every Catholic family in the country. It is impossible for us to honor the Mother of God sufficiently well. But in reading this book, or any like it, we must ever bear in mind that acts, not mere professions of piety, should be the distinctive marks of "the true servant of the Blessed Virgin," and that she is really honored, only in so far as we imitate her virtues for the sake of Him through whom alone we can hope for eternal life.

The name of Mrs. Sadlier is familiar to the public; her talents as an authoress are too well known to need any eulogy here; she is an accomplished lady, and has faithfully done her part. As to the publisher, Mr. Cunningham, we say, without flattery, that he has done a *good* work in presenting this excellent book to his fellow-Catholics, and with all our heart we wish him the fullest measure of success to which this noble enterprise entitles him.—*The Monthly*

www.ingramcontent.com/pod-product-compliance
Lightning Source LLC
Chambersburg PA
CBHW051734300426
44115CB00007B/559